**50% OFF!**

Free Video  Free Video

Essential Test Tips Video from Trivium Test Prep

Dear Customer,

Thank you for purchasing from Trivium Test Prep! We're honored to help you prepare for your HSPT exam.

To show our appreciation, we're offering a **FREE** *HSPT Essential Test Tips* **Video by Trivium Test Prep**.* Our video includes 35 test preparation strategies that will make you successful on the HSPT. All we ask is that you email us your feedback and describe your experience with our product. Amazing, awful, or just so-so: we want to hear what you have to say!

To receive your **FREE** *HSPT Essential Test Tips* **Video**, please email us at 5star@ triviumtestprep.com. Include "Free 5 Star" in the subject line and the following information in your email:

1.   The title of the product you purchased.

2.   Your rating from 1 – 5 (with 5 being the best).

3.   Your feedback about the product, including how our materials helped you meet your goals and ways in which we can improve our products.

4.   Your full name and shipping address so we can send your **FREE** *HSPT Essential Test Tips* **Video**.

If you have any questions or concerns please feel free to contact us directly at 5star@ triviumtestprep.com.

Thank you!

– Trivium Test Prep Team

*To get access to the free video please email us at 5star@triviumtestprep.com, and please follow the instructions above.

HSPT
PREP BOOK
2024-2025:

700+ Practice Questions and Study Guide for the Catholic High School Placement Test

Jonathan Cox

Table of Contents

Introduction

Congratulations on taking the High School Placement Test (HSPT)! By choosing this book and getting prepared, you're taking an important step in your education and journey to high school.

This guide will give you a detailed overview of the HSPT so that you know exactly what to expect on test day. We'll walk you through all the concepts covered on the exams and give you the opportunity to test your knowledge with practice questions. Even if you're a little nervous about taking a major test, don't worry; we'll make sure you're more than ready!

What is the HSPT?

The High School Placement Test (HSPT) is the most common of the three major Catholic school entrance exams. This test was developed by the Scholastic Testing Service. It is used around the United States and Canada to determine an eighth-grade student's skill level and potential in reading, math, and verbal and quantitative reasoning.

What's on the HSPT?

There are five sections on the HSPT: Verbal Skills, Quantitative Skills, Reading, Mathematics, and Language Skills. The HSPT tests not only on reading, language, and mathematical knowledge, but also on verbal and quantitative reasoning abilities. This means you will be asked to determine relationships between words, analyze situations to determine if a statement is true or false, figure out associations between numbers, guess the next number in a series, and more.

What's on the HSPT?

Section	Topics	Number of Questions	Number of Minutes
Verbal Skills	reasoning with words, verbal aptitude, vocabulary skills	60 multiple choice • 17 verbal classification • 12 synonyms • 10 analogies • 12 logic • 9 antonyms	16
Quantitative Skills	reasoning with numbers and quantities	52 multiple choice • 25 sequence • 10 reasoning • 9 geometric comparison • 8 nongeometric comparison	30
Reading	identifying and understanding main ideas and supporting details, drawing inferences, vocabulary in context, author's purpose and tone	62 multiple choice • 40 comprehension • 22 vocabulary	25
Mathematics	numbers and operations, algebraic patterns, data analysis, probability, statistics, geometry, measurement	64 multiple choice • 33 numbers and numeration • 4 measurements • 15 geometry • 5 algebra • 7 statistics and probability	45
Language Skills	punctuation, spelling, capitalization, usage, grammar	60 multiple choice • 15 incorrect usage • 5 correct usage • 17 punctuation • 3 capitalization • 10 spelling • 10 composition	25
Total:		**298 multiple-choice questions**	**2 hours and 21 minutes (141 minutes)**

You will have two hours and twenty-one minutes (141 minutes), to complete the exam. All the questions are multiple choice, with four answer choices each. The questions are numbered consecutively.

How is the HSPT Scored?

You cannot pass or fail the HSPT. Instead, you will receive a score report with several pieces of information. You will receive two important scores on the HSPT: your Standard Score and your Cognitive Skills Quotient. On the HSPT, points are not deducted for incorrect answers, so you should always guess even if you don't know the answer to a question: you may get it right!

Your Standard Score (SS) is determined by finding your raw score, which is simply the number of questions you answered correctly on the test. That number is scaled to a score from 200 – 800. The more questions you answered correctly, the closer your SS will be to 800. You will also receive a SS for each subject: Verbal Skills, Quantitative Reasoning, Reading Comprehension, Math, and Language Skills.

Your Cognitive Skills Quotient (CSQ) is measured only from the Verbal Skills and Quantitative Reasoning questions. The CSQ is a measure of your reasoning and cognitive abilities. It measures how you think, not what you know. When the test writers work out the score for the CSQ, they also factor in your age. CSQ scores range from 70 – 130.

The HSPT also offers percentile ranking information. This means that you will be able to find out how your scores compare to the scores of other students who took the exam. On your score report, you will receive a National Percentile (NP) rank and a Local Percentile (LP) rank. Your NP rank indicates how your score compares to the scores of other test-takers around the country, while your LP rank compares your score to the scores of other test-takers in your state or region. Both of these ranks will appear on your score report.

Finally, your HSPT score report will include grade equivalents (GE). GE show how well you do in a subject compared to students in other grade levels. So if you score a 10 in reading comprehension, for example, you read eighth-grade level reading questions as well as a tenth grader would.

How is the HSPT Administered?

The HSPT is administered to eighth-grade students in December and January. When you register, you may choose the high schools that you would like to receive your scores.

To register for the HSPT, sign up online through your local archdiocese or call the admissions office of your preferred testing site. After you register, you will receive an email confirmation of registration.

If you need an accommodation for the HSPT, you must submit supporting documentation by early November.

HELPFUL HINT:
Remember, scores and percentile rankings are just a few tools schools use to determine admission. It is important to do as well as you can, and this book is designed to support you. Even if you are stronger in some subjects than others, the scoring on the HSPT will help schools understand your strengths.

About This Guide

This guide will help you to master the most important test topics and develop critical test-taking skills. We have built features into our books to prepare you for your tests and increase your score. Along with a detailed summary of the format, content, and scoring of the HSPT, we offer an in-depth overview of the content knowledge required to pass the exams. In the review you'll find sidebars that provide interesting information, highlight key concepts, and review content so that you can solidify your understanding of each exam's concepts. You can also test your knowledge with sample questions throughout the text and practice questions that reflect the content and format of the exams. We're pleased that you've chosen Accepted, Inc. to be a part of your educational journey!

CHAPTER ONE
VERBAL SKILLS

The questions in this section will be mixed together, meaning you won't see all the questions of one type grouped together. Instead, you'll have to move between all five question types as you work through this part of the test. To prepare, make sure you are comfortable with the types of questions and how to answer them so you can move quickly between test questions.

Word Structure

All the questions in the verbal skills section will test your ability to recognize words and their relationships to each other. Having a large vocabulary will help you do well on the exam, but you don't have to memorize long lists of words to succeed. Instead, you can use word structure to figure out the definition of many words.

Many words can be broken down into three main parts to help determine their meaning:

prefix – root – suffix

PREFIXES are elements added to the beginning of a word, and **SUFFIXES** are elements added to the end of the word; together they are known as **AFFIXES**. They carry assigned meanings and can be attached to a word to completely change the word's meaning or to enhance the word's original meaning.

Let's use the word *prefix* itself as an example: *fix* means to place something securely, and *pre–* means before. Therefore, *prefix* means to place something before or in front of.

Now let's look at a suffix: in the word *fearful*, fear is the root word. The suffix *–ful* means "full of." Thus, *fearful* means "being full of fear" or "being afraid."

The **ROOT** is what is left when you take away the prefixes and suffixes from a word. For example, in the word *unclear*, if you take away the prefix *un–*, you have the root *clear*.

Roots are not always recognizable words because they often come from Latin or Greek words, such as *nat*, a Latin root meaning born. The word *native*, which means a person born in a referenced place, comes from this root.

Table 1.1 shows some common affixes and root words.

TABLE 1.1. Common Affixes and Root Words		
PREFIXES	**ROOT WORDS**	**SUFFIXES**
a–, an–, im–, in–, un– (without, not) ab– (away from) ante– (before) anti– (against) bi–, di– (two) dis– (not, apart) ex– (out) micro– (small) omni– (all) over– (excessively) pre– (before) re– (again) sym– (with) uni– (single)	ambi (both) aud (to hear) bell (combative) bene (good) contra (against) dys (bad, impaired) equ (equal) morph (shape)	–able, –ible (capable) –ian (related to) –dom (quality) –en (made of) –ful (full of) –ine (nature of) –ment (act of)

Word structures won't be directly tested on the HSPT, but you can use this knowledge to answer questions throughout the verbal skills and reading sections.

Synonyms

When different words mean the same thing, they are **SYNONYMS**. For the HSPT synonym questions, you will be given a word and then asked to choose a word that has the most similar meaning.

Microscopic most nearly means

A) tiny.

B) unusual.

C) enormous.

D) hungry.

Choice A is the correct answer. To answer this question, study the given word. The prefix *micro–* means "small." The word *tiny* also means "small," meaning it is a synonym for "microscopic."

Having a large vocabulary will obviously help with these questions, but you can also use root words and affixes to determine the meaning of unfamiliar words. Check the prefixes: does the prefix on the word correspond to the meaning of any of the answer choices? If so, you have a hint that the words might have a related meaning.

If you can't figure out the exact meaning of the word, try to figure out its tone. Does it have a positive or negative prefix? Is it a word you've seen in a positive or negative context before? Then, try to choose a word that matches the tone of the word in the question.

TEACHING TIPS:
Help students develop their understanding of synonyms by having them make lists of synonyms for common words (either out loud or on paper). You can turn it into a game by seeing who can list the most synonyms for a particular word.

PRACTICE QUESTIONS

1. Advance most nearly means

   A) promote.

   B) abduct.

   C) destroy.

   D) review.

2. Rudimentary most nearly means

   A) impolite.

   B) basic.

   C) juvenile.

   D) innovative.

3. Impartial most nearly means

   A) fond.

   B) incomplete.

   C) objective.

   D) mathematical.

4. Prudent most nearly means
   A) sensible.
   B) inquisitive.
   C) terrified.
   D) modest.

5. Acrimonious most nearly means
   A) bitter.
   B) inedible.
   C) rotten.
   D) loud.

Antonyms

When two words have opposite meanings, they are **ANTONYMS**. In antonym questions, you'll be given a word and asked which of the answer choices has the *opposite* meaning.

ANTONYM QUESTION FORMAT   **9 QUESTIONS**

Subtle means the opposite of
   A) obvious
   B) rapid
   C) happy
   D) large

Choice A is correct. *Subtle* means "difficult to observe," so the opposite of *subtle* is obvious.

Like synonym questions, antonym questions are really just vocabulary questions. The stronger your vocabulary, the better you will do on these questions.

You can use your knowledge of word structure if you're not sure of a word. Check the prefixes. Does the prefix on the word correspond to the meaning of any of the answer choices? If so, you have a hint that the words might have a related meaning. But that's not always so: be sure to study the roots of words as well.

PRACTICE QUESTIONS

6. Sensible means the opposite of
   A) opaque.
   B) prohibited.
   C) necessary.
   D) irrational.

7. Superficial means the opposite of
   A) deep.
   B) forgetful.
   C) unhappy.
   D) small.

8. Retain means the opposite of
   A) excrete.
   B) fill.
   C) allow.
   D) steady.

9. Diminish means the opposite of
   A) identify.
   B) intensify.
   C) stop.
   D) consume.

10. Adhere means the opposite of
    A) exit.
    B) clean.
    C) reject.
    D) heal.

Verbal Analogies

An **ANALOGY** presents two sets of words or objects that share a relationship. The relationship is set up using the following format:

_____ is to _____ as _____ is to _____

Let's look at an example.

Bird is to flock as wolf is to pack

In this analogy, the first word is an individual animal, and the second word represents a group of those animals. A group of birds is a flock, and a group of wolves is a pack.

Solving analogies requires you to determine the relationship between the first two words, and then use that relationship to fill in the missing word:

Sail is to boat as fly is to_____

Here, the missing word is *plane:* you sail on a boat and fly on a plane.

Bark is to dog as meow is to

A) puppy.

B) veterinarian.

C) cat.

D) turtle.

Choice C is correct. Dogs bark; cats meow.

The pairs of words in the analogy can have many different relationships. Some of the more common relationships are described below.

In a **SYNONYM ANALOGY,** the two words in each pair are synonyms.

> Confusing is to puzzling as intelligent is to smart.

Confusing and *puzzling* are synonyms (have the same or similar meaning), and *intelligent* and *smart* are synonyms, too.

In an **ANTONYM ANALOGY,** the two words in each pair are antonyms.

> Ugly is to pretty as hungry is to full.

Ugly and *pretty* are antonyms (words with opposite meanings), and *hungry* and *full* are antonyms, too.

In an **ACTION ANALOGY,** each pair contains a noun (person, animal, or thing) and a verb that describes an action that person, animal, or thing commonly performs. For example:

> Horse is to gallops as runner is to sprints.

A horse gallops, just as a runner sprints.

In a **FUNCTION ANALOGY,** each pair contains a noun and a verb that describes that person's, animal's, or thing's function (what it is supposed to do).

> Microphone is to amplify as wheelbarrow is to transport.

A microphone's function is to amplify sound, just as a wheelbarrow's function is to transport things.

TEACHING TIPS:
Encourage your student to explain why they chose a particular answer choice as you complete practice items. This will enable you to correct misconceptions and to understand the connections the student is making.

The word pair in an analogy can also have a relationship of **SIZE, DEGREE,** or **AMOUNT.** Here is an example of a degree analogy that shows increasing intensity:

> Sad is to despondent as happy is to ecstatic.

Someone who is *extremely* sad feels despondent; someone who is *extremely* happy feels ecstatic.

The example below also shows a relationship of degree/amount:

> Whispers is to bellows as drips is to gushes.

When a man whispers he speaks very softly, and when he bellows, he shouts very loudly. When a tap drips, a tiny amount of water comes out, and when a tap gushes, a large amount of water comes out.

In a **PART-TO-WHOLE ANALOGY,** the first word forms a part of the object described by the second word (or vice versa).

> Step is to staircase as key is to keyboard.

A step is one part of a staircase, just as a key is one part of a keyboard.

PRACTICE QUESTIONS

11. Durable is to sturdy as arid is to
    A) dry.
    B) thirst.
    C) resilient.
    D) flimsy.

12. Wheel is to car as wing is to
    A) road.
    B) runway.
    C) boat.
    D) airplane.

13. Scissors are to cut as tape is to
    A) sticky.
    B) transparent.
    C) device.
    D) attach.

14. Famished is to hungry as drenched is to
    A) damp.
    B) ravenous.
    C) tired.
    D) unsure.

15. Exhausted is to yawn as hot is to
    A) freeze.
    B) sweat.
    C) blink.
    D) shiver.

Logic

The HSPT logic questions will give you three statements. The first two statements will be true, and you will have to determine if the third statement is true, false, or uncertain.

LOGIC QUESTIONS FORMAT   **12 QUESTIONS**

Kenneth jumps higher than Shawn. Ronnie jumps higher than Kenneth. Shawn jumps higher than Ronnie.

If the first two statements are true, the third statement is

     A)   true.

     B)   false.

     C)   uncertain.

Choice B (false) is correct. Shawn does not jump higher than Ronnie.

There's no one way to solve logic questions. Because the questions often involve placing objects in order, it can be helpful to draw lists or diagrams. Let's use the question above as an example. Who jumps the highest? Make a list of the ordered names starting with the highest jumper. From sentence 1, we know that Kenneth jumps higher than Shawn:

> Kenneth
> Shawn

From sentence 2, we know that Ronnie jumps higher than Kenneth:

> Ronnie
> Kenneth

Remember the facts from sentence 1: "Kenneth jumps higher than Shawn." So we can order the boys like this:

> Ronnie: highest jumper
> Kenneth: second-highest jumper
> Shawn: third-highest jumper

Making this list shows that Ronnie jumps higher than both Kenneth *and* Shawn.

TEACHING TIPS:
Provide lots of positive reinforcement. These questions are different from the ones most students see in school, and students may take some time to figure out what they're being asked to do.

With this information, let's return to sentence 3, which states, "Shawn jumps higher than Ronnie." Looking at our list, we can see that Shawn doesn't jump higher than anyone: he is the third-highest jumper. That means that sentence 3 must be **FALSE**, making B the correct choice.

PRACTICE QUESTIONS

16. Jenny is older than Jason. Clyde is older than Jenny. Jason is older than Clyde. If the first two statements are true, the third statement is

    A) true.

    B) false.

    C) uncertain.

17. Mangoes cost more than oranges. Mangoes cost less than cantaloupes. Cantaloupes cost more than both oranges and mangoes. If the first two statements are true, the third statement is

    A) true.

    B) false.

    C) uncertain.

18. All the bushes in the park are flowering bushes. Some of the bushes in the park are lilacs. All lilacs in the park are flowering bushes. If the first two statements are true, the third statement is

    A) true.

    B) false.

    C) uncertain.

19. Moana runs faster than Tina. Nora runs faster than Moana. Tina runs faster than Nora. If the first two statements are true, the third statement is

    A) true.

    B) false.

    C) uncertain.

20. All girls like to run. Some girls like to swim. Some girls like to run and swim. If the first two statements are true, the third statement is

    A) true.

    B) false.

    C) uncertain.

Verbal Classifications

The verbal classification questions on the HSPT will gauge your knowledge of common vocabulary words and your understanding of word relationships. You will be given a list of four words, and you will have to choose the word that does NOT belong.

VERBAL CLASSIFICATIONS QUESTION FORMAT   17 QUESTIONS

Which word does NOT belong with the others?

    A) truck

    B) bus

    C) train

    D) bicycle

Choice D is correct. A bicycle is the only vehicle that is self-propelled; all the others have engines.

TEACHING TIPS:
Have your student cover up the answer they have chosen with a pencil, leaving only the similar words in view. Then have them state the relationship between the words out loud to reinforce the relationship.

You can use many of the techniques discussed above to answer verbal classification questions, including analyzing word structure and looking for relationships between words. The link between the answer choices will be different in each question, but some general guidelines are given here.

▶ If you aren't sure what a word means, look for a word that is different in tone from the others.

▶ If the answer choices are objects, ask yourself how those objects are used. Do they perform similar functions? Are they used in the same way?

▶ If the answer choices are places, ask yourself what those places are usually used for.

▶ Look for a quality (size, color, material) that three of the items share.

▶ Look for words that are a different part of speech (e.g., noun, verb) than the other choices.

PRACTICE QUESTIONS

21. Which word does NOT belong with the others?

A) bag

B) box

C) carton

D) jar

22. Which word does NOT belong with the others?

A) flour

B) milk

C) salt

D) sugar

23. Which word does NOT belong with the others?

A) cup

B) bottle

C) plastic

D) mug

24. Which word does NOT belong with the others?

A) calendar

B) sundial

C) clock

D) watch

25. Which word does NOT belong with the others?

A) distressed

B) worried

C) relaxed

D) stressed

Answer Key

1. **A)** *Advance* and *promote* both mean "to move something or someone forward." Note the prefix *ad–* in "advance." The prefix *ad–* means "toward." Likewise, the prefix *pro–* in "promote" means forward. That's a clue that the words are related. To advance something is to promote it, to push it forward.

2. **B)** *Rudimentary* means "basic or elementary." For example, familiarity with the alphabet is a rudimentary reading skill that children learn at a young age.

3. **C)** The prefix *im–* means "not," and the root word *partial* means "biased," so an impartial jury is one whose members are not biased and are therefore able to evaluate evidence in an objective, unprejudiced manner.

4. **A)** *Prudent* means "wise or judicious." For example, a prudent decision is a wise, practical one.

5. **A)** The root word *ācer* in a*crid*, *acrimony*, and *acrimonious* means "sharp and sour," and the suffix *–ous* means "possessing" or "full of." So, an acrimonious relationship is full of bitterness.

6. **D)** *Sensible* means having "good sense or reason." The opposite of sensible is irrational, which means "not following good reasoning."

7. **A)** *Superficial* means "shallow" or "on the surface," so the opposite of *superficial* is *deep*.

8. **A)** *Retain* means "to hold" or "to keep in possession." The opposite of *retain* is *excrete*, which means "to pass from the body."

9. **B)** *Diminish* means "become less in amount or intensity." The opposite of *diminish* is *intensify*, which means "to increase in intensity."

10. **C)** *Adhere* means "to follow devotedly," so the opposite of *adhere* is *reject*.

11. **A)** *Durable* is a synonym for *sturdy*; *arid* is a synonym for *dry*.

12. **D)** A *wheel* is one part of a car; a *wing* is one part of an *airplane*.

13. **D)** *Scissors* are used to *cut* materials. *Tape* is used to *attach* one thing to another.

14. **A)** Someone who is *famished* is extremely *hungry*; something that is *drenched* is extremely *damp*.

15. **B)** When you are *exhausted*, you *yawn*; when you are *hot*, you *sweat*.

16. **B)** If Clyde is older than Jenny—who is older than Jason—then Jason must be *younger* than both Clyde and Jenny.

17. **A)** Oranges are least expensive, followed by mangoes and finally cantaloupes.

18. **A)** If all of the bushes in the park have flowers and lilacs are in the park, then lilacs must be flowering bushes.

19. **B)** If Nora runs faster than Moana—who runs faster than Tina—then Nora runs faster than Tina as well.

20. **C)** It is not clear from the given statements whether there is overlap between girls who like to run and girls who like to swim.

21. **D)** A jar is made of glass; all the others are made from paper.

22. **B)** While all items are ingredients for cooking/baking, milk is the only liquid.

23. **C)** Plastic is a material; all the others are containers that hold liquids.

24. **A)** A calendar tells the days/months of the year; all the others tell smaller increments of time.

25. **C)** *Relaxed* means "at ease or peaceful," and the other four words describe the feeling of being upset.

CHAPTER TWO
Reading

On the HSPT reading comprehension section, you will be asked to read short passages and then answer questions about them. Passages will be both informational and literary. The questions will address the following general topics:

▶ **IDEAS AND DETAILS**

  ▷ Main idea: what is the overall message of the passage?

  ▷ Supporting details: how does the passage support the main idea?

  ▷ Inferences: what conclusions can you draw from the passage?

▶ **CRAFT AND STRUCTURE**

  ▷ Author's purpose: why did the author write the passage?

  ▷ Vocabulary: what do words in the passage mean?

▶ **INTEGRATION OF IDEAS**

  ▷ Organization: how is the passage organized?

  ▷ Reasoning: what is a fact and what is an opinion?

▶ **LITERARY ELEMENTS AND TECHNIQUES**

  ▷ Tone and style: how does the writer use language?

READING COMPREHENSION QUESTION FORMAT   40 QUESTIONS

Read the passage carefully and choose the best answer to each question.

It is negligence for an adult to be unable to swim. A person who can't swim is a danger to himself and to others. Every man, woman, and child should learn. Children as young as four can learn: no one is too young, and no one is too old. If you haven't learned yet, there is still time.

The primary purpose of the passage is to

    A) encourage the reader to learn to swim.

    B) explain how people who cannot swim are a danger to others.

    C) inform the reader that swimming is easy.

    D) argue that people who cannot swim should be punished.

Choice A is correct. The author argues that "every man, woman, and child should learn" to swim and addresses the reader directly by saying "there is still time" for them to learn to swim.

The reading comprehension section also includes vocabulary questions that will be similar to the synonym questions you will see in the verbal skills section.

The questions will present a phrase with an underlined word. You will need to identify the answer choice that is most similar to the underlined word. You can use the skills you practiced in the verbal skills section to answer these questions, such as learning word roots, matching the tone of the underlined word, and memorizing word lists to build your vocabulary. (See Chapter 1 "Verbal Skills" for more details.)

VOCABULARY QUESTION FORMAT   **22 QUESTIONS**

Choose the word that means the same or about the same as the underlined word.

a <u>futile</u> quest

    A) useful

    B) effective

    C) pointless

    D) special

Choice C is correct. The adjective "futile" means something that is useless or pointless.

Ideas and Details
THE MAIN IDEA

The **MAIN IDEA** of a text is the argument the author is trying to make about a particular **TOPIC**. Every sentence in a passage should support or address the main idea in some way.

The main idea is the author making an argument, just like you might do in conversation. Imagine you are hungry for dinner, and you want pizza. You need to talk to your family and convince them to eat pizza for dinner. The **TOPIC** of your conversation is dinner, and the **MAIN IDEA** is that the family should eat pizza for dinner.

Let's look at an example passage to see how to identify the topic and main idea.

Babe Didrikson Zaharias, one of the most decorated female athletes of the twentieth century, is an inspiration for everyone. Born in 1911 in Beaumont, Texas, Zaharias lived in a time when women were considered second class to men, but she never let that stop her from becoming a champion. Zaharias was one of seven children in a poor immigrant family and was competitive from an early age. As a child she excelled at most things she tried, especially sports, which continued into high school and beyond. After high school, Zaharias played amateur basketball for two years and soon after began training in track and field. Zaharias represented the United States in the 1932 Los Angeles Olympics. Even though women were only allowed to enter three events, she won two gold medals and one silver in track and field events.

The topic of this paragraph is obviously Babe Zaharias—the whole passage describes events from her life. To figure out the main idea, consider what the writer is saying about Zaharias. The passage describes her life but focuses mostly on her accomplishments and the difficulties she overcame. The writer is saying that Zaharias is someone who should be admired for her determination and skill. That is the main idea and what unites all the information in the paragraph.

The topic, and sometimes the main idea of a paragraph, is introduced in the **TOPIC SENTENCE**. The topic sentence usually appears early in a passage. The first sentence in the example paragraph above about Babe Zaharias states the topic and main idea: "Babe Didrikson Zaharias, one of the most decorated female athletes of the twentieth century, is an inspiration for everyone."

There may also be a **SUMMARY SENTENCE** at the end of a passage. As its name suggests, this sentence sums up the passage, often by restating the main idea and the author's key evidence supporting it.

TEACHING TIPS:

Use the "I say, we say, you say" method to help reinforce concepts. After you model the way to solve the problem, have the student solve the problem in unison with you. Then, have the student solve the problem on their own.

PRACTICE QUESTION

Read the passage carefully and choose the best answer to each question.

From far away it's easy to imagine the surface of our solar system's planets as enigmas—how could we ever know what those far-flung planets really look like? It turns out, however, that scientists have a number of tools that allow them to examine many planets' surfaces. The topography of Venus, for example, has been explored by several space probes, including the Russian Venera landers and NASA's Magellan orbiter.

In addition to these long-range probes, NASA has also used its series of "great observatories" to study distant planets. These four massively powerful orbiting telescopes are the famous Hubble Space Telescope, the Compton Gamma Ray Observatory, the Chandra X-Ray Observatory, and the Spitzer Space Telescope.

Such powerful telescopes aren't just found in space: NASA uses Earth-based telescopes as well. Scientists at the National Radio Astronomy Observatory in

Charlottesville, Virginia, have spent decades using radio imaging to build an incredibly detailed portrait of Venus's surface.

1. Which of the following sentences best describes the main idea of the passage?

   A) It's impossible to know what the surfaces of other planets are really like.

   B) Telescopes are an important tool for scientists studying planets in our solar system.

   C) Venus's surface has many of the same features as Earth's.

   D) Scientists use a variety of advanced technologies to study the surfaces of other planets.

Supporting Details

SUPPORTING DETAILS reinforce the author's main idea. Let's go back to the conversation about what to eat for dinner. If you want to convince your family to order pizza, you might present a number of supporting details: everybody in the family likes pizza, it's easy to clean up, and so on. The authors of the reading comprehension passages will similarly present details that support their main idea.

Let's look again at the passage about athlete Babe Zaharias.

> Babe Didrikson Zaharias, one of the most decorated female athletes of the twentieth century, is an inspiration for everyone. Born in 1911 in Beaumont, Texas, Zaharias lived in a time when women were considered second class to men, but she never let that stop her from becoming a champion. Babe was one of seven children in a poor immigrant family and was competitive from an early age. As a child she excelled at most things she tried, especially sports, which continued into high school and beyond. After high school, Babe played amateur basketball for two years and soon after began training in track and field. Zaharias represented the United States in the 1932 Los Angeles Olympics. Even though women were only allowed to enter three events, she won two gold medals and one silver in track and field events.

Remember that the main idea of the passage is that Zaharias is someone to admire—an idea introduced in the opening sentence. The remainder of the paragraph provides ideas or details that support this assertion. These details include the circumstances of her childhood, her childhood success at sports, and the medals she won at the Olympics.

When looking for supporting details, be alert for signal words. These signal words tell you that the author is about to introduce a supporting detail. Common **SIGNAL WORDS** include:

▶ for example

▶ specifically

- in addition
- furthermore
- for instance
- others
- in particular
- some

PRACTICE QUESTION

Read the passage carefully and choose the best answer to each question.

Exercise is critical for healthy development in children. Today in the United States, there is an epidemic of poor childhood health; many of these children will face further illnesses in adulthood that are due to poor diet and lack of exercise now. This is a problem for all Americans, especially with the rising cost of health care.

It is vital that school systems and parents encourage children to engage in a minimum of thirty minutes of cardiovascular exercise each day, mildly increasing their heart rate for a sustained period. This is proven to decrease the likelihood of developmental diabetes, obesity, and a multitude of other health problems. Also, children need a proper diet, rich in fruits and vegetables, so they can develop physically and learn healthy eating habits early on.

2. The author states that many adulthood illnesses are the result of
   A) a diet rich in fruits and vegetables.
   B) poor diet and lack of exercise in childhood.
   C) excessive cardiovascular exercise during childhood.
   D) children not being taken to the doctor.

Making Inferences

In addition to understanding the main idea and factual content of a passage, you will also be asked to make inferences about the passage. An **INFERENCE** is a conclusion that is not directly stated in the passage but is based on information found there. In an excerpt from a fictional work, for example, you might be asked to anticipate what the character would do next. In a nonfiction passage, you might be asked which statement the author of the passage would agree with.

To answer such questions, you need a solid understanding of the topic and main idea of the passage. Armed with this information, you can figure out which of the answer choices best fits the criteria (or, alternatively, which do not). For example, if the author of the passage is advocating for safer working conditions in factories, any details that could be added to the passage should support that idea. You might add sentences that contain information about the number of accidents that occur in factories or that outline a new plan for fire safety.

PRACTICE QUESTION

Read the passage carefully and choose the best answer to each question.

Alfie closed his eyes and took several deep breaths. He was trying to ignore the sounds of the crowd, but even he had to admit that it was hard not to notice the tension in the stadium. He could feel 50,000 sets of eyes burning through his skin—this crowd expected perfection from him. He took another breath and opened his eyes, setting his sights on the soccer ball resting peacefully in the grass. One shot, just one last shot, between his team and the championship. He didn't look up at the goalie, who was jumping nervously on the goal line just a few yards away. Afterward, he would swear he didn't remember anything between the referee's whistle and the thunderous roar of the crowd.

3. Which of the following conclusions is best supported by the passage?
    A) Alfie passed out on the field and was unable to take the shot.
    B) The goalie blocked Alfie's shot.
    C) Alfie scored the goal and won his team the championship.
    D) The referee declared the game a tie.

TEACHING TIPS:
Ask your student to come up with real life examples of narrative, persuasive, informational, and instructional writing. Then ask them to describe how they decided what category the writing belonged in.

Craft and Structure
AUTHOR'S PURPOSE

Authors typically write with a purpose. Sometimes referred to as "intention," an author's purpose lets us know why the author is writing and what he or she would like to accomplish. There are many reasons an author might write, but these reasons generally fall into four categories: narrative, persuasive, informational, or instructive.

▶ **NARRATIVE** writing tells a story to entertain. The writing may include vivid characters, exciting plot twists, or beautiful, figurative language.

▶ **PERSUASIVE** writing attempts to persuade the reader to accept an idea. The passage may present an argument or contain convincing examples that support the author's point of view.

▶ **INFORMATIONAL** writing describes something, such as a person, place, thing, or event. It is characterized by detailed descriptions and a lack of persuasive elements (meaning it is written to inform the reader, not persuade them).

▶ **INSTRUCTIONAL** writing explains a process or procedure. It may include step-by-step instructions or present information in a sequence.

PRACTICE QUESTION

Read the passage carefully and choose the best answer to each question.

One of my summer reading books was *Mockingjay*. I was captivated by the adventures of the main character and the complicated plot of the book. However, I would argue that the ending didn't reflect the excitement of the story. Given what a powerful personality the main character has, I felt like the ending didn't do her justice.

4. Which of the following best captures the author's purpose?

A) explain the plot of the novel *Mockingjay*

B) persuade the reader that the ending of *Mockingjay* is inferior

C) list the novels she read during the summer

D) explain why the ending of a novel is important

Vocabulary

TEACHING TIPS:

Cover the underlined word and have your student suggest words that would fit correctly in the blank. Then, have them look at the answers to see if any of the choices match their suggestions.

Reading questions may also ask you to figure out the meanings of words within passages. You may have never encountered some of these words before the test, but you can often use the same types of context clues you learned in the Verbal Reasoning Skills chapter to find their meaning.

RESTATEMENT CLUES state the definition of the word in the sentence. The definition is often set apart from the rest of the sentence by a comma, parentheses, or a colon.

Teachers often prefer teaching students with intrinsic motivation: these students have an internal desire to learn.
The meaning of *intrinsic* is restated as *internal*.

CONTRAST CLUES include the opposite meaning of a word. Words like *but, on the other hand*, and *however* are tip-offs that a sentence contains a contrast clue.

Janet was destitute after she lost her job, but her wealthy sister helped her get back on her feet.
Destitute is contrasted with *wealthy*, so the definition of destitute is "poor."

POSITIVE/NEGATIVE CLUES tell you whether a word has a positive or negative meaning.

The film was lauded by critics as stunning, and it was nominated for several awards.
The positive descriptions *stunning* and *nominated* for *several awards* suggest that *lauded* has a positive meaning.

PRACTICE QUESTION

Read the passage carefully and choose the best answer to each question.

In December of 1944 Germany launched its last major offensive campaign of World War II, pushing through the dense forests of the Ardennes region of Belgium, France, and Luxembourg. The attack, designed to block the Allies from the Belgian port of Antwerp and to split their lines, caught the Allied forces by surprise. Due to troop positioning, the Americans bore the brunt of the attack, incurring 100,000 deaths, the highest number of casualties of any battle during the war. However, after a month of grueling fighting in the bitter cold, a lack of fuel and a masterful American military strategy resulted in an Allied victory that sealed Germany's fate.

5. In the last sentence, the word *grueling* most nearly means
   A) exhausting.
   B) expensive.
   C) intermittent.
   D) ineffective.

Integration of Ideas
TEXT ORGANIZATION

Authors can organize their writing in many different ways. These distinct organizational patterns, referred to as **TEXT STRUCTURE**, use the logical relationships between ideas to improve the readability and coherence of a text. The most common ways passages are organized include:

▶ **PROBLEM-SOLUTION**: the author outlines a problem and then discusses a solution.

▶ **COMPARISON-CONTRAST**: the author presents two situations and then discusses the similarities and differences.

▶ **CAUSE-EFFECT**: the author recounts an action and then discusses the resulting effects.

▶ **DESCRIPTIVE**: the author describes an idea, object, person, or other item in detail.

PRACTICE QUESTION

Read the passage carefully and choose the best answer to each question.

The issue of public transportation has begun to haunt the fast-growing cities of the southern United States. Unlike their northern counterparts, cities like Atlanta, Dallas, and Houston have long promoted growth out and not up. These cities are full of sprawling suburbs and single-family homes, not densely concentrated skyscrapers and apartment buildings. What to do, then, when all those suburbanites need to get downtown for work? For a long time it seemed highways were the answer: twenty-lane–wide expanses of concrete that would allow commuters to move from home to work and back again. But these modern miracles have become time-sucking, pollution-spewing nightmares. The residents of these cities may not like it, but it's time for them to turn toward public transport like trains and buses if they want their cities to remain livable.

6. The organization of this passage can best be described as

   A) a comparison of two similar ideas.

   B) a description of a place.

   C) a discussion of several effects all related to the same cause.

   D) a discussion of a problem followed by a suggested solution.

Reasoning

On reading passages, you might be asked to identify a statement in a passage as either a fact or an opinion, so you'll need to know the difference between the two.

A **FACT** is a statement or thought that can be proven to be true. The statement "Wednesday comes after Tuesday" is a fact—you can point to a calendar to prove it.

In contrast, an **OPINION** is an assumption that is not based in fact and cannot be proven to be true. The assertion "television is more entertaining than feature films" is an opinion—people will disagree on this, and there's no reference you can use to prove or disprove it.

PRACTICE QUESTION

Read the passage carefully and choose the best answer to each question.

Exercise is critical for healthy development in children. Today in the United States, there is an epidemic of poor childhood health; many of these children will face further illnesses in adulthood that are due to poor diet and lack of exercise now. This is a problem for all Americans, especially with the rising cost of health care.

It is vital that school systems and parents encourage children to engage in a minimum of thirty minutes of cardiovascular exercise each day, mildly increasing their heart rate for a sustained period. This is proven to decrease the likelihood of developmental diabetes, obesity, and a multitude of other health problems. Also, children need a proper diet, rich in fruits and vegetables, so they can develop physically and learn healthy eating habits early on.

7. Which of the following is a fact in the passage, not an opinion?

   A) Fruits and vegetables are the best way to help children be healthy.

   B) Children today are lazier than they were in previous generations.

   C) The risk of diabetes in children is reduced by physical activity.

   D) Children should engage in thirty minutes of exercise a day.

Literary Elements and Techniques
TONE AND POINT OF VIEW

POINT OF VIEW is the perspective the author writes from. A reading passage may be in the first, second, or third person.

▶ **FIRST PERSON**: a narrative is described from the writer's point of view (uses *I, me, we, us*).

▶ **SECOND PERSON**: a narrative addressing the reader directly as you; it is rarely used.

▶ **THIRD PERSON**: a narrative is described by somebody who isn't the writer (uses *he, she, they, them*).

The **TONE** of a passage describes the author's attitude toward the topic. The **MOOD** is the pervasive feeling or atmosphere in a passage that provokes specific emotions in the reader. Put simply, tone is how the author feels about the topic, and mood is how the reader feels about the text. In general, mood and tone can be categorized as positive, neutral, or negative.

TABLE 2.1. Words to Describe Tone and Mood		
POSITIVE	**NEUTRAL**	**NEGATIVE**
admiring	casual	angry
approving	detached	annoyed
celebratory	formal	belligerent
encouraging	impartial	bitter
excited	informal	condescending
funny	objective	confused
hopeful	questioning	cynical
humorous	unconcerned	depressed
optimistic		disrespectful
playful		fearful
proud		gloomy
respectful		melancholy
sentimental		pessimistic
silly		skeptical
sympathetic		unsympathetic

Diction and Figurative Language

DICTION, or word choice, helps determine mood and tone in a passage. Many readers make the mistake of using the author's ideas alone to determine tone; a much better practice is to look at specific words and try to identify a pattern in the emotion they evoke. Does the writer choose positive words like *ambitious* and *confident*, which might be described as admiring? Or does she describe those concepts with negative words like *greedy* and *overbearing*, which might be described as disapproving?

When looking at tone, it's important to examine not just the dictionary definition of words. Many authors use **FIGURATIVE LANGUAGE**, which is the use of a word to imply something other than the word's literal definition. Common types of figurative language include:

▶ **SIMILE** and **METAPHOR**: comparing two things (e.g., *I felt like a butterfly when I got a new haircut*)

▶ **HYPERBOLE**: exaggeration (e.g., *I'm so tired I could sleep for three days*)

▶ **VERBAL IRONY**: when the narrator says something that is the opposite of what he or she means

▶ **SITUATIONAL IRONY**: when something happens that is the opposite of what the reader expected

▶ **PERSONIFICATION**: when human characteristics are attributed to objects or animals

---

PRACTICE QUESTION

Read the passage carefully and choose the best answer to each question.

East River High School has released its graduation summary for the class of 2016. Out of a total of 558 senior students, 525 (94 percent) successfully completed their degree program and graduated. Of these, 402 (representing 72 percent of the total class) went on to attend a two- or four-year college or university. According to the data, the majority of East River High School's college-attending graduates chose a large, public institution.

8. Which of the following best describes the tone of the passage?
   A) professional
   B) casual
   C) concerned
   D) congratulatory

Putting It All Together

The passage below will help you practice answering multiple reading questions from a single, long passage. Read the passage carefully and choose the best answer to each question.

PRACTICE QUESTION

Have you ever wondered why exactly we feel pain when we get hurt? Or why some patients feel phantom pain even in the absence of a real trauma or damage? Pain is a highly sophisticated biological mechanism, one that is often downplayed or misinterpreted. Pain is much more than a measure of tissue damage—it is a complex neurological chain reaction that sends sensory data to the brain.

Pain is not produced by the toe you stubbed; rather, it is produced once the information about the "painful" incident reaches the brain. The brain analyzes the sensory signals emanating from the toe you stubbed, but the toe itself is not producing the sensation of pain.

In most cases, the brain offers accurate interpretations of the sensory data that is sent to it via the neurological processes in the body. If you hold your hand too close to a fire, for instance, the brain triggers pain that causes you to jerk your hand away, preventing further damage.

Phantom pain, most commonly associated with the amputation or loss of a limb, on the other hand, is triggered even in the absence of any injury. One possible explanation is that the spinal cord is still processing sensations from that area.

The science of pain management is complex and still poorly understood. However, anesthetics or anti-inflammatory medications can reduce or relieve pain by disrupting the neurological pathways that produce it. The absence of pain, however, is a double-edged sword—sometimes pain is the only clue to an underlying injury or disease. Likewise, an injury or disease can dull or eliminate pain, making it impossible to sense when something is actually wrong.

9. It can be inferred from the passage that people who cannot feel pain
- **A)** have damaged spinal cords.
- **B)** are more likely to injure themselves.
- **C)** will need to take anti-inflammatory medications.
- **D)** may still experience phantom pain.

10. In the fourth paragraph "phantom pain" refers to pain that is
- **A)** imaginary.
- **B)** mild.
- **C)** associated with amputated limbs.
- **D)** caused by injury to hands and feet.

11. Which sentence best summarizes the passage's main idea?
- **A)** Many people wonder why people feel phantom pain.
- **B)** Pain is a complicated biological process, one that many people misjudge or do not understand.
- **C)** When you stub your toe, your brain analyzes the sensory signals coming from your injury.
- **D)** Anti-inflammatory medications can lessen or ease pain by affecting neurological processes.

12. According to the passage, what is true of phantom pain?

A) It can be controlled with anesthetics or anti-inflammatory medications.

B) Biologists do not know what causes this type of pain.

C) It occurs because the body remembers how painful it felt when a limb was severely injured.

D) It may happen because the spinal cord is still processing sensations from an amputated limb.

13. In the last paragraph, "a double-edged sword" means that the absence of pain can be

A) positive or negative.

B) mild or unbearable.

C) caused by knife wounds.

D) harder to endure than pain.

Answer Key

1. **D)** Choice A can be eliminated because it directly contradicts the rest of the passage. Choices B and C can also be eliminated because they state only specific details from the passage. While both choices contain details from the passage, neither is general enough to encompass the passage as a whole. Only Choice D provides an assertion that is both backed up by the passage's content and general enough to cover the entire passage.

2. **B)** The authors states that "children will face further illnesses in adulthood that are due to poor diet and lack of exercise." Choice A is incorrect because the author states that children should eat a diet rich in fruits and vegetables to prevent illness. Similarly, Choice C is wrong because the author is promoting cardiovascular exercise as healthy. The passage does not mention taking children to doctors.

3. **C)** The crowd's support for Alfie and their collective roar after the shot implies that Alfie scored the goal and won the championship.

4. **B)** The purpose of the passage is to persuade the reader of the author's opinion of the novel *Mockingjay*, specifically that the ending did not do the main character justice. The passage's use of the verb "argue" tells us that the author is presenting a case to the reader. The passage follows this statement with evidence—that the main character had a powerful personality.

5. **A)** The context implies that the fighting was intense and tiring. The author describes the fight as lasting "a month" in the "bitter cold."

6. **D)** Choice C is wrong because the author provides no root cause or a list of effects. Choices A and B are tricky because the passage contains structures similar to those described above. For example, it compares two things (cities in the North and South) and describes a place (a sprawling city). However, if you look at the overall organization of the passage, you can see that it starts by presenting a problem (transportation) and then suggests a solution (trains and buses), making Choice D the only option that encompasses the entire passage.

7. **C)** This sentence is a simple fact stated by the author. According to the passage, exercise "is proven to decrease the likelihood of developmental diabetes, obesity, and a multitude of other health problems."

8. **A)** The passage is written in a neutral, professional tone. It does not include any informal, emotional, or first-person language.

9. **B)** In the final paragraph, the author states that a lack of pain can make it "impossible to sense when something is actually wrong," implying that people without pain will not know when they have an injury.

10. **C)** In the fourth paragraph, the author writes that phantom pain is "most commonly associated with the amputation or loss of a limb."

11. **B)** The passage is mainly about the fact that pain is a complicated process. The other sentences provide details from the passage.

12. **D)** The author writes, "Phantom pain [may be caused when] the spinal cord [continues to process] sensations from that area."

13. **A)** In the last paragraph, the author writes, "The absence of pain ... is a double-edged sword—sometimes pain is the only clue to an underlying injury or disease. Likewise, an injury or disease can dull or eliminate pain, making it impossible to sense when something is actually wrong." Readers can infer that the author is using the metaphor of a double-edged sword to show that the absence of pain is not always positive.

CHAPTER THREE
Language Skills

THE HSPT LANGUAGE SKILLS SECTION TESTS WILL INCLUDE QUESTIONS ON THE FOLLOWING TOPICS:

1. Usage (rules of grammar)
2. Punctuation and Capitalization
3. Spelling
4. Composition

Most of the questions on this section will ask you to identify a sentence with an error. If there is no error, choose "No mistakes." You may be asked to find a specific type of error, such as spelling. In other questions, you will not be told which type of error to look for.

USAGE, PUNCTUATION, CAPITALIZATION, AND SPELLING QUESTION FORMAT   50 QUESTIONS

Find the sentence that has an error in usage, punctuation, capitalization, or spelling. If there is no error, choose D) No mistakes.

A) My dad will bring their van to pick us up.

B) The university is having its tenth fundraiser tonight.

C) Alicia bought herself a big lunch today.

D) No mistakes

Choice A is the correct answer. The singular subject "dad" does not agree with the plural pronoun "their." The sentence should be "My dad will bring <u>his</u> van to pick us up."

For the composition questions, you will be tested on how to construct sentences and paragraphs. For example, you may be asked to choose a word that correctly connects two sentences or to choose which answer choice is written most clearly. Questions may also ask about the order of sentences in a short paragraph.

Choose the best work to join the thoughts together.

I can't go with you to the meeting tonight _____ I have too much work to complete for class.

- **A)** yet
- **B)** nor
- **C)** because
- **D)** although

Choice C is the correct answer. The conjunction *because* correctly connects the opening independent clause "I can't go with you to the meeting tonight" to the dependent clause "because I have too much work to complete for class." It describes a cause-and-effect relationship between the two clauses.

The HSPT will test your understanding of the basic rules of grammar. The first step in getting ready for the test is to review the parts of speech and the rules that accompany them. The good news is that you have been using these rules since you first began to speak. Even if you do not know a lot of the technical terms, many of these rules will be familiar to you. Some of the topics you might see include:

- ▶ matching pronouns with their antecedents
- ▶ matching verbs with their subjects
- ▶ ensuring that verbs are in the correct tense
- ▶ spelling irregular, hyphenated, and commonly misspelled words
- ▶ using correct capitalization
- ▶ distinguishing between types of sentences
- ▶ correcting sentence structure

Verbs

A **VERB** is the action of a sentence: it describes what the subject of the sentence is or is doing. Verbs must match the subject of the sentence in person and number.

PERSON describes the relationship of the speaker to the subject of the sentence.

- ▶ first (I, we)
- ▶ second (you)
- ▶ third (he, she, it, they).

NUMBER refers to whether the subject of the sentence is singular or plural. Verbs are conjugated to match the person and number of the subject.

TABLE 3.1. Conjugating Verbs for Person		
PERSON	**SINGULAR**	**PLURAL**
First	I jump	we jump
Second	you jump	you jump
Third	he/she/it jumps	they jump

> Wrong: The cat chase the ball while the dogs runs in the yard.
> Correct: The cat chases the ball while the dogs run in the yard.

Cat is singular, so it takes a singular verb which confusingly ends with an *s*; dogs is plural, so it needs a plural verb.

> Wrong: The cars that had been recalled by the manufacturer was returned within a few months.
> Correct: The cars that had been recalled by the manufacturer were returned within a few months.

Sometimes, the subject and verb are separated by clauses or phrases. Here, the subject cars is separated from the verb by the relatively long phrase "that had been recalled by the manufacturer," making it more difficult to determine how to correctly conjugate the verb.

> Correct: The doctor and nurse work in the hospital.
> Correct: Neither the nurse nor her boss was scheduled to take a vacation.
> Correct: Either the patient or her parents need to sign the release forms.

When the subject contains two or more nouns connected by *and*, that subject becomes plural and requires a plural verb. Singular subjects joined by *or, either/or, neither/nor*, or *not only/but also* remain singular; when these words join plural and singular subjects, the verb should match the closest subject.

Verbs must also be in the proper **TENSE**—past, present, or future. Finally, verbs must be conjugated for tense, which shows *when* the action happened. Some conjugations include helping verbs like *was, have, have been*, and *will have been*.

TABLE 3.2. Verb Tenses

Tense	Past	Present	Future
Simple	I <u>gave</u> her a gift yesterday.	I <u>give</u> her a gift every day.	I <u>will give</u> her a gift on her birthday.
Continuous	I <u>was giving</u> her a gift when you got here.	I <u>am giving</u> her a gift; come in!	I <u>will be giving</u> her a gift at dinner.
Perfect	I <u>had given</u> her a gift before you got there.	I <u>have given</u> her a gift already.	I <u>will have given</u> her a gift by midnight.
Perfect continuous	Her friends <u>had been giving</u> her gifts all night when I arrived.	I <u>have been giving</u> her gifts every year for nine years.	I <u>will have been giving</u> her gifts on holidays for ten years next year.

Tense must also be consistent throughout the sentence and the passage. For example, the sentence *I was baking cookies and eat some dough* sounds strange. That is because the two verbs, *was baking* and *eat*, are in different tenses. *Was baking* occurred in the past; *eat*, on the other hand, occurs in the present. To make them consistent, change *eat* to *ate*.

> Wrong: Because it will rain during the party last night, we had to move the tables inside.
> Correct: Because it rained during the party last night, we had to move the tables inside.

All the verb tenses in a sentence need to agree both with each other and with the other information in the sentence. In the first sentence above, the tense does not match the other information in the sentence: *last night* indicates the past *(rained)*, not the future *(will rain)*.

PRACTICE QUESTIONS

1. Which of the following sentences contains an incorrectly conjugated verb?
   A) The brother and sister runs very fast.
   B) Neither Anne nor Suzy likes the soup.
   C) The mother and father love their new baby.
   D) Either Jack or Jill will pick up the pizza.

2. Which of the following sentences contains an incorrect verb tense?
   A) After the show ended, we drove to the restaurant for dinner.
   B) Natasha went to the mall before she headed home.
   C) Johnny went to the movies after he cleans the kitchen.
   D) Before the alarm sounded, smoke filled the cafeteria.

Nouns and Pronouns

Nouns are people, places, or things. The subject of a sentence is typically a noun. For example, in the sentence, "The *hospital* was very clean," the subject, hospital, is a noun; it is a place.

Pronouns stand in for nouns and can be used to make sentences sound less repetitive. Take the sentence, "Sam stayed home from school because Sam was not feeling well." The word *Sam* appears twice in the same sentence. Instead, you can use the pronoun *he* to stand in for *Sam* and say, "Sam stayed home from school because he was not feeling well."

TABLE 3.3 Pronouns		
	Singular	**Plural**
First person	I, me, my, mine	we, us, our, ours
Second person	you, your, yours	---
Third person	she, her, hers, it, its	they, them, their, theirs

Because pronouns take the place of nouns, they need to agree both in number and gender with the noun they replace. So, a plural noun needs a plural pronoun, and a noun referring to something feminine needs a feminine pronoun. There will usually be several questions on the exam that cover pronoun agreement, so it's good to get comfortable spotting pronouns.

> Wrong: When nurses prepare for surgery, you should wash your hands.
> Correct: When nurses prepare for surgery, they should wash their hands.

This sentence begins in third-person perspective and then switches to second-person perspective. So, this sentence is incorrect. To correct it, use a third-person pronoun in the second clause.

> Wrong: After the teacher spoke to the student, she realized her mistake.
> Correct: After Mr. White spoke to his student, she realized her mistake.
> (She and her refer to the student.)
> Correct: After speaking to the student, the teacher realized her own mistake.
> (Her refers to the teacher.)

This sentence refers to a teacher and a student. But whom does *she* refer to, the teacher or the student? To eliminate the ambiguity, use specific names or state more specifically who made the mistake.

3. Which pronoun correctly completes the sentence?

My wife taught me to drive so ____ could use her car.

A) you

B) I

C) my

D) his

4. Find the sentence that has an error in usage.

A) After we walked inside, we took off our hats and shoes and hung them in the closet.

B) The members of the band should leave her instruments in the rehearsal room.

C) The janitor on duty should rinse out his or her mop before leaving for the day.

D) When you see someone in trouble, you should always try to help them.

Adjectives and Adverbs

ADJECTIVES provide more information about a noun in a sentence. Take the sentence, "The boy hit the ball." If you want your readers to know more about the noun *boy*, you could use an adjective to describe him: "the <u>little</u> boy," "the <u>young</u> boy," "the <u>tall</u> boy."

ADVERBS describe verbs, adjectives, and even other adverbs. For example, in the sentence "The doctor had recently hired a new employee," the adverb recently tells us more about how the action *hired* took place.

Adjectives, adverbs, and **MODIFYING PHRASES** (groups of words that together modify another word) should be placed as close as possible to the word they modify. Separating words from their modifiers can create incorrect or confusing sentences.

> Wrong: Running through the hall, the bell rang and the student knew she was late.
> Correct: Running through the hall, the student heard the bell ring and knew she was late.
> The phrase "running through the hall" should be placed next to *student*, the noun it modifies.

The suffixes *–er* and *–est* are often used to modify adjectives when a sentence is making a comparison. The suffix *–er* is used when comparing two things, and the suffix *–est* is used when comparing more than two.

> Anne is taller than Steve, but Steve is more coordinated.
> Of the five brothers, Billy is the funniest, and Alex is the most intelligent.

Adjectives longer than two syllables are compared using *more* (for two things) or *most* (for three or more things).

> Wrong: Of my two friends, Clara is the smartest.
> Correct: Of my two friends, Clara is smarter.

More and *most* should not be used in conjunction with *–er* and *–est* endings.

> Wrong: My most warmest sweater is made of wool.
> Correct: My warmest sweater is made of wool.

PRACTICE QUESTIONS

5. Identify the adverb in this sentence.

   He carelessly sped around the flashing yellow light.

   A) flashing

   B) yellow

   C) around

   D) carelessly

6. Find the sentence that has an error in usage.

   A) The new red car was faster than the old blue car.

   B) Reggie's apartment is in the tallest building on the block.

   C) The slice of cake was tastier than the brownie.

   D) Of the four speeches, Jerry's was the most long.

Other Parts of Speech

PREPOSITIONS express the location of a noun or pronoun in relation to other words and phrases described in a sentence. For example, in the sentence "The nurse parked her car in a parking garage," the preposition *in* describes the position of the car in relation to the garage.

Together, the preposition and the noun that follow it are called a **PREPOSITIONAL PHRASE.** In this example, the prepositional phrase is "in a parking garage."

CONJUNCTIONS connect words, phrases, and clauses. The conjunctions comprising the acronym FANBOYS—For, And, Nor, But, Or, Yet, So—are called coordinating conjunctions. They are used to join **INDEPENDENT CLAUSES** (clauses that can stand alone

TEACHING TIPS:

An independent (or main) clause can stand alone as its own sentence. A dependent (or subordinate) clause must be attached to an independent clause to make a complete sentence.

as a complete sentence). For example, in the following sentence, the conjunction *and* joins together two independent clauses:

> The nurse prepared the patient for surgery, <u>and</u> the doctor performed the surgery.

Other conjunctions, like *although, because,* and *if,* connect an independent clause to a **DEPENDENT CLAUSE** (which cannot stand on its own). Take the following sentence:

> She had to ride the subway <u>because her car was broken.</u>

The clause "because her car was broken" cannot stand on its own: it is a dependent clause.

INTERJECTIONS, like *wow* and *hey,* express emotion and are most commonly used in conversation and casual writing.

PRACTICE QUESTIONS

7. Choose the word that best completes the sentence.

    Her love _____ blueberry muffins kept her coming back to the bakery every week.

    A) to

    B) with

    C) of

    D) about

8. Choose the word that best completes the sentence.

    Christine left her house early on Monday morning, _____ she was still late for work.

    A) but

    B) and

    C) for

    D) or

Phrases

To understand what a phrase is, you have to know about subjects and predicates. The **SUBJECT** is what the sentence is about; the **PREDICATE** contains the verb and its modifiers.

> The person at the front desk will answer any questions you have.
> Subject: the person at the front desk
> Predicate: will answer any questions you have

A **PHRASE** is a group of words that communicates only part of an idea because it lacks either a subject or a predicate. Phrases are categorized based on the main word in the phrase.

TABLE 3.4. Types of Phrases		
TYPE	DESCRIPTION	EXAMPLE
Prepositional phrase	begins with a preposition and ends with an object of the preposition	The dog is hiding <u>under the porch.</u>
Verb phrase	the main verb along with any helping verbs	The chef <u>wanted to cook</u> a different dish.
Noun phrase	a noun and its modifiers	<u>The big red barn</u> rests beside <u>the vacant chicken house.</u>

PRACTICE QUESTIONS

9. Identify the prepositional phrase in the following sentence.

Wrapping packages for the soldiers, the kind woman tightly rolled the t-shirts to see how much space remained for the homemade cookies.

A) Wrapping packages for the soldiers

B) the kind woman

C) to see how much space

D) for the homemade cookies

Clauses

CLAUSES contain both a subject and a predicate. They can be either independent or dependent. An **INDEPENDENT** (or main) **CLAUSE** can stand alone as its own sentence.

> The dog ate her homework.

DEPENDENT (or subordinate) **CLAUSES** cannot stand alone as their own sentences. They start with a subordinating conjunction or other transition words that make them sound incomplete.

> <u>Because</u> the dog ate her homework

Clauses can be joined together to form sentences. A sentence always needs at least one independent clause. Other clauses can be added to make the sentence more complex.

When writing sentences, independent clauses should be joined using commas and coordinating conjunctions (FANBOYS). Alternately, a semicolon may be used.

> The game was canceled, <u>but </u>we will still practice on Saturday.
> My family eats turkey at Thanksgiving; we eat ham at Christmas.

Dependent clauses are added to independent clauses using subordinating conjunctions (*e.g., because, although, while*).

> I love listening to the radio in the car <u>because</u> I can
> sing along as loud as I want.
> <u>Although </u>we love pizza, we chose to get hamburgers for lunch.

PRACTICE QUESTIONS

10. Which of the following sentences includes two independent clauses?
  A) Elsa drove while Erica navigated.
  B) Betty ordered a fruit salad, and Sue ordered eggs.
  C) Because she was late, Jenny ran down the hall.
  D) John ate breakfast with his mother, brother, and father.

11. Find the sentence that has an error in usage.
  A) I don't know whether I'll be available tomorrow.
  B) Although she was cold, she hesitated before turning off the air-conditioning.
  C) Neither my mother nor my father has been to Canada.
  D) Because I was hungry and didn't bring any lunch.

Punctuation

Punctuation questions are likely on all the HSPT exams, and it is a good idea to review your knowledge. The basic rules for using the major punctuation marks are given in Table 3.5.

TABLE 3.5. How to Use Punctuation		
PUNCTUATION	USED FOR	EXAMPLE
Period	ending sentences	Periods go at the end of complete sentences.
Question mark	ending questions	What's the best way to end a sentence?
Exclamation point	ending sentences that show extreme emotion	I'll never understand how to use commas!

Punctuation	Used for	Example
Comma	joining two independent clauses (always with a coordinating conjunction)	Commas can be used to join clauses, but they must always be followed by a coordinating conjunction.
	setting apart introductory and nonessential words and phrases	Commas, when used properly, set apart extra information in a sentence.
	separating items in a list	My favorite punctuation marks include the colon, semicolon, and period.
Semicolon	joining together two independent clauses (never used with a conjunction)	I love exclamation points; they make sentences seem so exciting!
Colon	introducing a list, explanation, or definition	When I see a colon I know what to expect: more information.
Apostrophe	forming contractions	It's amazing how many people can't use apostrophes correctly.
	showing possession	Parentheses are my sister's favorite punctuation; she finds commas' rules confusing.
Quotation marks	indicating a direct quote	I said to her, "Tell me more about parentheses."

PRACTICE QUESTIONS

12. Which of the following sentences contains an error in punctuation?

A) I love apple pie! John exclaimed with a smile.

B) Jennifer loves Adam's new haircut.

C) Billy went to the store; he bought bread, milk, and cheese.

D) Alexandra hates raisins, but she loves chocolate chips.

13. Which punctuation mark correctly completes the sentence?

Sam, why don't you come with us for dinner_

A) .

B) ?

C) ;

D) :

Capitalization

Capitalization questions on the exam will ask you to spot errors in capitalization within a phrase or sentence. Below are the most important rules for capitalization you are likely to see on the test.

The first word of a sentence is always capitalized.

> We will be having dinner at a new restaurant tonight.

The first letter of a proper noun is always capitalized.

> We're going to Chicago on Wednesday.

Titles are capitalized if they precede the name they modify.

> Harry Truman, the vice president, met with President Roosevelt.

Months are capitalized, but not the names of the seasons.

> Snow fell in March even though winter was over.

The names of major holidays should be capitalized. The word *day* is only capitalized if it is part of the holiday's name.

> We always go to a parade on Memorial Day, but Christmas day we stay home.

The names of specific places should always be capitalized. General location terms are not capitalized.

> We're going to San Francisco next weekend so I can see the ocean.

Titles for relatives should be capitalized when they precede a name, but not when they stand alone.

> Fred, my uncle, will make fried chicken, and Aunt Wanda is going to make spaghetti.

PRACTICE QUESTION

14. Find the sentence that has an error in capitalization.
- **A)** My two brothers are going to New Orleans for Mardi Gras.
- **B)** On Friday we voted to elect a new class president.
- **C)** Janet wants to go to Mexico this Spring.
- **D)** Peter complimented the chef on his cooking.

Homophones and Spelling

You may encounter questions that ask you to choose between **HOMOPHONES,** words that are pronounced the same but have different meanings. *Bawl* and *ball*, for example, are homophones: they sound the same, but the first means to cry, and the second is a round toy.

Here is a list of common homophones:
- ▶ bare/bear
- ▶ brake/break
- ▶ die/dye
- ▶ effect/affect
- ▶ flour/flower
- ▶ heal/heel
- ▶ insure/ensure
- ▶ morning/mourning
- ▶ peace/piece
- ▶ poor/pour
- ▶ principal/principle
- ▶ sole/soul
- ▶ stair/stare
- ▶ suite/sweet
- ▶ their/there/they're
- ▶ wear/where

The HSPT tests on spelling, so it is good to familiarize yourself with commonly misspelled words and special spelling rules.

Special Spelling Rules

i comes before e except after *c*

> belief, thief, receive, ceiling

TEACHING TIPS:
Be cautious of the rule "*i* comes before e except after *c*," for it has exceptions. Your foreign neighbors weighed the iciest beige glaciers!

Double a final consonant when adding suffixes if the consonant is preceded by a single vowel.

> run → running
> admit → admittance

Drop the final vowel when adding a suffix.

> sue → suing
> observe → observance

Change the final y to an i when adding a suffix.

lazy → laziest
tidy → tidily

Regular nouns are made plural by adding s. Irregular nouns can follow many different rules for pluralization, which are summarized in Table 3.6.

TABLE 3.6. Irregular Plural Nouns		
ENDS WITH . . .	MAKE IT PLURAL BY . . .	EXAMPLE
y	changing y to i and adding –es	baby → babies
f	changing f to v and adding –es	leaf→ leaves
fe	changing f to v and adding –s	knife→ knives
o	adding –es	potato → potatoes
us	changing –us to –i	nucleus → nuclei
Always the same	**Doesn't follow the rules**	
sheep	man → men	
deer	child → children	
fish	person → people	
moose	tooth → teeth	
pants	goose → geese	
binoculars	mouse → mice	
scissors	ox → oxen	

Commonly Misspelled Words

accommodate

across

argument

believe

committee

completely

conscious

discipline

experience

foreign

government

guarantee

height

immediately

intelligence

judgment

knowledge

license

lightning

lose

maneuver

misspell

noticeable

occasionally

occurred

opinion

personnel

piece

possession

receive

separate

successful

technique

tendency

unanimous

until

usually

vacuum

whether

which

PRACTICE QUESTIONS

15. Find the sentence that has an error in spelling.
- **A)** It was unusually warm that winter, so we didn't need to use our fireplace.
- **B)** Our garden includes tomatos, squash, and carrots.
- **C)** The local zoo will be opening a new exhibit that includes African elephants.
- **D)** My sister is learning to speak a foreign language so she can travel abroad.

16. Choose the word that best completes the sentence.

The nurse has three _____ to see before lunch.
- **A)** patents
- **B)** patience
- **C)** patients
- **D)** patience

Answer Key

1. **A)** Choice A should read "The brother and sister run very fast." When the subject contains two or more nouns connected by *and*, the subject is plural and requires a plural verb.

2. **C)** Choice C should read "Johnny will go to the movies after he cleans the kitchen." It does not make sense to say that Johnny does something in the past *(went to the movies)* after doing something in the present *(after he cleans)*.

3. **B)** The pronoun "I" refers to the writer. It agrees with the verb "could use." The pronouns "me" and "mine" also refer to the writer, so first-person singular makes the most sense.

4. **B)** "The members of the band" is plural, so it should be replaced by the plural pronoun *their* instead of the singular *her*.

5. **D)** *Carelessly* is an adverb modifying *sped* and explaining *how* the driving occurred.

6. **D)** Choice D should read, "Of the four speeches, Jerry's was the longest." The word *long* has only one syllable, so it should be modified with the suffix –est, not the word *most*.

7. **C)** The correct preposition is *of*.

8. **A)** In this sentence, the conjunction is joining together two contrasting ideas, so the correct answer is *but*.

9. **D)** This phrase begins with the preposition *for*. (The phrase "to see how much space" is not a prepositional phrase because it contains an infinitive: the infinitive form of the verb "to see.")

10. **B)** Choice B contains two independent clauses joined by a coordinating conjunction.

11. **D)** This is a sentence fragment that begins with the subordinating conjunction "because." There is no independent clause.

12. **A)** Choice A should use quotation marks to set off a direct quote: *"I love apple pie!" John exclaimed with a smile.*

13. **B)** The sentence is a question, so it should end with a question mark.

14. **C)** *Spring* is the name of a season and should not be capitalized.

15. **B)** *Tomatos* should be spelled tomatoes.

16. **C)** *Patients* is the correct spelling and the correct homophone. *Patients* are people in a hospital and patience is the ability to avoid getting upset in negative situations.

CHAPTER FOUR
Mathematics

The HSPT includes two sections that measure mathematical abilities: quantitative skills and mathematics. You will need to study the same concepts and skills for both sections. However, you will use your skills differently on each section.

The **QUANTITATIVE SKILLS** section tests your number sense (an understanding of how numbers are related to each other) and mathematical reasoning skills. You will only need to perform simple calculations to answer these questions. There are four types of questions in this section: sequences, reasoning, geometric comparison, and nongeometric comparison.

SEQUENCE QUESTIONS will present you with a sequence—a list of numbers that follow a pattern—and ask you to find another number in the sequence.

QUANTITATIVE SKILLS (SEQUENCE) QUESTION FORMAT   **18 QUESTIONS**

62, 60, 58, 56, ...

Which number should come next in the series?

  A) 52
  B) 57
  C) 50
  D) 54

The correct answer is D. The numbers in the series are decreasing by 2 (62 – 60 = 2, 60 – 58 = 2). Subtract 2 from the last value to find the next number in the series: 56 – 2 = 54.

REASONING questions require you to interpret a mathematical statement and perform simple calculations.

What number is 5 more than $\frac{2}{3}$ of 27?

- **A)** 14
- **B)** 23
- **C)** 9
- **D)** 32

The correct answer is B. The solution can be found in two steps. First, find $\frac{2}{3}$ of 27: $\frac{2}{3}$ × 27 = 18. Then, add 5: 18 + 5 = 23.

GEOMETRIC COMPARISON questions will ask you to look at three geometric quantities (such as shaded shapes or parts of a triangle) and decide which one is greater than the others.

QUANTITATIVE SKILLS (GEOMETRIC COMPARISON)   **9 QUESTIONS**
QUESTION FORMAT

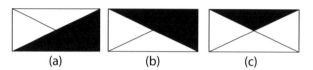

(a)   (b)   (c)

Examine (a), (b), and (c), and then choose the best answer.

- **A)** (a) is more shaded than (c)
- **B)** (a), (b), and (c) are equally shaded
- **C)** (b) is less shaded than (c)
- **D)** (c) is more shaded than (a)

The correct answer is A. Half the area of (a) and (b) are shaded, (c) has less than half of its area shaded.

NONGEOMETRIC COMPARISON questions will be structured similarly to geometric comparisons, but you will be comparing mathematical terms or expressions.

QUANTITATIVE SKILLS (NONGEOMETRIC COMPARISON)   **8 QUESTIONS**
QUESTION FORMAT

Examine (a), (b), and (c) to determine the correct answer.

(a) 6 – (2 × 3)

(b) (6 – 2) × 3

(c) 6 – 2 × 3

- **A)** (a), (b), and (c) are equal
- **B)** (a) is greater than (b)
- **C)** (b) is greater than (c)
- **D)** (b) and (c) are equal

The correct answer is C. Use the order of operations to simplify each expression.

(a): Simplify the expression in the parentheses, $2 \times 3 = 6$. Solve by subtracting, $6 - 6 = 0$.

(b): Simplify the parentheses, $6 - 2 = 4$. Solve by multiplying, $4 \times 3 = 12$.

(c): Multiply first and then subtract: $6 - 2 \times 3 = 6 - 6 = 0$.

$12 > 0$: (b) is greater than (c)

The **MATHEMATICS** section focuses on mathematical thinking and calculations. It includes two types of questions: concepts and problem-solving. **CONCEPT** problems will test your knowledge of mathematical terms and ideas.

MATHEMATICS (CONCEPTS) QUESTION FORMAT   **24** QUESTIONS

What is 498,235 rounded to the nearest thousands?

    A)   498,000

    B)   498,200

    C)   499,000

    D)   500,000

The correct answer is A. The 8 is in the thousands place. Because the value to the right of the 8 is less than 5, the 8 remains the same and all values to its right become zero. The result is 498,000.

Problem-solving questions will require you to find the solution to a mathematical problem. You will likely need to perform calculations to find the correct answer.

MATHEMATICS (PROBLEM-SOLVING) QUESTION FORMAT   **40** QUESTIONS

Solve: $12x + 5 = 77$

    A)   −6

    B)   6

    C)   10

    D)   8

The correct answer is B. Isolate x by subtracting 5 from both sides and dividing by 12.

$12x + 5 = 77$

$12x = 72$

$x = 6$

Numbers and Operations
ARITHMETIC OPERATIONS

The four basic arithmetic operations are addition, subtraction, multiplication, and division.

▶ **ADD** to combine two or more quantities (6 + 5 = 11).

▶ **SUBTRACT** to find the difference of two or more quantities (10 – 3 = 7).

▶ **MULTIPLY** to add a quantity multiple times (4 × 3 = 12 ⇔ 3 + 3 + 3 + 3 = 12).

▶ **DIVIDE** to determine how many times one quantity goes into another (10 ÷ 2 = 5).

Word problems contain **CLUE WORDS** that help you determine which operation to use.

TABLE 4.1. Operations Word Problems

OPERATION	CLUE WORDS	EXAMPLE
Addition	sum together (in) total all in addition increased give	Leslie has 3 pencils. If her teacher **gives** her 2 pencils, how many does she now have **in total**? 3 + 2 = 5 pencils
Subtraction	minus less than take away decreased difference How many left? How many more/less?	Sean has 12 cookies. His sister **takes** 2 cookies. **How many** cookies does Sean have **left**? 12 – 2 = 10 cookies
Multiplication	product times of each/every groups of twice	A hospital department has 10 patient rooms. If **each** room holds 2 patients, how many patients can stay in the department? 10 × 2 = 20 patients
Division	divided per each/every distributed average How many for each? How many groups?	A teacher has 150 stickers to **distribute** to her class of 25 students. If each student gets the same number of stickers, **how many** stickers will **each** student get? 150 ÷ 25 = 6 stickers

PRACTICE QUESTIONS

1. A case of pencils contains 10 boxes. Each box contains 150 pencils. How many pencils are in the case?

    A) 15

    B) 160

    C) 1500

    D) 16,000

2. Solve: $(12 - 8 \div 4)^2$

    A) 0.25

    B) 1

    C) 16

    D) 100

OPERATIONS WITH POSITIVE AND NEGATIVE NUMBERS

POSITIVE NUMBERS are greater than zero, and **NEGATIVE NUMBERS** are less than zero. Use the rules in the table below to determine the sign of the answer when performing operations with positive and negative numbers.

TABLE 4.2. Operations with Positive and Negative Numbers	
ADDITION AND SUBTRACTION	**MULTIPLICATION AND DIVISION**
positive + positive = positive $4 + 5 = 9$	positive × positive = positive $5 \times 3 = 15$
negative + negative = negative $-4 + (-5) = -9 \rightarrow -4 - 5 = -9$	negative × negative = positive $-6 \times (-5) = 30$
negative + positive = sign of the larger number $-15 + 9 = -6$	negative × positive = negative $-5 \times 4 = -20$

A **NUMBER LINE** shows numbers increasing from left to right (usually with zero in the middle). When adding positive and negative numbers, a number line can be used to find the sign of the answer. When adding a positive

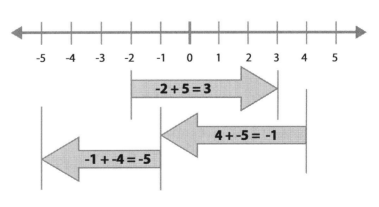

Figure 4.1. Adding Positive and Negative Numbers

number, count to the right; when adding a negative number, count to the left. Note that adding a negative value is the same as subtracting.

PRACTICE QUESTIONS

3. The wind chill on a cold day in January was −3°F. When the sun went down, the temperature fell 5°F. What was the temperature after the sun went down?

A) −2°F

B) −8°F

C) 2°F

D) 8°F

4. Examine (a), (b), and (c) and find the best answer.

(a) −5 + 25   (b) 13 − (−10)   (c) 2 × 14

A) (a), (b), and (c) are equal

B) (a) is greater than (b)

C) (c) is greater than (a)

D) (b) is less than (a)

EXPONENTS AND RADICALS

Exponential expressions, such as 5^3, contain a base and an exponent. The **EXPONENT** indicates how many times to use the **BASE** as a factor. In the expression 5^3, 5 is the base and 3 is the exponent. The value of 5^3 is found by multiplying 5 by itself 3 times: $5^3 = 5 \times 5 \times 5 = 125$. Rules for working with exponents are given in the table below.

TABLE 4.3. Operations with Exponents	
RULE	**EXAMPLE**
$a^0 = 1$	$5^0 = 1$
$a^{-n} = \dfrac{1}{a^n}$	$5^{-3} = \dfrac{1}{5^3}$
$a^m a^n = a^{m+n}$	$5^3 5^4 = 5^{3+4} = 5^7$
$(a^m)^n = a^{m \times n}$	$(5^3)^4 = 5^{3(4)} = 5^{12}$
$\dfrac{a^m}{a^n} = a^{m-n}$	$\dfrac{5^4}{5^3} = 5^{4-3} = 5^1$
$(ab)^n = a^n b^n$	$(5 \times 6)^3 = 5^3 6^3$
$\left(\dfrac{a}{b}\right)^n = \dfrac{a^n}{b^n}$	$\left(\dfrac{5}{6}\right)^3 = \dfrac{5^3}{6^3}$
$\left(\dfrac{a}{b}\right)^{-n} = \left(\dfrac{b}{a}\right)^n$	$\left(\dfrac{5}{6}\right)^{-3} = \left(\dfrac{6}{5}\right)^3$
$\dfrac{a^{-m}}{b^{-n}} = \dfrac{b^n}{a^m}$	$\dfrac{5^{-3}}{6^{-4}} = \dfrac{6^4}{5^3}$

Finding the **ROOT** of a number is the inverse of raising a number to a power. In other words, the root is the number of times a value should be multiplied by itself to reach a given value. Roots are named for the power on the base:

- 5 is the **SQUARE ROOT** of 25 because $5^2 = 25$
- 5 is the **CUBE ROOT** of 125 because $5^3 = 125$
- 5 is the **FOURTH ROOT** of 625, because $5^4 = 625$

The symbol for finding the root of a number is the radical: $\sqrt{}$. By itself, the radical indicates a square root: $\sqrt{36} = 6$ because $6^2 = 36$. Other numbers can be included in front of the radical to indicate different roots: $\sqrt[4]{1,296} = 6$ because $6^4 = 1,296$. The number under the radical is called the **RADICAND**. Rules for working with radicals are given in the table below.

TABLE 4.4. Operations with Radicals

RULE	EXAMPLE
$\sqrt[b]{ac} = \sqrt[b]{a}\,\sqrt[b]{c}$	$\sqrt[3]{81} = \sqrt[3]{27}\,\sqrt[3]{3} = 3\sqrt[3]{3}$
$\sqrt[b]{\dfrac{a}{c}} = \dfrac{\sqrt[b]{a}}{\sqrt[b]{c}}$	$\sqrt{\dfrac{4}{81}} = \dfrac{\sqrt{4}}{\sqrt{81}} = \dfrac{2}{9}$
$\sqrt[b]{a^c} = (\sqrt[b]{a})^c = a^{\frac{c}{b}}$	$\sqrt[3]{6^2} = (\sqrt[3]{6})^2 = 6^{\frac{2}{3}}$

PRACTICE QUESTIONS

5. Which of the following values is equivalent to $\sqrt{48}$?

   A) $4\sqrt{3}$

   B) $24\sqrt{2}$

   C) $4\sqrt{12}$

   D) $3\sqrt{16}$

6. Examine (a), (b), and (c) to determine the correct answer.

   (a) 2^0

   (b) 2^{-1}

   (c) 2^1

   A) (a), (b), and (c) are equal

   B) (a) is greater than (b)

   C) (b) is greater than (c)

   D) (b) and (c) are equal

SCIENTIFIC NOTATION

SCIENTIFIC NOTATION is a method of representing very large and very small numbers in the form $a \times 10^n$, where a is a value between 1 and 10, and n is a nonzero integer. For example, the number 927,000,000 is written in scientific notation as 9.27×10^8. The rules of exponents are used to perform operations with numbers in scientific notation.

- ► When adding and subtracting numbers in scientific notation, write all numbers with the same n value and add or subtract the a values.

- ► When multiplying numbers in scientific notation, multiply the a values and add the n values (exponents).

- ► To divide numbers in scientific notation, divide the a values and subtract the n values (exponents).

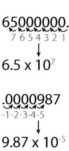

Figure 4.2. Scientific Notation

PRACTICE QUESTION

7. Which of the following shows the expression $(3.8 \times 10^3) + (4.7 \times 10^2)$ written correctly in scientific notation?

A) 42.7×10^2

B) 4.27×10^3

C) 85×10^4

D) 8.5×10^5

ORDER OF OPERATIONS

When performing multiple operations, the order of operations must be used to obtain the correct answer. The problem should be worked in the following order:

Please **E**xcuse (**M**y **D**ear) (**A**unt **S**ally)

1. **P** — Parentheses: Calculate expressions inside parentheses, brackets, braces, etc.

2. **E** — Exponents: Calculate exponents and square roots.

3. **M** — Multiply and **D** — Divide: Calculate any remaining multiplication and division in order from left to right.

4. **A** — Add and **S** — Subtract: Calculate any remaining addition and subtraction in order from left to right.

The steps "Multiply/Divide" and "Add/Subtract" are completed from left to right. In other words, divide before multiplying if the division is to the left of the multiplication.

For example, the expression $(3^2 - 2)^2 + (4)5^3$ is simplified using the following steps:

1. Parentheses: Because the parentheses in this problem contain two operations (exponents and subtraction), use the order of operations within the parentheses. Exponents come before subtraction. $(3^2 - 2)^2 + (4)5^3 = (9 - 2)^2 + (4)5^3 = (7)^2 + (4)5^3$

2. Exponents: $(7)^2 + (4)5^3 = 49 + (4)125$

3. Multiplication and division: $49 + (4)125 = 49 + 500$

4. Addition and subtraction: $49 + 500 = 549$

TEACHING TIP:
When working with complicated expressions, ask your student to underline or highlight the operation being performed in each step to avoid confusion.

PRACTICE QUESTIONS

8. Simplify: $-3^2 + 4(5) + (5 - 6)^2 - 8$
   A) 2
   B) 22
   C) 4
   D) 29

9. Examine (a), (b), and (c) and find the best answer.
   (a) $6 - (2 \times 3)$
   (b) $(6 - 2) \times 3$
   (c) $6 - 2 \times 3$
   A) (a), (b), and (c) are equal
   B) (a) is greater than (b)
   C) (b) is greater than (c)
   D) (b) and (c) are equal

FRACTIONS

A **FRACTION** represents parts of a whole. The top number of a fraction, called the **NUMERATOR**, indicates how many equal-sized parts are present. The bottom number of a fraction, called the **DENOMINATOR**, indicates how many equal-sized parts make a whole.

Fractions have several forms:

▶ **PROPER FRACTION**: the numerator is less than the denominator

▶ **IMPROPER FRACTION**: the numerator is greater than or equal to the denominator

▶ **MIXED NUMBER**: the combination of a whole number and a fraction

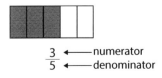

Figure 4.3. Parts of Fractions

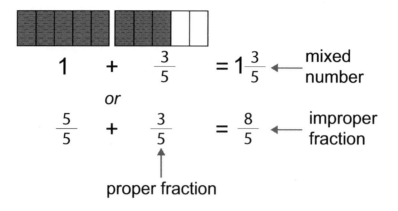

$$1 \quad + \quad \frac{3}{5} \quad = 1\frac{3}{5} \longleftarrow \text{mixed number}$$

or

$$\frac{5}{5} \quad + \quad \frac{3}{5} \quad = \frac{8}{5} \longleftarrow \text{improper fraction}$$

proper fraction

Figure 4.4. Types of Fractions

Improper fractions can be converted to mixed numbers by dividing. In fact, the fraction bar is also a division symbol.

$$\frac{14}{3} = 14 \div 3 = 4 \ \text{(with 2 left over)}$$

$$\frac{14}{3} = 4\frac{2}{3}$$

To convert a mixed number to a fraction, multiply the whole number by the denominator of the fraction, and add the numerator. The result becomes the numerator of the improper fraction; the denominator remains the same.

$$5\frac{2}{3} = \frac{(5 \times 3) + 2}{3} = \frac{17}{3}$$

To **MULTIPLY FRACTIONS**, multiply numerators and multiply denominators. Reduce the product to lowest terms. To **DIVIDE FRACTIONS**, multiply the first fraction by the reciprocal of the second fraction. (The **RECIPROCAL** of a fraction is just the fraction with the top and bottom numbers switched.) When multiplying and dividing mixed numbers, the mixed numbers must be converted to improper fractions.

$$\frac{a}{b} \times \frac{c}{d} = \frac{ac}{bd}$$

$$\frac{a}{b} \div \frac{c}{d} = \left(\frac{a}{b}\right)\left(\frac{d}{c}\right) = \frac{ad}{bc}$$

Adding or subtracting fractions requires a common denominator. To find a **COMMON DENOMINATOR**, multiply the denominators of the fractions. Then, to add the fractions, add the numerators and keep the denominator the same.

$$\frac{a}{b} + \frac{c}{b} = \frac{a+c}{b}$$

$$\frac{a}{b} - \frac{c}{b} = \frac{a-c}{b}$$

PRACTICE QUESTIONS

10. Ari and Teagan each ordered a pizza. Ari has $\frac{1}{4}$ of his pizza left, and Teagan has $\frac{1}{3}$ of her pizza left. How much total pizza do they have left?

A) $\frac{2}{7}$ pizza

B) $\frac{1}{12}$ pizza

C) $\frac{3}{4}$ pizza

D) $\frac{7}{12}$ pizza

11. Twenty-four students recently took a math test and were given a grade of "pass" or "fail." If $\frac{1}{4}$ of the students failed the test, how many students passed the test?

A) 6

B) 96

C) 18

D) 16

DECIMALS

In the base-10 system, each digit (the numeric symbols 0 – 9) in a number is worth ten times as much as the number to the right of it. For example, in the number 321 each digit has a different value based on its position: 321 = 300 + 20 + 1. The value of each place is called **PLACE VALUE**.

TABLE 4.5. Place Value Chart									
1,000,000	100,000	10,000	1,000	100	10	1		$\frac{1}{10}$	$\frac{1}{100}$
10^6	10^5	10^4	10^3	10^2	10^1	10^0	.	10^{-1}	10^{-2}
millions	hundred thou-sands	ten thou-sands	thou-sands	hundreds	tens	ones	decimal	tenths	hun-dredths

Decimals can be added, subtracted, multiplied, and divided:

▶ To add or subtract decimals, align at the decimal point, and perform the operation. Keep the decimal point in the same place in the answer.

▶ To multiply decimals, multiply the numbers without the decimal points. Add the number of decimal places to the right of the decimal point in the original numbers. Place the decimal point in the answer so that there are that many places to the right of the decimal.

TEACHING TIP:
To determine which way to move the decimal after multiplying, remember that changing the decimal should always make the final answer smaller.

▶ When dividing decimals, move the decimal point to the right in order to make the divisor a whole number. Move the decimal the same number of places in the dividend. Divide the numbers without regard to the decimal. Then, place the decimal point of the quotient directly above the decimal point of the dividend.

PRACTICE QUESTIONS

12. A customer at a restaurant ordered a drink that cost $2.20, a meal that cost $32.54, and a dessert that cost $4. How much was the total bill?

A) $38.74

B) $34.74

C) $30.24

D) $26.34

13. Examine (a), (b), and (c) to determine the correct answer.

(a) 0.79   (b) 0.0122 + 0.7778   (c) 0.3 × 0.4

A) (a) and (b) are equal

B) (c) is greater than (a)

C) (b) and (c) are equal

D) (b) is greater than (a)

RATIOS AND PROPORTIONS

A **RATIO** is a comparison of two quantities. For example, if a class consists of 15 women and 10 men, the ratio of women to men is 15 to 10. This ratio can also be written as 15:10 or $\frac{15}{10}$. Ratios, like fractions, can be reduced by dividing by common factors.

A **PROPORTION** is a statement that two ratios are equal. For example, the proportion $\frac{5}{10} = \frac{7}{14}$ is true because both ratios are equal to $\frac{1}{2}$.

The cross product is found by multiplying the numerator of one fraction by the denominator of the other (*across* the equal sign).

$$\text{Cross product: } \frac{a}{b} = \frac{c}{d} \rightarrow ad = bc$$

The fact that the cross products of proportions are equal can be used to solve proportions in which one of the values is missing. Use x to represent the missing value, then cross multiply and solve.

$$\frac{5}{x} = \frac{7}{14}$$
$$5(14) = x(7)$$
$$70 = 7x$$
$$x = 10$$

14. The dosage for a particular medication is proportional to the weight of the patient. If the dosage for a patient weighing 60 kg is 90 mg, what is the dosage for a patient weighing 80 kg?

A) 120 mg

B) 53.3 mg

C) 106.7 mg

D) 68 mg

15. Jacob is running for class president at his high school and received 250 votes. If 40% of the students in the class voted for Jacob, how many students are in Jacob's class?

A) 100

B) 625

C) 290

D) 500

PERCENTS

A **PERCENT** (or percentage) means *per hundred* and is expressed with the percent symbol, %. For example, 54% means 54 out of 100. Percentages are converted to decimals by moving the decimal point two places to the left; 54% = 0.54. Percentages can be solved by setting up a proportion:

$$\frac{\text{part}}{\text{whole}} = \frac{\%}{100}$$

PERCENT CHANGE involves a change from an original amount. Often percent change problems appear as word problems that include discounts, growth, or markups. In order to solve percent change problems, it is necessary to identify the percent change (as a decimal), the amount of change, and the original amount. (Keep in mind that one of these will be the value being solved for.) These values can then be substituted in the equations below:

$$\text{amount of change} = \text{original amount} \times \text{percent change}$$

$$\text{percent change} = \frac{\text{amount of change}}{\text{original amount}}$$

$$\text{original amount} = \frac{\text{amount of change}}{\text{percent change}}$$

16. On Tuesday, a radiology clinic had 80% of patients come in for their scheduled appointments. If they saw 16 patients, how many scheduled appointments did the clinic have on Tuesday?
- **A)** 11
- **B)** 12
- **C)** 20
- **D)** 22

17. A TV that originally cost $1500 is on sale for 45% off. What is the sale price for the TV?
- **A)** $675
- **B)** $825
- **C)** $1455
- **D)** $2727

18. Kevin is planning to host a party in a room that can hold 120 people. If he expects 30% of the people he invites not to attend, what is the maximum number of invitations he should send?
- **A)** 36
- **B)** 84
- **C)** 171
- **D)** 400

ESTIMATION AND ROUNDING

ESTIMATION is the process of rounding numbers before performing operations to make operations easier. Estimation can be used when an exact answer is not necessary or to check work.

To **ROUND** a number, first identify the digit in the specified place value. Then look at the digit one place to the right. If that digit is 4 or less, keep the digit in the specified place value the same. If that digit is 5 or more, add 1 to the digit in the specified place value. All the digits to the right of the specified place value become zeros.

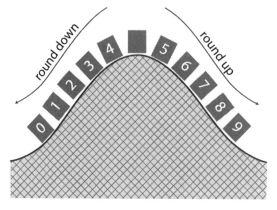

Figure 4.5. Rounding

19. Voter turnout in a city election is estimated to be 80%. If Hank earns 4000 or 40% of the vote, how many registered voters live in the city? (Round to the nearest 100.)

    A) 5000

    B) 8000

    C) 10,000

    D) 12,500

20. The populations of five local towns are given below.

TOWN	POPULATION
A	12,341
B	8975
C	9431
D	10,521
E	11,427

Which of the following values is closest to the total population of the five towns?

    A) 50,000

    B) 53,000

    C) 55,000

    D) 58,000

Algebra
ALGEBRAIC PROPERTIES

The algebraic properties describe basic rules related to addition, subtraction, multiplication, and division. The names of the properties will not be included on the test, but it's important to understand what the properties are and how they are used.

TABLE 4.6. Algebraic Properties		
PROPERTY	EXPLANATION	EXAMPLE
Commutative property of addition	Changing the order of the addends does not change the result.	$4 + 8 = 8 + 4$
Commutative property of multiplication	Changing the order of the factors does not change the result.	$5 \times 9 = 9 \times 5$

continued on next page

Algebraic Properties (continued)

PROPERTY	EXPLANATION	EXAMPLE
Associative property of addition	Changing the grouping of the addends does not change the result.	$(2 + 6) + 4 = 2 + (6 + 4)$
Associative property of multiplication	Changing the grouping of the factors does not change the result.	$(3 \times 5) \times 4 = 3 \times (5 \times 4)$
Distributive property of multiplication over addition	A factor outside parentheses enclosing a sum can be distributed to the terms inside the parentheses.	$7(10 + 3) = 7(10) + 7(3)$

PRACTICE QUESTION

21. Which equation demonstrates the associative property of addition?
  A) $2 + (1 + 5) = (2 + 1) + 5$
  B) $2(1 \times 5) = (2 \times 1)5$
  C) $1 \times 3 = 3 \times 1$
  D) $2(7 + 4) = 2 \times 7 + 2 \times 4$

EVALUATING EXPRESSIONS

The foundation of algebra is the **VARIABLE**, an unknown number represented by a symbol (usually a letter such as x or a). Variables can be preceded by a **COEFFICIENT**, which is a constant in front of the variable, such as $4x$ or $-2a$. An **ALGEBRAIC EXPRESSION** is any sum, difference, product, or quotient of variables and numbers (for example, $3x^2$, $2x + 7y - 1$, and $5/x$ are all algebraic expressions). The value of an expression is found by replacing the variable with a given value and simplifying the result.

PRACTICE QUESTIONS

22. Evaluate the following expression for $a = -10$:
  $\frac{a^2}{4} - 3a + 4$
  A) 59
  B) −1
  C) −51
  D) 9

23. Evaluate the following expression for $a = xy$ and $b = x^2$:

$2a + 3b$

   A) $2xy + 3x^2$

   B) $3xy + 2x^2$

   C) $5xy + 5x^2$

   D) $6x^3y$

ADDING AND SUBTRACTING ALGEBRAIC EXPRESSIONS

TERMS are any quantities that are added or subtracted in an expression. For example, the terms of the expression $x^2 + 5$ are x^2 and 5. **LIKE TERMS** are terms with the same variable part. For example, in the expression $2x + 3xy - 2z + 6y + 2xy$, the like terms are $3xy$ and $2xy$.

Expressions can be added or subtracted by simply adding and subtracting like terms. The other terms in the expression will not change.

$$2x + \underline{3xy} - 2z + 6y + \underline{2xy} \rightarrow 2x - 2z + 6y + (\underline{3xy} + \underline{2xy}) \rightarrow 2x - 2z + 6y + \underline{5xy}$$

PRACTICE QUESTIONS

24. Simplify the expression: $4x - 3y + 12z + 2x - 7y - 10z$

   A) $6x - 10y + 2z$

   B) $6x + 10y - 2z$

   C) $-2xyz$

   D) $-x + 14z - 17y$

25. At the arcade, games give out green tickets or red tickets. The arcade also gives out small boxes to store tickets. Paul and Paula both play numerous games, and at the end of the day, Paul has 3 boxes of green tickets and 8 boxes of red tickets, while Paula has 6 boxes of green tickets and 2 boxes of red tickets. If the green box holds g tickets and the red box hold r tickets, write an expression that describes how many tickets they have together.

   A) $11g + 8r$

   B) $5g + 14r$

   C) $9g + 10r$

   D) $10g + 9r$

DISTRIBUTING AND FACTORING

Often, simplifying expressions requires distributing and factoring, which are opposite processes. To **DISTRIBUTE**, multiply the term outside the parentheses by each term inside the parentheses. For each term, coefficients are multiplied, and exponents are added (following the rules of exponents).

$$2x(3x^2 + 7) = 6x^3 + 14x$$

FACTORING is the reverse process: taking a polynomial and writing it as a product of two or more factors. The first step in factoring a polynomial is always to "undistribute," or factor out, the greatest common factor (GCF) among the terms. The remaining terms are placed in parentheses. Factoring can be checked by multiplying the GCF through the parentheses.

$$14a^2 + 7a = 7a(2a + 1)$$

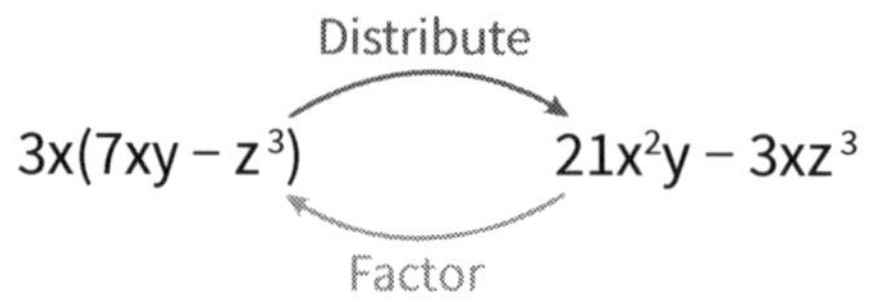

Distribute
$$3x(7xy - z^3) \qquad 21x^2y - 3xz^3$$
Factor

Figure 4.6. Distribution and Factoring

To multiply binomials (expressions with two terms), use FOIL: First – Outer – Inner – Last. Multiply the first term in each expression, the outer terms, the inner terms, and the last term in each expression. Then simplify the expression.

$$(2x + 3)(x - 4)$$
$$= (2x)(x) + (2x)(-4) + (3)(x) + 3(-4)$$
$$= 2x^2 - 8x + 3x - 12$$
$$= 2x^2 - 5x - 12$$

PRACTICE QUESTIONS

26. Expand the following expression: $5x(x^2 - 2c + 10)$
    A) $5x^3 + 10xc + 50x$
    B) $5x^3 - 10xc + 50x$
    C) $5x^2 - 10c + 50$
    D) $5x^3 - 2xc + 10x$

27. Evaluate $-3(b + 8c)$ if $b = -2$ and $c = -3$
    A) −78
    B) −18
    C) 78
    D) 498

EQUATIONS

An **EQUATION** states that two expressions are equal to each other. Solving an equation means finding the value(s) of the variable that make the equation true. To solve a linear equation (which has two variables with no exponents), manipulate the terms so that the variable being solved for is isolated on one side of the equal sign. All other terms should be on the other side of the equal sign.

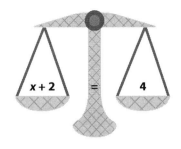

Figure 4.7. Equations

The way to solve linear equations is to "undo" all the operations that connect numbers to the variable of interest. Follow these steps:

1. Eliminate fractions by multiplying each side by the least common multiple of any denominators.

2. Distribute to eliminate parentheses, braces, and brackets.

3. Combine like terms.

4. Use addition or subtraction to collect all terms containing the variable of interest to one side and all terms not containing the variable to the other side.

5. Use multiplication or division to remove coefficients from the variable being solved for.

$2(2x - 8) = x - 7$	
$4x - 16 = x - 7$	Distribute.
$4x - 16 - x = x - 7 - x$ $3x - 16 = -7$	Subtract x to isolate the variable on one side.
$3x - 16 + 16 = -7 + 16$ $3x = 9$	Add 16 to both sides.
$\frac{3x}{3} = \frac{9}{3}$ $x = 3$	Divide both sides by 3.

PRACTICE QUESTIONS

28. Solve for x: $5(x + 3) - 12 = 43$

 A) $x = 14$

 B) $x = 3$

 C) $x = 10.4$

 D) $x = 8$

29. Mandy babysits for families and charges $8 an hour for one child plus $3 an hour per additional child. The Buxton family has 4 children, and they ask Mandy to babysit for 5 hours. How much will Mandy make for babysitting the Buxton children?

   A) $163

   B) $104

   C) $220

   D) $85

INEQUALITIES

INEQUALITIES are similar to equations, except both sides of the problem are not necessarily equal (≠). Inequalities may be represented as follows:

▶ greater than (>)

▶ greater than or equal to (≥)

▶ less than (<)

▶ less than or equal to (≤)

Inequalities may be represented on a number line, as shown below. A circle is placed on the end point with a filled circle representing ≤ and ≥ and an empty circle representing < and >. An arrow is then drawn to show either all the values greater than or less than the value circled.

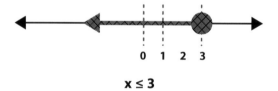

x ≤ 3

Figure 4.8. Inequality Line Graph

Inequalities can be solved by manipulating, just like equations. The only difference is that the direction of the inequality sign must be reversed when the inequality is divided by a negative number.

$$10 - 2x > 14$$
$$-2x > 4$$
$$x < -2$$

The solution to an inequality is a *set* of numbers, not a single value. For example, simplifying $4x + 2 \le 14$ gives the inequality $x \le 3$, meaning every number less than or equal to 3 would be included in the set of correct answers.

30. Solve the inequality: $4x + 10 > 58$

  A) $x > 11$

  B) $x < 12$

  C) $x > 19.5$

  D) $x > 12$

31. The students on the track team are buying new uniforms. T-shirts (t) cost $12, pants ($p$) cost $15, and a pair of shoes (s) costs $45. If the team has a budget of $2500, write a mathematical sentence that represents how many of each item they can buy.

  A) $t + p + s < 2500$

  B) $\frac{t}{12} + \frac{p}{15} + \frac{s}{45} > 2500$

  C) $12t + 15p + 45s \leq 2500$

  D) $12t + 15p + 45s \geq 2500$

GRAPHING LINEAR EQUATIONS ON A COORDINATE PLANE

A **COORDINATE PLANE** is a plane containing the x- and y-axes. The **X-AXIS** is the horizontal line on a graph where $y = 0$. The **Y-AXIS** is the vertical line on a graph where $x = 0$. The x-axis and y-axis intersect to create four **QUADRANTS**. The first quadrant is in the upper right, and other quadrants are labeled counterclockwise using the roman numerals

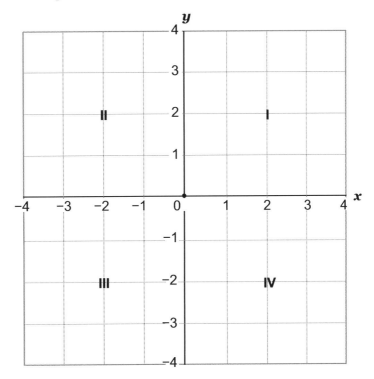

Figure 4.9. Four Quadrants

I, II, III, and IV. **POINTS**, or locations, on the graph are written as **ORDERED PAIRS**, (x, y), with the point (0, 0) called the **ORIGIN**. Points are plotted by counting over x places from the origin horizontally and y places from the origin vertically.

The most common way to write a linear equation is **SLOPE-INTERCEPT FORM**:

$$y = mx + b$$

TEACHING TIP:
Use the phrase *begin, move* to remember that *b* is the *y*-intercept (where to begin) and *m* is the slope (how the line moves).

In this equation, m is the slope, and b is the y-intercept. The y-**INTERCEPT** is the point where the line crosses the y-axis, or where x equals zero. **SLOPE** is often described as "rise over run" because it is calculated as the difference in y-values (rise) over the difference in x-values (run).

$$m = \frac{y_2 - y_1}{x_2 - x_1} = \frac{\text{rise}}{\text{run}}$$

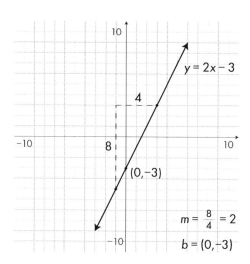

Figure 4.10. Linear Equation

To graph a linear equation, identify the y-intercept and place that point on the y-axis. Then, starting at the y-intercept, use the slope of "rise over run" to go "up and over" and place the next point. The numerator of the slope tells you how many units to go up, the "rise." The denominator of the slope tells you how many units to go to the right, the "run." However, if the slope is negative, reverse the process and go down and over to the left before placing the next point. You can repeat the process to plot additional points. These points can then be connected to draw the line. To find the equation of a line, identify the y-intercept, if possible, on the graph and use two easily identifiable points to find the slope.

PRACTICE QUESTIONS

32. What is the slope of the line whose equation is $6x - 2y - 8 = 0$?

   A) −3

   B) $\frac{3}{4}$

   C) $-\frac{1}{3}$

   D) 3

33. In which quadrant is the point (−5, 2) located?

A) I

B) II

C) III

D) IV

Geometry and Measurement

UNITS

The United States uses **CUSTOMARY UNITS**, sometimes called *standard units*. In this system, several different units can be used to describe the same variable. These units and the relationships between them are shown in the table below.

TABLE 4.7. US Customary Units		
VARIABLE MEASURED	**UNIT**	**CONVERSIONS**
Length	inches, foot, yard, mile	12 inches = 1 foot 3 feet = 1 yard 5280 feet = 1 mile
Weight	ounces, pound, ton	16 ounces = 1 pound 2000 pounds = 1 ton
Volume	fluid ounces, cup, pint, quart, gallon	8 fluid ounces = 1 cup 2 cups = 1 pint 2 pints = 1 quart 4 quarts = 1 gallon
Time	second, minute, hour, day	60 seconds = 1 minute 60 minutes = 1 hour 24 hours = 1 day
Area	square inch, square foot, square yard	144 square inches = 1 square foot 9 square feet = 1 square yard

Most other countries use the metric system, which has its own set of units for variables like length, weight, and volume. These units are modified by prefixes that make large and small numbers easier to handle. These units and prefixes are shown in the table below.

TABLE 4.8. Metric Units and Prefixes	
VARIABLE MEASURED	**BASE UNIT**
length	meter
weight	gram
volume	liter

continued on next page

TABLE 4.8. Metric Units and Prefixes (continued)

Metric Prefix	Conversion
kilo	base unit × 1000
hecto	base unit × 100
deka	base unit × 10
deci	base unit × 0.1
centi	base unit × 0.01
milli	base unit × 0.001

Conversion factors are used to convert one unit to another (either within the same system or between different systems). A conversion factor is simply a fraction built from two equivalent values. For example, there are 12 inches in 1 foot, so the conversion factor is $\frac{12 \text{ in}}{1 \text{ ft}}$ or $\frac{1 \text{ ft}}{12 \text{ in}}$.

To convert from one unit to another, multiply the original value by a conversion factor. Choose a conversion factor that will eliminate the unwanted unit with the desired unit.

TEACHING TIP:

Have your student practice unit conversion with measurements from their daily lives to help them learn metric units (e.g., convert their weight in pounds to kilograms, find the number of milliliters in a 1 liter water bottle).

How many inches are in 6 feet?

$$\frac{6 \text{ ft} \times 12 \text{ in}}{1\text{ft}} = \frac{6 \text{ ft} \times 12 \text{ in}}{1\text{ft}} = 72 \text{ in}$$

PRACTICE QUESTIONS

34. How many centimeters are in 2.5 m?

A) 25
B) 250
C) 2500
D) 25,000

35. Examine (a), (b), and (c) to determine the correct answer.

(a) 2 cups
(b) 0.5 quarts
(c) 16 fluid ounces

A) (a), (b), and (c) are equal
B) (b) and (c) are equal and less than (a)
C) (c) is greater than (a) and (b)
D) (b) is greater than (a)

GEOMETRIC FIGURES

GEOMETRIC FIGURES are shapes made up of points, lines, or planes. A **POINT** is simply a location in space; it does not have any dimensional properties like length, area, or volume. A collection of points that extend infinitely in both directions is a **LINE**, and one that extends infinitely in only one direction is a **RAY**. A section of a line with a beginning and end point is a **LINE SEGMENT**. Lines, rays, and line segments are examples of **ONE-DIMENSIONAL** objects because they can only be measured in one dimension (length).

Figure 4.11. One-Dimensional Object

Lines, rays, and line segments can intersect to create **ANGLES**, which are measured in degrees or radians. Angles between 0° and 90° are **ACUTE**, and angles between 90° and 180° are **OBTUSE**. An angle of exactly 90° is a **RIGHT ANGLE**, and two lines that form right angles are **PERPENDICULAR**. Lines that do not intersect are described as **PARALLEL**. Any two angles whose sum is 90° are called **COMPLEMENTARY ANGLES**. **SUPPLEMENTARY ANGLES** have a sum of 180°.

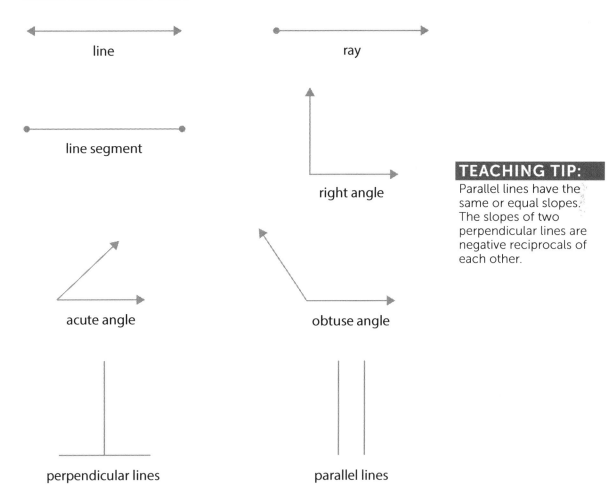

TEACHING TIP:
Parallel lines have the same or equal slopes. The slopes of two perpendicular lines are negative reciprocals of each other.

Figure 4.12. Lines and Angles

TWO-DIMENSIONAL objects can be measured in two dimensions (length and width). A **PLANE** is a two-dimensional object that extends infinitely in both dimensions.

Figure 4.13. Two-Dimensional Object

THREE-DIMENSIONAL objects, such as cubes, can be measured in three dimensions (length, width, and height). Three-dimensional objects are also called **SOLIDS**, and the shape of a flattened solid is called a **NET**.

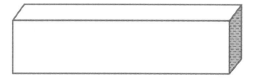

Figure 4.14. Three-Dimensional Object

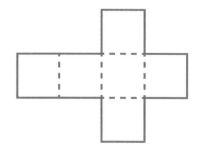

Figure 4.15. Net

PRACTICE QUESTIONS

36. Angle *M* measures 36°. What is the measure of an angle supplementary to angle *M*?

A) 180°

B) 144°

C) 36°

D) 54°

37. Which points and lines are contained in plane *M* in the figure below?

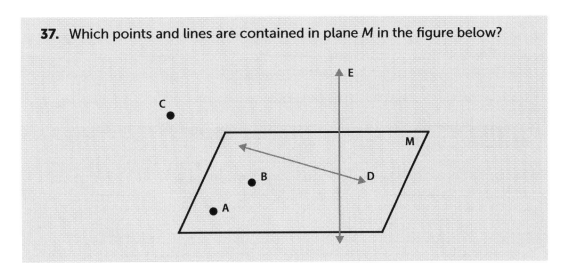

PERIMETER AND AREA

POLYGONS are two-dimensional shapes, such as triangles and squares, that have three or more straight sides. Regular polygons are polygons whose sides are all the same length. Angles inside a polygon are **INTERIOR ANGLES**. Angles formed by one side of the polygon and a line extending outside the polygon are **EXTERIOR ANGLES**.

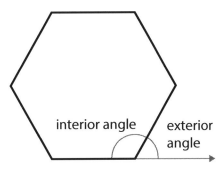

Figure 4.16. Interior and Exterior Angles

PERIMETER is the distance around a shape. It can be determined by adding the lengths of all sides of the shape. **AREA** is the amount of space a shape occupies. The area of an object is its length times its width and is measured in square units. For example, if a wall is 3 feet long and 2 feet wide, its area would be 6 square feet (ft²).

The table below gives the formulas for the area and perimeter of basic shapes. To find the area and perimeter of a circle, use the constant *pi* (π = 3.14).

TABLE 4.9. Area and Perimeter of Basic Shapes		
SHAPE	**AREAS**	**PERIMETER**
Triangle	$A = \frac{1}{2} bh$	$P = s_1 + s_2 + s_3$
Square	$A = s^2$	$P = 4s$
Rectangle	$A = l \times w$	$P = 2l + 2w$
Circle	$A = \pi r^2$	$C = 2\pi r$ (circumference)

TEACHING TIPS:
Don't worry about having students memorize these formulas—they'll be given on the test. Just make sure they understand all the terms.

An **EQUILATERAL** figure has sides that are all the same length. In an **EQUIANGULAR** figure, all the angles have the same measurement. To find the length of a side in an equilateral figure, divide the perimeter by the number of sides. To find the measure of each angle, divide the sum of all the interior angles by the number of angles.

PRACTICE QUESTIONS

38. What is the perimeter of the regular polygon shown below?

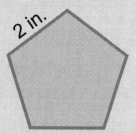

    A)   6.88 inches

    B)   8 inches

    C)   10 inches

    D)   12 inches

39. Examine (a), (b), and (c) to determine the best answer

    (a)   the perimeter of a square with side length of 6

    (b)   the perimeter of a rectangle with a width of 4 and length of 8

    (c)   the perimeter of an equilateral triangle of side length of 7

    A)   (a) is greater than (c)

    B)   (a) is equal to (c)

    C)   (b) is equal to (c)

    D)   (a), (b), and (c) are equal

VOLUME AND SURFACE AREA

Three-dimensional shapes have depth in addition to width and length. **VOLUME** is the number of cubic units any solid can hold—that is, what it takes to fill it. **SURFACE AREA** is the sum of the areas of the two-dimensional figures that are found on its surface. Some three-dimensional shapes also have a unique property called a **SLANT HEIGHT** (*l*), which is the distance from the base to the apex along a lateral face.

TABLE 4.10. Three-Dimensional Shapes and Formulas

Term	Shape	Formula	
Prism		$V = Bh$ $SA = 2lw + 2wh + 2lh$	B = area of base h = height l = length w = width
Cube		$V = s^3$ $SA = 6s^2$	s = cube edge
Sphere		$V = \frac{4}{3}\pi r^3$ $SA = 4\pi r^2$	r = radius
Cylinder		$V = Bh = \pi r^2 h$ $SA = 2\pi r^2 + 2\pi rh$	B = area of base h = height r = radius
Cone		$V = \frac{1}{3}\pi r^2 h$ $SA = \pi r^2 + \pi rl$	r = radius h = height l = slant height
Pyramid		$V = \frac{1}{3}Bh$ $SA = B + \frac{1}{2}(p)l$	B = area of base h = height p = perimeter l = slant height

PRACTICE QUESTIONS

40. What is the surface area of a cube with a side length of 5 meters?

A) 75 m²

B) 125 m²

C) 100 m²

D) 150 m²

SIMILARITY AND CONGRUENCE

When discussing shapes in geometry, the term **CONGRUENT** is used to mean that two shapes have the same shape and size (but not necessarily the same orientation or location). For example, if the length of two lines are equal, the two lines themselves are called congruent. Congruence is written using the symbol ≅. On figures, congruent parts are denoted with hash marks.

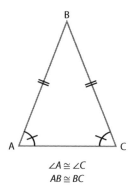

$$\angle A \cong \angle C$$
$$AB \cong BC$$

Figure 4.17. Congruent Parts of a Triangle

Shapes that are **SIMILAR** have the same shape but not the same size, meaning their corresponding angles are the same, but their lengths are not. For two shapes to be similar, the ratio of their corresponding sides must be a constant (usually written as k). Similarity is described using the symbol ~.

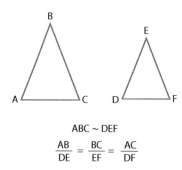

$$ABC \sim DEF$$
$$\frac{AB}{DE} = \frac{BC}{EF} = \frac{AC}{DF}$$

Figure 4.18. Similar Triangles

Statistics and Probability

DESCRIPTIVE STATISTICS

Statistics is the study of data. Analyzing data requires using **MEASURES OF CENTRAL TENDENCY** (mean, median, and mode) to identify trends or patterns.

The **MEAN** is the average; it is determined by adding all values and then dividing by the total number of values. For example, the average of the data set {16, 19, 19, 25, 27, 29, 75} is found by adding the values and dividing by 7.

$$\frac{16 + 19 + 19 + 25 + 27 + 29 + 75}{7} = \frac{210}{7} = 30$$

The **MEDIAN** is the number in the middle when the data set is arranged in order from least to greatest. For example, in the data set {16, 19, 19, $\underline{25}$, 27, 29, 75}, the median is 25. When a data set contains an even number of values, finding the median requires averaging the two middle values. In the data set {75, 80, 82, 100}, the two numbers in the middle are 80 and 82. Consequently, the median will be the average of these two values: $\frac{80 + 82}{2} = 81$.

The **MODE** is the most frequent outcome in a data set. In the set {16, $\underline{19}$, $\underline{19}$, 25, 27, 29, 75}, the mode is 19 because it occurs twice, which is more than any of the other numbers. If several values appear an equally frequent number of times, both values are considered the mode. If every value in a data set appears only once, the data set has no mode.

> **TEACHING TIP:**
> Mode is <u>most</u> common. Median is in the middle (like a median in the road). Mean is average.

Other useful indicators include range and outliers. The **RANGE** is the difference between the highest and the lowest values in a data set. For example, the range of the set {16, 19, 19, 25, 27, 29, 75} is 75 – 16 = 59.

OUTLIERS, or data points that are much different from other data points, should be noted as they can skew the central tendency. In the data set {16, 19, 19, 25, 27, 29, 75}, the value 75 is far outside the other values and raises the value of the mean. Without the outlier, the mean is much closer to the other data points.

$$\frac{16 + 19 + 19 + 25 + 27 + 29 + 75}{7} = \frac{210}{7} = 30$$

$$\frac{16 + 19 + 19 + 25 + 27 + 29}{6} = \frac{135}{6} = 22.5$$

43. In 2016, LeBron James scored 1954 points over 74 games. What was the mean number of points that he scored per game? (Round to the nearest tenth.)

A) 74

B) 26.4

C) 3.8

D) 25

44. In his class, Bart surveyed his classmates to determine their favorite pizza topping. The data he found was as follows:

Anchovy	1
Pineapple	2
Olives	4
Pepperoni	9
Bacon	2
Canadian Bacon	1

Which topping represents the mode?

A) Anchovy

B) Pineapple

C) Olives

D) Pepperoni

SET THEORY

A **SET** is any collection of items. In mathematics, a set is represented using a capital letter; it may include numbers, ordered pairs, or other mathematical objects.

The **UNION** of two sets, denoted $A \cup B$, contains all the data that is in either set A or set B, or both sets. The **INTERSECTION** of two sets, denoted $A \cap B$, includes only elements that are in both A and B.

$$A = \{1, 4, 7\} \text{ and } B = \{2, 4, 5, 8\}$$
$$A \cup B = \{1, 2, 4, 5, 7, 8\}$$
$$A \cap B = \{4\}$$

Unions and intersections can be understood in terms of a **VENN DIAGRAM**. The Venn diagram in Figure 4.19 shows two sets, A and B. The union of A and B is the entire area of the diagram; the intersection of sets is the shaded area where they overlap.

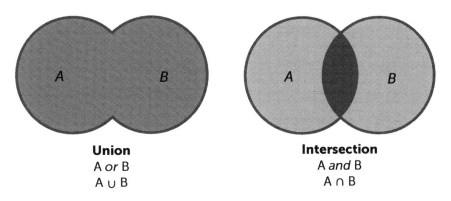

Union
A *or* B
A ∪ B

Intersection
A *and* B
A ∩ B

Figure 4.19. Unions and Intersections

PRACTICE QUESTION

45. Which of the following represents the intersection of sets *D* and *E* below?

$D = \{3, 7, 9, 12, 15\}$

$E = \{5, 9, 11, 15, 22\}$

A) $D \cap E = \{15\}$

B) $D \cap E = \{9, 15\}$

C) $D \cap E = \{3, 7, 9, 12, 15\}$

D) $D \cap E = \{3, 5, 7, 9, 11, 12, 15, 22\}$

PROBABILITY

PROBABILITY describes how likely something is to happen. In probability, an **EVENT** is the single result of a trial, and an **OUTCOME** is a possible event that results from a trial. The collection of all possible outcomes for a particular trial is called the **SAMPLE SPACE**. For example, when rolling a die, the sample space is the numbers 1 – 6. Rolling a single number, such as 4, would be a single event.

COUNTING PRINCIPLES are methods used to find the number of possible outcomes for a given situation. The **FUNDAMENTAL COUNTING PRINCIPLE** states that, for a series of independent events, the number of outcomes can be found by multiplying the number of possible outcomes for each event. For example, if a die is rolled (6 possible outcomes) and a coin is tossed (2 possible outcomes), there are 6 × 2 = 12 total possible outcomes.

The probability of a single event occurring is the number of outcomes in which that event occurs (called favorable events) divided by the number of items in the sample space (total possible outcomes):

$$P \text{ (an event)} = \frac{\text{number of favorable outcomes}}{\text{number of possible outcomes}}$$

The probability of any event occurring will always be a fraction or decimal between 0 and 1. A probability may also be expressed as a percent (e.g., a probability of 0.75 is 75%). An event with 0 probability will never occur, and an event with a probability of 1 is certain to occur. The probability of an event not occurring is referred to as that event's **COMPLEMENT**. The sum of an event's probability and the probability of that event's complement will always be 1.

To find the probability of multiple **INDEPENDENT EVENTS**—events whose outcomes do not affect each other—multiply the probability of each separate event. For example, the probability of getting the same number on a die during two consecutive rolls is

$$\frac{1}{6} \times \frac{1}{6} = \frac{1}{36}.$$

PRACTICE QUESTIONS

46. What is the probability that an even number results when a six-sided die is rolled?

A) $\frac{1}{6}$

B) $\frac{1}{3}$

C) $\frac{1}{2}$

D) $\frac{2}{3}$

47. In a particular game, a person must draw a uniquely colored marble to win money. There are 12 blue marbles, 3 red marbles, and 1 yellow marble in a bag. If you draw a blue marble, then you lose your money; if you draw a red marble, you get your money back; if you draw a yellow marble, you win $5. What is the probability Marcia will not win $5?

A) $\frac{15}{16}$

B) $\frac{1}{16}$

C) $\frac{3}{4}$

D) $\frac{3}{16}$

Number Series

To answer number series questions, it's helpful to know the two basic types of number series. Other types of series may appear on the test, but most of the series will be either arithmetic or geometric.

In an **ARITHMETIC** number series, the difference between each term is the same (a value called the **COMMON DIFFERENCE**). For example, the number series {20, 30, 40, 50} is arithmetic because the difference between the terms is 10. To determine if a number series is arithmetic, subtract consecutive terms to determine if the difference is the same.

15, 21, 27, 33, ...

21 – 15 = 6

27 – 21 = 6

33 – 27 = 6

The series is arithmetic with a common difference of 6.

33 + 6 = 39

The next term in the series is 39.

In a **GEOMETRIC** number series, the ratio between consecutive terms is constant (a value called the **COMMON RATIO**). For example, the number series {2, 4, 8, 16, 32, 64} is geometric, with a common ratio of 2. To find the common ratio, choose any term in the series and divide it by the previous term. To find the next term in the number series, multiply the previous term by the common ratio.

3, 9, 27, 81, ...

$$\frac{9}{3} = 3$$

$$\frac{27}{9} = 3$$

$$\frac{81}{27} = 3$$

The number series is geometric with a common ratio of 3.

$81 \times 3 = 243$

The next term in the series is 243.

PRACTICE QUESTIONS

48. 110, 99, 88, 77, ...

Which number should come next in the series?

A) 56

B) 66

C) 88

D) 82

49. $\frac{1}{5}, \frac{1}{25}, \frac{1}{125}, \frac{1}{625}, \cdots$

Which number should come next in the series?

A) $\frac{1}{15625}$

B) $\frac{1}{525}$

C) $\frac{1}{3125}$

D) $\frac{1}{625}$

50. 74, 78, 82, __ , 90, 94

Which number should fill in the blank in the series?

A) 98

B) 84

C) 88

D) 86

51. 1, 3, 9, 27, 81, ...

Which number should come next in the series?

A) 108

B) 243

C) 810

D) 9

52. 3, 7, 15, 31, ...

Which number should come next in the series?

A) 46

B) 93

C) 63

D) 87

Answer Key

1. **C**

   Multiply the number of boxes by the number of pencils in each box to find the total number of pencils.

   10 × 150 = **1500 pencils**

2. **D**

   Use order of operations (PEMDAS) to solve the equation.

   First, complete the operations in the parentheses. Divide, then subtract.

   8 ÷ 4 = 2

   12 − 2 = 10

   Complete the exponents outside the parentheses.

   10^2 = **100**

3. **A**

   Because the temperature went down, add a negative number.

   −3 + (−5) = **−8°F**

4. **C**

   Simplify each expression.

   (a): −5 + 25 = 20

   (b): 13 − (−10) = 23

   (c): 2 × 14 = 28

   (c) > (b) > (a)

5. **A**

   Determine the largest square number that is a factor of the radicand, 48. Write the radicand as a product using that square number as a factor.

   $\sqrt{48}$ = $\sqrt{16 \times 3}$ = $\sqrt{16}\sqrt{3}$ = **$4\sqrt{3}$**

6. **B**

   Calculate each value.

   (a): 2^0 = 1

   (b): 2^{-1} = $\frac{1}{2^1}$ = $\frac{1}{2}$

   (c): 2^1 = 2

   (c) > (a) > (b)

   a is greater than b

7. **B**

   To add, the powers of 10 must be the same. Convert the first value so the power of 10 is 2.

   $3.8 \times 10^3 = 3.8 \times 10 \times 10^2 = 38 \times 10^2$

   Add the *a* terms together and write the answer in proper scientific notation, where $1 \leq a < 10$.

   $(38 \times 10^2) + (4.7 \times 10^2) = (38 + 4.7) \times 10^2 = 42.7 \times 10^2 = \textbf{4.27} \times \textbf{10}^3$

8. **C**

   $-(3)^2 + 4(5) + (5 - 6)^2 - 8$

   $= -(3)^2 + 4(5) + (-1)^2 - 8$

   $= -9 + 4(5) + 1 - 8$

   $= -9 + 20 + 1 - 8$

   $= 11 + 1 - 8$

   $= 12 - 8$

   $= \textbf{4}$

9. **C**

   Use the order of operation to simplify each expression.

   (a): Simplify the expression in the parentheses, $2 \times 3 = 6$. Solve by subtracting, $6 - 6 = 0$.

   (b): Simplify the parentheses, $6 - 2 = 4$. Solve by multiplying, $4 \times 3 = 12$.

   (c): Multiply first and then subtract: $6 - 2 \times 3 = 6 - 6 = 0$.

   (b) is greater than (c): 12 > 0

10. **D**

    The common denominator is $4 \times 3 = 12$.

    Convert each fraction to the common denominator.

    $\frac{1}{4}\left(\frac{3}{3}\right) = \frac{3}{12}$

    $\frac{1}{3}\left(\frac{4}{4}\right) = \frac{4}{12}$

    Add the numerators and keep the denominator the same.

    $\frac{3}{12} + \frac{4}{12} = \frac{7}{12}$ **pizza**

11. **C**

    Multiply 24 by $\frac{1}{4}$ to find the number of students who failed the test.

    $24 \times \frac{1}{4} = \frac{24}{4} = 6$

    Subtract to find the number of students who passed the test.

    $24 - 6 = \textbf{18 students}$

12. **A**

    Rewrite the numbers vertically, lining up the decimal points.

    Add:

2.20
32.54
+ 4.00
38.74

The total bill was **$38.74**.

13. **A**

Convert each value to a decimal value.

(a): 0.79

(b): 0.0122 + 0.7778 = 0.79

(c): 0.3 × 0.4 = 0.08

(a) = (b) > (c)

14. **A**

Write a proportion using x for the missing value.

$$\frac{60 \text{ kg}}{90 \text{ mg}} = \frac{80 \text{ kg}}{x \text{ mg}}$$

Cross multiply.

$60(x) = 80(90)$

Divide by 60.

$60x = 7200$

$x = 120$

The proper dosage is **120 mg**.

15. **B**

Convert the percentage to a decimal.

$40\% = 0.4$

Write the proportion.

$$\frac{250}{x} = \frac{0.4}{1}$$

Cross multiply.

$250(1) = 0.4(x)$

$250 = 0.4x$

Divide both sides by 0.4.

$625 = x$

There are **625** students in Jacob's class.

16. **C**

Set up a proportion and solve.

$$\frac{\text{part}}{\text{whole}} = \frac{\%}{100}$$

$$\frac{16}{x} = \frac{80}{100}$$

$16(100) = 80(x)$

$x = 20$

17. B

Identify the known values, then substitute in the percentage equation.

Original amount = $1500

Percent change = 45% = 0.45

Amount of change = ?

Amount of change = original amount × percent change → $1500 × 0.45 = $675

Original price − amount of change = new price

$1500 − $675 = **$825**

18. C

Kevin can only have 120 people attend. More than 120 people can be invited if he expects 30% to decline his invitation.

Convert the percentage to a decimal.

Accept invitation → 70% = 0.7

Let x = the number of people he can invite.

$x(0.7) = 120$

$x = \frac{120}{0.7}$

$x = \mathbf{171}$

19. D

Hank earned 40% or 4000 of the vote.

Write and solve the proportion.

$\frac{4000}{x} = \frac{40}{100} \rightarrow x = 10{,}000$

If voter turnout was 80%, then the number of registered voters is equivalent to:

$\frac{10{,}000}{x} = \frac{80}{100} \rightarrow x = \mathbf{12{,}500}$

20. B

Round each town population to the nearest thousand.

12,341 ≈ 12,000

8975 ≈ 9000

9431 ≈ 9000

10,521 ≈ 11,000

11,627 ≈ 12,000

Add to find the total population.

12,000 + 9000 + 9000 + 11,000 + 12,000 = **53,000**

21. A

When using the associative property, the answer will remain the same in an addition problem regardless of where the parentheses are placed. 2 + (1 + 5) = (2 + 1) + 5 is the correct answer.

22. A

Substitute the value −10 for a in the expression and simplify.

$\frac{a^2}{4} - 3a + 4$

$= \frac{(-10)^2}{4} - 3(-10) + 4$

$= \frac{100}{4} + 30 + 4$

$= 25 + 30 + 4 = \mathbf{59}$

23. A

Substitute the given terms for a and b.

$2a + 3b$

$= 2(xy) + 3(x^2)$

$= \mathbf{2xy + 3x^2}$

24. A

Combine like terms.

$4x - 3y + 12z + 2x - 7y - 10z$

$= (4x + 2x) + (-3y - 7y) + (12z - 10z)$

$= \mathbf{6x - 10y + 2z}$

25. C

Write an expression for each person's tickets and then combine like terms.

Paul = 3 boxes of green tickets and 8 boxes of red tickets: $3g + 8r$.

Paula = 6 boxes of green tickets and 2 boxes of red tickets: $6g + 2r$.

Combining like terms gives $\mathbf{9g + 10r}$.

26. B

Distribute the term $5x$ by multiplying by each of the three terms inside the parentheses:

$5x(x^2 - 2c + 10)$

$(5x)(x^2) = 5x^3$

$(5x)(-2c) = -10xc$

$(5x)(10) = 50x$

$5x(x^2 - 2c + 10) = \mathbf{5x^3 - 10xc + 50x}$

27. C

Plug $b = -2$ and $c = -3$ into the expression $-3(b + 8c)$ and simplify.

$-3(b + 8c)$

$= -3(-2 + 8(-3))$

$= -3(-2 + (-24))$

$= -3(-26)$

$= \mathbf{78}$

28. D

Distribute the 5 and combine like terms:

$5(x + 3) - 12 = 43$

$5x + 15 - 12 = 43$

$5x + 3 = 43$

Subtract 3 from both sides:

$5x + 3 - 3 = 43 - 3$

$5x = 40$

Divide both sides by 5:

$\frac{5x}{5} = \frac{40}{5}$

$\mathbf{x = 8}$

29. D

Determine the amount per hour Mandy will charge this family.

Charges: $8 for one child plus $3 each for additional children.

4 children → $8 + 3 \times 3 = \$17$ per hour.

If she babysits for 5 hours, then she should expect to earn $17 \times 5 = \mathbf{\$85}$.

30. D

Inequalities can be solved just like equations.

$4x + 10 > 58$

Subtract 10 from both sides:

$4x + 10 - 10 > 58 - 10$

$4x > 48$

Divide by 4 to isolate x:

$\frac{4x}{4} > \frac{48}{4}$

$\mathbf{x > 12}$

31. C

Identify the quantities:

number of shirts = t

total cost of shirts = $12t$

number of pants = p

total cost of pants = $15p$

number of pairs of shoes = s

total cost of shoes = $45s$

The cost of all the items must be less than $2500: $\mathbf{12t + 15p + 45s \leq 2500}$

32. D

$6x - 2y - 8 = 0$

Write in slope-intercept form (solve for y).

$-2y = -6x + 8$

$\frac{-2y}{-2} = \frac{-6x}{-2} + \frac{8}{-2}$

$y = 3x - 4$

The slope is the coefficient of x, which is **3**.

33. B

Starting at the origin, move 5 units to the left and then up 2 units. The point is located in the top left quadrant, which is **quadrant II**.

34. B

Use a conversion factor to convert centimeters to meters.

$2.5 \text{ m} \times \frac{100 \text{ cm}}{1 \text{ m}} = \frac{2.5 \text{ m} \times 100 \text{ cm}}{1 \text{ m}} = \textbf{250 cm}$

35. A

Convert each value to a common unit.

(a): $2 \text{ c} \times \frac{8 \text{ oz}}{1 \text{ c}} = 16$ ounces

(b): $0.5 \text{ qt} \times \frac{4 \text{ c}}{1 \text{ qt}} \times \frac{8 \text{ oz}}{1 \text{ c}} = 16$ ounces

(c): 16 ounces

(a) = (b) = (c)

36. B

Supplementary angles have a sum of 180°. Subtract the measure of angle M from 180°.

$180° - 36° = \textbf{144°}$

37. $\dot{A}, \dot{B}, \overleftrightarrow{D}$

Points A and B and line D all lie on plane M.

38. C

Add the lengths of all the sides.

$2 \text{ in} + 2 \text{ in} + 2 \text{ in} + 2 \text{ in} + 2 \text{ in} = \textbf{10 in}$

39. A

Calculate each value.

(a): $P(square) = 4s = 4(6) = 24$

(b): $P(rectangle) = 2w + 2l = 2(4) + 2(8) = 24$

(c): $P(triangle) = s_1 + s_2 + s_3 = 7 + 7 + 7 = 21$

(a) > (c)

40. D

A cube has six faces, each of which is a square.

Find the area of each side using the formula for the area of a square:

$A = s^2 = 5^2 = 25 \text{ m}^2$

Multiply the area by 6 (because the cube has six faces):

$SA = 25(6) = \textbf{150 m}^2$

41. A

Plug the given values into the formula for the cylinder.

$V(cylinder) = \pi r^2 h = 300$ cubic meters

Because the radius and height are the same, $\pi r^2 h = 300$ cubic meters can be substituted into the formula for the volume of a cone.

$V(cone) = \frac{1}{3}\pi r^2 h = \frac{1}{3}(300 \text{ m}^2) =$ **100 cubic meters**

42. A

Find the length of a side in square *ABCD* using the formula for the area of a square.

$A = s^2 = 100 \text{ mm}^2$

$A = 10 \text{ mm}$

The side length of square *MNOP* is $\frac{1}{2}$ the side length of square *ABCD*.

$10 \text{ mm} \div 2 = 5 \text{ mm}$

Find the area of square *MNOP* using the formula for the area of a square.

$A = s^2 = 5^2 =$ **25 mm²**

43. B

The mean is the average number of points per game. Divide the total number of points by the number of games played:

$\frac{1954}{74} \approx$ **26.4**

44. D

The mode occurs the most often. The mode is **Pepperoni**.

45. B

The intersection of two sets of numbers is all the numbers that appear in both sets.

$D = \{3, 7, \underline{9}, 12, \underline{15}\}$

$E = \{5, \underline{9}, 11, \underline{15}, 22\}$

$D \cap E = \{9, 15\}$

46. C

$P(\text{rolling even}) = \frac{number\ of\ favorable\ outcomes}{total\ number\ of\ possible\ outcomes} = \frac{3}{6} = \frac{1}{2}$

47. A

Win \$5 = yellow marble

There are 16 possible marbles and only 1 yellow marble.

The probability of drawing a yellow marble $= \frac{1}{16}$.

The probability she would not win $= 1 - \frac{1}{16} = \frac{15}{16}$.

48. B

The series is arithmetic with a difference of −11.

110, 99, 88, 77, ...

99 − 110 = −11

88 − 99 = −11

77 − 89 = − 11

The next number is 77 − 11 = **66**.

49. C

The series is geometric with a common ratio of $\frac{1}{5}$.=

$\frac{1}{5}$, $\frac{1}{25}$, $\frac{1}{125}$, $\frac{1}{625}$, ...

$\frac{1}{5} \times \frac{1}{5} = \frac{1}{25}$

$\frac{1}{25} \times \frac{1}{5} = \frac{1}{125}$

$\frac{1}{125} \times \frac{1}{5} = \frac{1}{625}$

The next number is $\frac{1}{625} \times \frac{1}{5} = \mathbf{\frac{1}{3125}}$.

50. D

The series is arithmetic with a difference of 4.

74, 78, 82, _____, 90, 94

78 − 74 = 4

82 − 78 = 4

94 − 90 = 4

To find the missing number, add 4 to the previous term.

82 + 4 = **86**

51. B

The series is geometric with a common ratio of 3.

1, 3, 9, 27, 81, ...

$\frac{3}{1} = 3$

$\frac{9}{3} = 3$

$\frac{27}{9} = 3$

$\frac{81}{27} = 3$

The next number is 81 × 3 = **243**

52. C

The next number in the series is found by multiplying the previous term by 2 and adding 1.

3, 7, 15, 31, ...

1 × 2 + 1 = 3

3 × 2 + 1 = 7

7 × 2 + 1 = 15

15 × 2 + 1 = 31

The next number in the series is 31 × 2 + 1 = **63**.

CHAPTER FIVE
PRACTICE TEST ONE

Verbal Skills

1. Classroom is to teaching as park is to
   A) sleeping.
   B) eating.
   C) playing.
   D) dancing.

2. Which word does NOT belong with the others?
   A) mouse
   B) keyboard
   C) internet
   D) screen

3. All baseball players wear caps. Caps are hats. All baseball players wear hats. If the first two statements are true, the third statement is
   A) true.
   B) false.
   C) uncertain.

4. Which word does NOT belong with the others?
   A) oven
   B) freezer
   C) microwave
   D) grill

5. Divisive means the opposite of
   A) troublesome.
   B) contentious.
   C) artificial.
   D) unifying.

6. Joey is to kangaroo as puppy is to
   A) cat.
   B) fish.
   C) frog.
   D) dog.

7. Maria wanted to lose weight. After several weeks, she tried on pants that used to be too tight and that are now too loose. Maria lost weight. If the first two statements are true, the third statement is
   A) true.
   B) false.
   C) uncertain.

8. Which word does NOT belong with the others?
   A) lively
   B) dull
   C) gloomy
   D) somber

9. Tremble most nearly means
   A) squeak.
   B) shiver.
   C) steadfast.
   D) calm.

10. Tornadoes are dangerous. Hurricanes are dangerous. Hurricanes are more dangerous than tornadoes. If the first two statements are true, the third statement is
    A) true.
    B) false.
    C) uncertain.

11. Which word does NOT belong with the others?
    A) tired
    B) exhausted
    C) weary
    D) energetic

12. Swooped means the opposite of
    A) plunged.
    B) dove.
    C) swept.
    D) risen.

13. Computer is to typing as phone is to
    A) social media.
    B) texting.
    C) ringing.
    D) watching.

14. Hesitate most nearly means
    A) persevere.
    B) continue.
    C) pause.
    D) resolve.

15. All candy costs between 5 and 10 cents. Some candy is made from chocolate. Some candy costs less than 5 cents. If the first two statements are true, the third statement is
    A) true.
    B) false.
    C) uncertain.

16. Which word does NOT belong with the others?
    A) ordinary
    B) miraculous
    C) magical
    D) different

17. Assurance means the opposite of
    A) promise.
    B) word.
    C) timidity.
    D) poise.

18. Clean is to dirty as small is to
    A) smelly.
    B) sparkly.
    C) big.
    D) shady.

19. Nicole likes sandwiches from the local deli. There are only vegetarian and meat-filled sandwiches at the local deli. Nicole likes vegetarian and meat-filled sandwiches. If the first two statements are true, the third statement is
    A) true.
    B) false.
    C) uncertain.

20. John always tells the truth. Mary sometimes lies. Mary says that sometimes John lies. If the first two statements are true, the third statement is
    A) true.
    B) false.
    C) uncertain.

21. Which word does NOT belong with the others?
    A) destroy
    B) finish
    C) create
    D) shatter

22. Entail means the opposite of
    A) require.
    B) obfuscate.
    C) necessitate.
    D) exclude.

23. Puzzle is to piece as team is to
    A) player.
    B) soccer.
    C) base.
    D) goal.

24. Meager most nearly means
    A) sufficient.
    B) plentiful.
    C) inadequate.
    D) substantial.

25. Marlen has five animals. Marlen has two dogs. Marlen has three cats. If the first two statements are true, the third statement is
    A) true.
    B) false.
    C) uncertain.

26. Which word does NOT belong with the others?
    A) unhappy
    B) miserable
    C) cheerful
    D) depressed

27. Dormant most nearly means
    A) awake.
    B) modern.
    C) inactive.
    D) loud.

28. Which word does NOT belong with the others?
    A) recent
    B) new
    C) ancient
    D) modern

29. Vexation means the opposite of
    A) satisfaction.
    B) anger.
    C) taxation.
    D) exasperation.

30. Feather is to bird as fur is to
    A) frog.
    B) dog.
    C) scales.
    D) turkey.

31. Pacify most nearly means
    A) soothe.
    B) transport.
    C) motivate.
    D) nurture.

32. Which word does NOT belong with the others?
    A) cat
    B) dog
    C) horse
    D) chameleon

33. Acclaim most nearly means
    A) pity.
    B) praise.
    C) interest.
    D) assistance.

34. Max played soccer this weekend. Max's team has never won. Max's team lost today. If the first two statements are true, the third statement is
    A) true.
    B) false.
    C) uncertain.

35. Which word does NOT belong with the others?
    A) pleased
    B) angry
    C) furious
    D) outraged

36. Consistent means the opposite of
    A) reliable.
    B) uneven.
    C) unswerving.
    D) stable.

37. Facilitate is to assist as obliterate is to
    A) create.
    B) question.
    C) bother.
    D) destroy.

38. Haphazard most nearly means
    A) dangerous.
    B) chaotic.
    C) cautious.
    D) creative.

39. The Sears Tower is in Chicago. Anthony went to Chicago last year. Anthony visited the Sears Tower. If the first two statements are true, the third statement is
    A) true.
    B) false.
    C) uncertain.

40. Which word does NOT belong with the others?
    A) water
    B) ice
    C) lemonade
    D) soda

41. Insightful means the opposite of
    A) visionary.
    B) unperceptive.
    C) openminded.
    D) aware.

42. Pedal is to bicycle as zipper is to
    A) closure.
    B) metal.
    C) button.
    D) jacket.

43. Meander most nearly means
    A) relax.
    B) whimper.
    C) sprint.
    D) wander.

44. Which word does NOT belong with the others?
    A) rake
    B) shovel
    C) pitchfork
    D) broom

45. Ascend most nearly means
    A) rise.
    B) imagine.
    C) find.
    D) recline.

46. Max bought a lollipop. The strawberry-flavored lollipop he chose was his favorite. Max likes strawberry-flavored lollipops. If the first two statements are true, the third statement is
    A) true.
    B) false.
    C) uncertain.

47. Which word does NOT belong with the others?
    A) pine needles
    B) tree trunks
    C) seagulls
    D) mushrooms

48. Partial means the opposite of
    A) fair.
    B) biased.
    C) subjective.
    D) broken.

49. Stomach is to digestion as lungs are to
    A) organ.
    B) chest.
    C) oxygen.
    D) breathing.

50. Quench most nearly means
    A) stimulate.
    B) ignite.
    C) satisfy.
    D) encourage.

51. Walter went to the water fountain. He drank water. Walter prefers soda. If the first two statements are true, the third statement is
    A) true.
    B) false.
    C) uncertain.

52. Which word does NOT belong with the others?
    A) shells
    B) sea glass
    C) lobsters
    D) rocks

53. Aptitude most nearly means
    A) talent for socializing.
    B) constant hunger.
    C) capacity to learn.
    D) lofty height.

54. Which word does NOT belong with the others?
    A) white board
    B) desk
    C) chair
    D) marker

55. Revelation means the opposite of
    A) surprise.
    B) admission.
    C) secret.
    D) disclosure.

56. Knife is to slice as fork is to
    A) slurp.
    B) pierce.
    C) gorge.
    D) spoon.

57. Abolish most nearly means
    A) eliminate.
    B) establish.
    C) continue.
    D) inaugurate.

58. Which word does NOT belong with the others?
    A) medal
    B) certificate
    C) trophy
    D) award

59. Jose plays lacrosse. Juanita plays soccer. Jose doesn't like soccer. If the first two statements are true, the third statement is
    A) true.
    B) false.
    C) uncertain.

60. Which word does NOT belong with the others?
    A) beep
    B) ring
    C) weight
    D) snort

Quantatative Skills

1. 1, 1, 2, 3, 5, 8, ...
   Which number should come next in the series?
    A) 11
    B) 13
    C) 16
    D) 9

2. Examine (a), (b), and (c), and then choose the best answer.

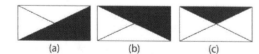

    A) (a) is more shaded than (c)
    B) (a), (b), and (c) are equally shaded
    C) (b) is less shaded than (c)
    D) (c) is more shaded than (a)

3. 73, 67, 61, _____, 49, 43
   Which number should fill in the blank in the series?
    A) 53
    B) 54
    C) 55
    D) 56

4. 8127, 8021, 7915, 7809, ...
   Which number should come next in the series?
    A) 7703
    B) 7721
    C) 7697
    D) 7715

5. What number is 75% of 24?
    A) 6
    B) 30
    C) 18
    D) 75

6. 71, 69, ___, ___, 63, 61
Which two numbers should fill in the blanks in the series?

   A) 65, 64

   B) 68, 64

   C) 67, 65

   D) 68, 65

7. $\frac{2}{3}$ of what number is equal to 12?

   A) 24

   B) 8

   C) 18

   D) 6

8. 0.04, 0.08, 0.16, 0.32, ...
Which number should come next in the series?

   A) 0.48

   B) 0.6

   C) 0.64

   D) 0.36

9. ___, 5, 6.1, 7.2, 8.3
Which number should fill in the blank in the series?

   A) 4.1

   B) 3.5

   C) 3.9

   D) 4.9

10. $\frac{3}{5}$ of what number is 300?

   A) 180

   B) 120

   C) 500

   D) 300

11. Examine (a), (b), and (c), and then choose the best answer.

   (a) the area of a square with a side length of 10

   (b) the area of a rectangle with a length of 5 and a width of 2

   (c) the area of a triangle with a base of 12 and a height of 3

   A) (c) is greater than (a)

   B) (c) is less than (b)

   C) (b) and (c) are each less than (a)

   D) (a) and (b) are equal

12. What number is $\frac{3}{5}$ of 500?

   A) 180

   B) 120

   C) 500

   D) 300

13. Examine (a), (b), and (c), and then choose the best answer.

   (a) the perimeter of a square with a side of 6

   (b) the perimeter of an equilateral triangle with a side of 8

   (c) the perimeter of an equilateral hexagon with a side of 3

   A) (a) is less than (c)

   B) (c) and (b) are both less than (a)

   C) (b) is less than (a)

   D) (a) and (b) are each greater than (c)

14. 4848, 2424, 1212, 606, ...
Which number should come next in the series?

   A) 353

   B) 202

   C) 909

   D) 303

15. Examine (a), (b), and (c), and then choose the best answer.

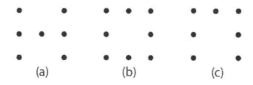

(a)   (b)   (c)

- **A)** (a) and (b) have the same number of circles
- **B)** (a) and (c) each have more circles than (b)
- **C)** (b) has more circles than (a)
- **D)** (c) has fewer circles than (a)

16. 1, 0, −1, 0, 1, 0, …
Which number should come next in the series?
- **A)** −1
- **B)** 0
- **C)** 1
- **D)** $\frac{1}{2}$

17. 13, 14, 16, 19, …
Which two numbers should come next in the series?
- **A)** 23, 27
- **B)** 23, 28
- **C)** 22, 25
- **D)** 24, 27

18. 24, 12, 6, 3, …
Which number should come next in the series?
- **A)** 2
- **B)** 1
- **C)** 1.5
- **D)** 0

19. Examine the triangle and choose the best answer.

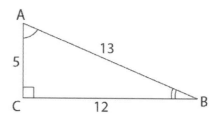

- **A)** ∠A is equal to ∠B
- **B)** ∠C is less than ∠A
- **C)** ∠C is greater than ∠B
- **D)** ∠B is greater than ∠A

20. 1.3, 2.6, 3.9, 5.2, …
Which number should come next in the series?
- **A)** 6.1
- **B)** 6.3
- **C)** 6.7
- **D)** 6.5

21. 1234, 2345, 3456, _____, 5678, 6789
Which number should fill in the blank in the series?
- **A)** 3567
- **B)** 4678
- **C)** 4680
- **D)** 4567

22. 567, 579, 592, 606, 621, _____
Which number should come next in the series?
- **A)** 637
- **B)** 636
- **C)** 638
- **D)** 635

23. Examine (a), (b), and (c) to determine the correct answer.

(a) 3.48×10^{-3}

(b) -3×-48

(c) $-2 - (-4)$

A) (a), (b), and (c) are all negative

B) only (c) is negative

C) (a), (b), and (c) are positive

D) (a) and (b) are negative

24. Examine (a), (b), and (c) to determine the correct answer.

(a) 30%

(b) 0.3

(c) $\frac{3}{100}$

A) (a) and (b) are equal and greater than (c)

B) (b) and (c) are equal and less than (a)

C) (a) and (c) are equal and less than (b)

D) (a), (b), and (c) are all equal

25. 710, 720, 740, 770, 810, ...
Which number should come next in the series?

A) 850

B) 860

C) 870

D) 855

26. What number is 21 more than 4 squared?

A) 13

B) 5

C) 37

D) 25

27. Examine (a), (b), and (c) to determine the correct answer.

(a) $\frac{2}{3} \times 42$

(b) $\frac{7}{10} \times 40$

(c) $\frac{5}{4} \times 24$

A) (a) is greater than (c)

B) (c) is greater than (a) and (b)

C) (b) is greater than (c)

D) (c) is less than (a) but not (b)

28. 15, ___, 23, ____, 31
Which two numbers should fill in the blanks in the series?

A) 17, 27

B) 19, 27

C) 19, 28

D) 18, 25

29. $\frac{5}{7}$ of what number is equal to 35?

A) 2

B) 49

C) 25

D) 5

30. What number is $\frac{1}{3}$ of 36?

A) 18

B) 6

C) 12

D) 24

31. What number is 11 less than 6 squared?

A) 47

B) 25

C) 1

D) −25

32. What number is 2 multiplied by the sum of 11 and 3?

A) 28

B) 18

C) 196

D) 7

33. 83.5, 80, _____, 73, 69.5

Which number should fill in the blank in the series?

A) 76

B) 76.5

C) 77

D) 75.5

34. $\frac{2}{3}$ of what number is equal to 150?

A) 100

B) 200

C) 225

D) 250

35. The sum of what number and 4 is equal to 10?

A) 10

B) 14

C) 6

D) 156

36. What number is $\frac{3}{5}$ of 100?

A) 35

B) 53

C) 60

D) 6

37. What number is the difference between two consecutive odd integers?

A) 8

B) 7

C) 1

D) 2

38. Examine (a), (b), and (c) to determine the correct answer.

(a) $0 + (3 - 2)$

(b) $0 \times (3 - 2)$

(c) $0 - (3 - 2)$

A) (a) is equal to 0

B) both (a) and (b) are positive

C) (a), (b), and (c) are equal

D) (a) is greater than (c)

39. What number is 20% of 25% of 80?

A) 4

B) 5

C) 36

D) 16

40. What number is $\frac{2}{3}$ of 60 divided by 8?

A) 60

B) 5

C) 25

D) 4

41. _____, −12, −14, −16, −18

Which number should fill in the blank in the series?

A) −8

B) −10

C) 10

D) −9

42. What number is 12 more than $\frac{2}{3}$ of 33?

A) 10

B) 33

C) 34

D) 30

43. What number is 12 less than 8 squared?

   A) 4

   B) 76

   C) 52

   D) 32

44. Examine (a), (b), and (c), and then choose the best answer.

   (a) circumference of a circle with a radius of 4

   (b) circumference of a circle with a diameter of 4

   (c) circumference of a circle with a radius of 2

   A) (a) is less than (b)

   B) (a), (b), and (c) are all equal

   C) (c) is greater than (b)

   D) (b) and (c) are equal

45. Examine (a), (b), and (c), and then choose the best answer.

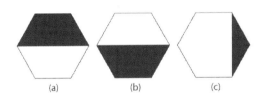

      (a)   (b)   (c)

   A) (a) is more shaded than (c)

   B) (a), (b), and (c) are equally shaded

   C) (b) is less shaded than (c)

   D) (c) is more shaded than (a)

46. Examine (a), (b), and (c) to determine the correct answer.

   (a) 30% of 50

   (b) 50% of 30

   (c) 3% of 500

   A) (a) = (b) = (c)

   B) (a) = (b) > (c)

   C) (b) > (a) > (c)

   D) (a) > (b) = (c)

47. Examine the rectangular prism below and choose the best answer.

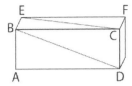

   A) AD is equal to BD

   B) AB is greater than AD

   C) BD is equal to CE

   D) CF is less than AB

48. Examine (a), (b), and (c) to determine the correct answer.

   (a) 8 + (3 − 2)

   (b) (8 + 3) − 2

   (c) 8 − (3 − 2)

   A) (b) and (c) are equal

   B) (b) is greater than (c)

   C) (c) is greater than (a)

   D) (a), (b), and (c) are equal

49. Examine (a), (b), and (c) to determine the correct answer.

   (a) $\frac{35}{35}$

   (b) 35^0

   (c) 35×0

   A) (a) = (b) > c

   B) (b) = (c) > (a)

   C) (a) = (b) = (c)

   D) (a) = (b) < c

50. −8, −3, ___, 7, 12

   Which number should fill in the blank in the series?

   A) 2

   B) 3

   C) −2

   D) 0

51. Examine the rectangle below and choose the best answer.

- **A)** BE is greater than DE
- **B)** BEC is equal to AED
- **C)** AD is greater than AC
- **D)** EBA is equal to EBC

52. Examine (a), (b), and (c) to determine the correct answer.

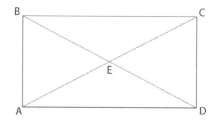

- (a)   0.6
- (b) $\frac{3}{5}$
- (c) $\frac{1}{2}$ of 1.2
- **A)**   (a), (b), and (c) are equal
- **B)**   (a) is greater than (b)
- **C)**   (b) is greater than (c)
- **D)**   (c) is greater than (a)

Reading

Have you ever devoured a tasty snow cone only to experience the agony of "brain freeze"? Have you ever wondered why or how that happens? Well, scientists now believe they understand the mechanism of these so-called ice cream headaches.

It begins with the icy temperature of the snow cone (or any cold food, or sometimes even exposure to cold air). When a cold substance (delicious or otherwise) presses against the roof of your mouth, it causes blood vessels there to begin to constrict, and your body starts to sense that something is awry. In response, blood is pumped to the affected region to try to warm it up, causing rapid dilation of the same vessels. This causes the neighboring trigeminal nerve to send rapid signals to your brain. Because the trigeminal nerve also serves the face, the brain misinterprets these signals as coming from your forehead. The duration of the pain varies from a few seconds up to about a minute.

Regardless of the time spent wincing, the danger of the ice cream headache certainly will not stop people for screaming for their favorite frozen treat in the future.

1. Readers can infer from the passage that the author is trying to _____ us.

- **A)**   inform and persuade
- **B)**   inform and entertain
- **C)**   warn and persuade
- **D)**   amuse and entertain

2. Which body part is NOT mentioned in the passage?

- **A)**   the roof of the mouth
- **B)**   the tongue
- **C)**   the face
- **D)**   the forehead

3. Why does the author use the word screaming in the last sentence?

A) to show how painful "brain freeze" can be

B) to show that ice cream headaches are dangerous

C) to jokingly refer to a play on words: "I scream for ice cream"

D) to rhyme with the word creaming in a traditional poem

4. Which sentence best summarizes the passage's main idea?

A) "Have you ever devoured a tasty snow cone only to experience the agony of 'brain freeze'?"

B) "Well, scientists now believe they understand the mechanism of these so-called ice cream headaches."

C) "When a cold substance (delicious or otherwise) presses against the roof of your mouth, it causes blood vessels there to begin to constrict, and your body starts to sense that something is awry."

D) "Because the trigeminal nerve also serves the face, the brain misinterprets these signals as coming from your forehead."

5. According to the passage, what happens immediately after the roof of the mouth grows cold?

A) Blood vessels on the roof of the mouth begin to expand.

B) The body pumps blood to the roof of the mouth to warm it up.

C) The trigeminal nerve sends rapid signals to the brain.

D) Blood vessels on the roof of the mouth begin to narrow.

6. In the last sentence, what does the word duration mean?

A) time period

B) skin surface

C) intensity

D) strength

Many snakes produce a toxic fluid in their salivary glands called venom. The two key ingredients in all snake venoms are enzymes and polypeptides. Some enzymes help the snake disable its prey, and others help the snake digest its prey. The victim of the snakebite has a much less beneficial experience with these enzymes: snake venoms can speed up chemical reactions that lower blood pressure, paralyze muscles, destroy tissues, deconstruct red blood cells, or cause internal bleeding.

CONTINUE

There are many different types of snake venom, composed of various combinations of toxic and nontoxic substances. Toxins in snake venom are often divided into three categories: hemotoxins, neurotoxins, and cytotoxins. Hemotoxins affect the blood by interfering with the process of blood coagulation. In some cases, hemotoxins inhibit the process of blood clotting, and in other cases they cause excessive clotting. Neurotoxins target the nervous system rather than body tissues; they disrupt the messages sent by neurotransmitter production and reception throughout the body. Neurotoxins can paralyze muscles, causing respiratory failure and possibly death. Cytotoxins cause liquefactive necrosis of body cells; they dissolve cells, leading to the death of tissues or organs. Some cytotoxins target specific types of cells—myotoxins affect muscles, cardiotoxins attack the heart, and nephrotoxins damage the kidneys.

In addition to research on various antivenoms to combat the potentially deadly effects of snake venom, scientists have also been looking at the venom itself as a possible source of medical benefits. Researchers have been studying the chemical compositions of these venoms and have been making strides in using the science behind the toxins to combat major diseases such as cancer, heart disease, and Alzheimer's. For instance, a drug called captopril, used to treat hypertension, is based on a toxin in the venom of a pit viper found in Brazil.

7. Which of the following statements can the reader infer from the passage?

A) All snakes produce venom.

B) Some snakes are not venomous.

C) A venomous snake never bites other members of its own species.

D) A Brazilian pit viper's venom is not poisonous to humans.

8. What is the author's primary purpose in writing this essay?

A) to advise readers on ways to treat patients with snakebites

B) to warn readers that most snakes are venomous

C) to inform readers about the contents of snake venom

D) to tell a story about a scientist who used venom as a medicine

9. In the last sentence in the second paragraph, what does the word part *nephro* in the word nephrotoxins probably mean?

A) poison

B) heart

C) muscle

D) kidney

10. In the last paragraph, what does the word *strides* mean?

A) long steps

B) heavy stomping

C) improvements

D) experiments

11. Which sentence best summarizes the passage's main idea?

A) "Many snakes produce a toxic fluid in their salivary glands called venom."

B) "There are many different types of snake venom, composed of various combinations of toxic and nontoxic substances."

C) "Some cytotoxins target specific types of cells—myotoxins affect muscles, cardiotoxins attack the heart, and nephrotoxins damage the kidneys."

D) "Researchers have been studying the chemical compositions of these venoms and have been making strides in using the science behind the toxins to combat major diseases such as cancer, heart disease, and Alzheimer's."

12. According to the passage, how does venom benefit snakes, besides the fact that this fluid allows snakes to kill their prey?

A) It helps snakes to disable and digest their prey.

B) It can heal snakes' diseases such as cancer and Alzheimer's.

C) It terrifies snakes' prey, momentarily paralyzing these creatures.

D) It discourages other predators from pursuing and eating snakes.

The history of vaccines dates back further than one might imagine—all the way to tenth-century China, where smallpox scabs were ground up and blown into a person's nostrils. However, what we recognize as the precursor to the modern vaccine came in 1796. English surgeon Edward Jenner built on the knowledge that people who worked with cows and had been exposed to cowpox, which has a mild effect on humans, did not catch smallpox. Jenner deliberately exposed a child to cowpox by taking some of the serum from a pustule on the hand of a milkmaid and scratching it into the child's skin. Six weeks later, he exposed the child to smallpox—and the child remained healthy.

Vaccines work by stimulating the immune system to produce antibodies against a particular disease. How does this happen? A minute amount of the disease-producing pathogen is injected into the bloodstream (although some vaccines can be taken orally or even as a nasal spray). The pathogen is either present in such a small amount that it will not cause illness or the pathogen is "dead." Either way, you cannot get sick, but your immune system will ramp up to repel the invaders. Your immune system hangs on to the antibodies it creates; if you are exposed to the pathogen in the future, your body is ready to fight it off.

CONTINUE

Vaccines have been a crucial component in the long history of public health efforts in the United States—they have helped eradicate or almost eradicate previously widespread diseases such as whooping cough, polio, rubella, tetanus, tuberculosis, smallpox, diphtheria, and measles. The creation of the National Vaccine Agency in 1813 encouraged many states to adopt mandatory immunizations for schoolchildren for the first time. Today, every state requires some immunizations for children entering public schools, though all allow medical exemptions and most allow exemptions on religious or philosophical grounds.

13. What does the first paragraph mainly concern?

   A) smallpox vaccines in tenth-century China

   B) Jenner's smallpox vaccine in 1796

   C) a cure for cowpox in the late 1700s

   D) wiping out widespread diseases in the United States

14. What is the meaning of the word *immunizations* in the last paragraph?

   A) immune systems

   B) pathogens

   C) pustules

   D) vaccinations

15. What is the author's primary purpose in writing this essay?

   A) to warn parents about possible side effects of vaccines

   B) to persuade parents to have their children vaccinated

   C) to advise people about different treatments for infectious diseases

   D) to inform readers about the history of vaccines, including how they work

16. Which of the following statements can be considered a statement of FACT according to the content offered in the paragraphs above?

   A) Chinese doctors were the first to successfully cure smallpox.

   B) A vaccine works with the body's immune system to prevent someone from getting a disease.

   C) Thanks to Edward Jenner, diseases such as whooping cough and polio no longer exist.

   D) Thanks to worldwide vaccination programs, most infectious diseases will soon be eradicated.

17. According to the passage, what is true about state laws on vaccinating schoolchildren?

   A) There are no exceptions to these requirements.

   B) The only exceptions to these laws are for medical reasons.

   C) Everyone should obey these laws, because diseases are infectious.

   D) Most states have religious and philosophical exemptions to these laws.

18. Readers can infer that neither
_____ nor the common cold
have been eradicated or close to
eradicated in the United States.

A) all flu viruses

B) the measles

C) tetanus

D) tuberculosis

In recent decades, jazz has been associated with New Orleans and festivals like Mardi Gras, but in the 1920s, jazz was a booming trend whose influence reached into many aspects of American culture. In fact, the years between World War I and the Great Depression were known as the Jazz Age, a term coined by F. Scott Fitzgerald in his famous novel *The Great Gatsby*. Sometimes also called the Roaring Twenties, this time period saw major urban centers experiencing new economic, cultural, and artistic vitality. In the United States, musicians flocked to cities like New York and Chicago, which would become famous hubs for jazz musicians.

Ella Fitzgerald, for example, moved from Virginia to New York City to begin her much-lauded singing career, and jazz pioneer Louis Armstrong got his big break in Chicago.

Jazz music was played by and for a more expressive and freed populace than the United States had previously seen. Women gained the right to vote and were openly seen drinking and dancing to jazz music. This period marked the emergence of the flapper, a woman determined to make a statement about her new role in society. Jazz music also provided the soundtrack for the explosion of African American art and culture now known as the Harlem Renaissance. In addition to Fitzgerald and Armstrong, numerous musicians, including Duke Ellington, Fats Waller, and Bessie Smith, promoted their distinctive and complex music as an integral part of the emerging African American culture.

19. What is the main idea of the passage?

A) People should associate jazz music with the 1920s, not modern New Orleans.

B) Jazz music played an important role in many cultural movements of the 1920s.

C) Many famous jazz musicians began their careers in New York City and Chicago.

D) African Americans were instrumental in launching jazz into mainstream culture.

20. What is a reasonable inference that can be drawn from this passage?

A) Jazz music was important to minority groups struggling for social equality in the 1920s.

B) Duke Ellington, Fats Waller, and Bessie Smith were the most important jazz musicians of the Harlem Renaissance.

C) Women gained the right to vote with the help of jazz musicians.

D) Duke Ellington, Fats Waller, and Bessie Smith all supported women's right to vote.

21. What is the author's primary purpose in writing this essay?

    A) to explain the role jazz musicians played in the Harlem Renaissance

    B) to inform the reader about the many important musicians playing jazz in the 1920s

    C) to discuss how jazz influenced important cultural movements in the 1920s

    D) to provide a history of jazz music in the 20th century

22. Which of the following is NOT a fact stated in the passage?

    A) The years between World War I and the Great Depression were known as the Jazz Age.

    B) Ella Fitzgerald and Louis Armstrong both moved to New York City to start their music careers.

    C) Women danced to jazz music during the 1920s to make a statement about their role in society.

    D) Jazz music was an integral part of the emerging African American culture of the 1920s.

23. What can the reader conclude from the passage above?

    A) F. Scott Fitzgerald supported jazz musicians in New York and Chicago.

    B) Jazz music is no longer as popular as it once was.

    C) Both women and African Americans used jazz music as a way of expressing their newfound freedom.

    D) Flappers and African American musicians worked together to produce jazz music.

Sugar is an essential fuel for the human body. However, Americans, on average, are consuming twenty more teaspoons of sugar daily than the American Heart Association's recommendation of six teaspoons for women and nine for men. The reason for this excess is twofold: humans may have an evolutionary hunger for sugar, and food companies are capitalizing on this human sweet tooth. As a result, millions of Americans are suffering from obesity, diabetes, and tooth decay.

When the body breaks down food, it only uses some simple sugars for immediate energy; the rest of the sugar is stored as fat that can be called upon for energy later. The issue is that millions of people are storing too much fat because they are simply eating too much sugar.

In addition to its obvious sources—cake, cookies, soda—added sugar lurks in many supposedly healthy foods, such as tomato sauce, yogurt, granola, and fruit snacks. In particular, low-fat versions of some of these foods are packed with extra sugar to improve the flavor lost by reducing the fat content.

Foods that naturally contain sugar offer a healthy alternative to processed foods with added sugar. The naturally occurring sugar in fruits and vegetables is accompanied by fiber and other nutritional elements. That is why health professionals recommend that children trade in their cans of soda for a handful of grapes or a plate of sweet potatoes. These so-called smart sweets help Americans satiate their sugar fix while also giving them the appropriate fuel to enjoy a healthy life.

24. What is the main idea of the passage?

   A) Sugar provides fuel for the human body.

   B) Consuming too much sugar causes obesity, diabetes, and tooth decay.

   C) Americans are eating too much sugar, experts say.

   D) Foods such as tomato sauce, yogurt, and granola contain added sugar.

25. What is the author's primary purpose in writing this essay?

   A) to inform readers about Americans' overconsumption of sugar

   B) to warn patients that they are in grave danger of becoming obese or diabetic

   C) to criticize the food industry for cynically taking advantage of Americans' sugar addiction

   D) to reassure Americans that a little more sugar than the recommended amount is usually OK

26. Which of the following is NOT listed as a detail in the passage?

   A) The American Heart Association recommends that women consume only six teaspoons of sugar per day.

   B) Human beings may have evolved to crave sugar.

   C) Some sugar is stored as fat; the body can use fat for energy at a later time.

   D) Corn syrup, an ingredient in some foods, contains a great deal of sugar.

27. What is the meaning of the word *fuel* in the first sentence?

   A) energy source

   B) gas or gasoline

   C) petroleum

   D) stimulate

28. Which of the following statements can readers infer from the passage?

   A) If you are a man and you consume ten teaspoons of sugar per day, you are certainly endangering your health.

   B) If you are a woman and you consume twenty-six teaspoons of sugar per day, you are likely to be—or to become—overweight.

   C) If you are a child and you drink one sugary soda drink per day, you are sure to have tooth decay.

   D) Homo sapiens living in prehistoric times were unable to find enough sugar to fuel their bodies.

Influenza (also called the flu) has historically been one of the most common, and deadliest, human infections. While many people who contract the virus will recover, many others will not. Over the past 150 years, tens of millions of people have died from the flu, and millions more have been left with lingering complications such as secondary infections.

CONTINUE

Although it's a common disease, the flu is not actually highly infectious, meaning it's relatively difficult to contract. The flu can only be transmitted when individuals come into direct contact with bodily fluids of people infected with the flu or when they are exposed to expelled aerosol particles (which result from coughing and sneezing). Because the viruses can only travel short distances as aerosol particles and will die within a few hours on hard surfaces, the virus can be contained with fairly simple health measures like hand washing and face masks.

However, the spread of the flu can only be contained when people are aware such measures need to be taken. One of the reasons the flu has historically been so deadly is the amount of time between when people become infectious and when they develop symptoms.

Viral shedding—the process by which the body releases viruses that have been successfully reproducing during the infection—takes place two days after infection, while symptoms do not usually develop until the third day of infection. Thus, infected individuals have at least twenty-four hours in which they may unknowingly infect others.

29. What is the main idea of the passage?

   A) The flu is a deadly disease that's difficult to control because people become infectious before they show symptoms.

   B) For the flu to be transmitted, individuals must come in contact with bodily fluids from infected individuals.

   C) The spread of the flu is easy to contain because the viruses do not live long either as aerosol particles or on hard surfaces.

   D) The flu has killed tens of millions of people and can often cause deadly secondary infections.

30. What is the meaning of the word *measures* in the second paragraph?

   A) a plan of action
   B) a standard unit
   C) an adequate amount
   D) a rhythmic movement

31. Which of the following correctly describes the flu?

   A) The flu is easy to contract and always fatal.

   B) The flu is difficult to contract and always fatal.

   C) The flu is easy to contract and sometimes fatal.

   D) The flu is difficult to contract and sometimes fatal.

32. Which statement is not a detail from the passage?

   A) Tens of millions of people have been killed by the flu virus.

   B) There is typically a twenty-four hour window during which individuals are infectious but not showing flu symptoms.

   C) Viral shedding is the process by which people recover from the flu.

   D) The flu can be transmitted by direct contact with bodily fluids from infected individuals or by exposure to aerosol particles.

33. Why is the flu considered to not be highly infectious?

A) Many people who get the flu will recover and have no lasting complications, so only a small number of people who become infected will die.

B) The process of viral shedding takes two days, so infected individuals have enough time to implement simple health measures that stop the spread of the disease.

C) The flu virus cannot travel far or live for long periods of time outside the human body, so its spread can easily be contained.

D) Twenty-four hours is a relatively short period of time for the virus to spread among a population.

34. What can the reader conclude from the passage?

A) Preemptively implementing health measures like hand washing and face masks could help stop the spread of the flu virus.

B) Doctors are not sure how the flu virus is transmitted, so they are unsure how to stop it from spreading.

C) The flu is dangerous because it is both deadly and highly infectious.

D) Individuals stop being infectious three days after they are infected.

If you frequent your local Whole Foods, you will likely come across a popular international spice: turmeric. Turmeric comes from the bulbous root of a plant known as Curcuma longa. It is related to ginger, but the fleshy inside of the root is a deep yellow. Once the root is boiled, dried, and ground, it creates a bitter yellow powdered spice that gives Indian curry its distinctive color. Turmeric has been used medicinally—as well as in cooking, as a dye, and in religious rituals—in India and Southeast Asia for millennia. Its anti-inflammatory properties have gained the adoration of Western health and wellness gurus in recent years.

Today, many Americans are touting turmeric as a holistic medicinal replacement for anti-inflammatory drugs. Small-scale studies have shown that curcumin, a key compound found in turmeric, can help with both skin inflammation and joint inflammation.

Companies are adding turmeric to topical creams for skin care, and patients with rheumatoid arthritis are taking their daily dose of turmeric pills to help decrease pain and stiffness in their joints. Larger-scale clinical studies have not provided conclusive evidence for these benefits.

Regardless of its true health benefits, expect to see turmeric continue to impact the health food and holistic medicine industries in the near future. It is hard to walk through any upscale health food store without seeing the buzzword *turmeric* plastered on trendy juices and vegan powder canisters.

35. Readers can infer from the passage that the author
    A) believes in turmeric's anti-inflammatory health properties.
    B) is not sure that turmeric is an effective anti-inflammatory aid.
    C) uses turmeric at home to add spice to Indian cuisine.
    D) has used turmeric to dye cloth a deep yellow.

36. What is the author's primary purpose in writing this essay?
    A) to persuade readers with arthritis to buy turmeric
    B) to criticize health food businesses for selling turmeric
    C) to explain what turmeric is and why it has become popular
    D) to warn consumers not to be gullible enough to buy turmeric

37. According to the passage, which types of studies have shown that turmeric is an effective medicine?
    A) studies run by wellness gurus
    B) small-scale studies
    C) larger-scale clinical studies
    D) studies run by the health food and holistic medicine industries

38. Which sentence best summarizes the passage's main idea?
    A) "Turmeric comes from the bulbous root of a plant known as Curcuma longa."
    B) "Once the root is boiled, dried, and ground, it creates a bitter yellow powdered spice that gives Indian curry its distinctive color."
    C) "Small-scale studies have shown that curcumin, a key compound found in turmeric, can help with both skin inflammation and joint inflammation."
    D) "Regardless of its true health benefits, expect to see turmeric continue to impact the health food and holistic medicine industries in the near future."

39. According to the passage, when did people first begin to use turmeric medicinally?
    A) thousands of years ago
    B) in the mid-1900s
    C) in the early 2000s
    D) a few years ago

40. In paragraph 1, what does the word *distinctive* mean?
    A) deep yellow
    B) characteristic
    C) fluorescent
    D) bright

VOCABULARY

1. a strong <u>affinity</u> for ice cream
   A) repulsion
   B) likeness
   C) allergy
   D) history

2. a <u>sustainable</u> food source
   A) supportable
   B) forsaken
   C) sensitive
   D) abandoned

3. a <u>vast</u> expanse of land
   A) empty
   B) enormous
   C) useless
   D) wild

4. an <u>adequate</u> amount of money
   A) meager
   B) unsatisfactory
   C) sufficient
   D) sparse

5. the heat is making him <u>irritable</u>
   A) content
   B) restless
   C) bothered
   D) cordial

6. in <u>subsequent</u> years
   A) prior
   B) antecedent
   C) missing
   D) later

7. the <u>proprietor</u> of a pet shop
   A) owner
   B) renter
   C) customer
   D) thief

8. surrounded by <u>throngs</u> of citizens
   A) separatists
   B) crowds
   C) disassembly
   D) spread

9. <u>uncharacteristically</u> nice of him
   A) typically
   B) unusually
   C) perfectly
   D) classically

10. the <u>scruffy</u> dogs in the yard
    A) tidy
    B) neat
    C) messy
    D) organized

11. the <u>notorious</u> bank robber
    A) infamous
    B) well-known
    C) popular
    D) famous

12. risen from <u>obscurity</u>
    A) fame
    B) clarity
    C) insignificance
    D) light

13. a frayed dress hem
    A) tattered
    B) mended
    C) perfect
    D) restored

14. its eyes darted back and forth
    A) sauntered
    B) flickered
    C) moved
    D) gazed

15. an integrated classroom
    A) separated
    B) disjointed
    C) combined
    D) intelligent

16. the limber gymnasts
    A) talented
    B) flexible
    C) dynamic
    D) strong

17. a sufficient supply of food
    A) scarce
    B) inadequate
    C) satisfactory
    D) delicious

18. after being jolted awake by the thunder
    A) jerked
    B) steadied
    C) enlightened
    D) confused

19. to delegate a task
    A) retain
    B) choose
    C) assign
    D) enact

20. to meet the most exalted person
    A) unwise
    B) happy
    C) lowly
    D) dignified

21. a prominent location
    A) flat
    B) subtle
    C) conspicuous
    D) obscure

22. the alien landscape
    A) unfamiliar
    B) unique
    C) happy
    D) recognizable

Mathematics

1. If the following expression is written in the form 10^n, what is the value of n?
$$\frac{(10^2)^3}{(10^{-2})^2}$$
    A) 2
    B) 5
    C) 6
    D) 10

2. Which of the following is closest to $15{,}886 \times 210$?
    A) 33,000
    B) 330,000
    C) 3,300,000
    D) 33,000,000

3. Mr. Smith has decided to curve his tests by adding 7 points to each of the test scores in his class. Which of the following values will remain the same after he curves the scores?

A) mean

B) median

C) mode

D) range

4. Which of the following statements is true for the line $x = 3$?

A) It has a slope of 3.

B) It has a y-intercept of 3.

C) It does not have an x-intercept.

D) It has an undefined slope.

5. Which expression is equivalent to dividing 400 by 16?

A) $2(200 - 8)$

B) $(400 \div 4) \div 12$

C) $(216 \div 8) + (184 \div 8)$

D) $(216 \div 16) + (184 \div 16)$

6. Justin has a summer lawn care business and earns $40 for each lawn he mows. He also pays $35 per week in business expenses. Which of the following expressions represents Justin's profit after x weeks if he mows m number of lawns?

A) $40m - 35x$

B) $40m + 35x$

C) $35x(40 + m)$

D) $35(40m + x)$

7. Which of the following problems has the same mathematical structure as the problem given below?

Selena had 7 pencils. She gave 2 pencils to her friend Amy. How many pencils does she have now?

A) Selena brought 3 friends to the end-of-summer party. Amy brought 2 friends. How many friends did they bring together?

B) Selena brought 10 carrot sticks for lunch. How many carrots sticks were left after she ate 6?

C) Selena earned 2 stickers every school day this week, Monday through Friday. How many stickers did she earn?

D) Selena has 7 markers. Amy has 3 more markers than Selena does. How many markers does Amy have?

8. Which of the following is listed in order from greatest to least?

A) $\frac{1}{2} \ \frac{1}{3} \ \frac{1}{7} \ -\frac{1}{5} \ -\frac{1}{6} \ -\frac{1}{4}$

B) $\frac{1}{2} \ \frac{1}{3} \ \frac{1}{7} \ -\frac{1}{6} \ -\frac{1}{5} \ -\frac{1}{4}$

C) $\frac{1}{2} \ \frac{1}{7} \ \frac{1}{3} \ -\frac{1}{4} \ -\frac{1}{5} \ -\frac{1}{6}$

D) $\frac{1}{2} \ \frac{1}{3} \ \frac{1}{7} \ -\frac{1}{6} \ -\frac{1}{4} \ -\frac{1}{5}$

9. If the value of y is between 0.0047 and 0.0162, which of the following could be the value of y?

A) 0.0035

B) 0.0055

C) 0.0185

D) 0.0238

10. Which of the following sequences follows the same rule as the sequence below?

    30, 27, 24, 21, ...

    A) 41, 39, 37, 35, ...
    B) 41, 44, 47, 50, ...
    C) 41, 37, 33, 29, ...
    D) 41, 38, 35, 32, ...

11. Students are asked if they prefer vanilla, chocolate, or strawberry ice cream. The results are tallied on the table below.

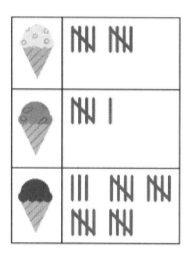

    Four students then display the information from the table in a bar graph. Which student completes the bar graph correctly?

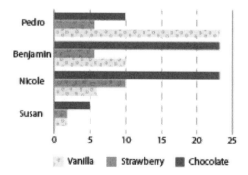

    A) Pedro
    B) Benjamin
    C) Nicole
    D) Susan

12. If $a + b$ is an even number, then both a and b must be even.

    Which of the following statements is a counterexample to the statement above?

    A) $6 + 9 = 15$
    B) $8 + 3 = 11$
    C) $10 + 14 = 24$
    D) $17 + 15 = 32$

13. A set of numbers contains all the prime factors of 42. What is the range of the set?

    A) 1
    B) 5
    C) 19
    D) 41

14. A circular swimming pool has a circumference of 50 feet. Which of the following is the diameter of the pool in feet?

    A) $\frac{25}{\pi}$
    B) $\frac{50}{\pi}$
    C) 25π
    D) 50π

15. If $4x = 3$, what is the value of $8x$?

    A) 0.75
    B) 6
    C) 12
    D) 24

16. If $x + y$ is an odd number, which of the following must be true?

    A) Both x and y must be odd numbers.
    B) Neither x nor y can equal 0.
    C) Either x or y is odd, while the other is even.
    D) The product of x and y is odd.

17. The table below shows the number of hours employees worked during the week. Which of the following is the median number of hours the employees worked per week?

EMPLOYEE	No. HOURS WORKED
Suzanne	42
Joe	38
Mark	26
Ellen	50
Jill	45
Rob	46
Nicole	17
Sean	41
Maria	46

A) 39
B) 41
C) 42
D) 46

18. A whole number is divided by 3. Which of the following CANNOT be the remainder?

A) 0
B) 1
C) 2
D) 3

19. Which expression has only prime factors of 3, 5, and 11?

A) 66 × 108
B) 15 × 99
C) 42 × 29
D) 28 × 350

20. The pie graph below shows how a state's government plans to spend its annual budget of $3 billion. How much more money does the state plan to spend on infrastructure than education?

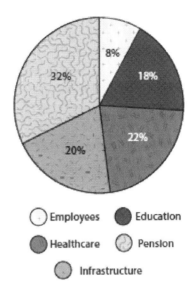

- ⚪ Employees
- ⚫ Education
- ⚫ Healthcare
- ⚫ Pension
- ⚫ Infrastructure

A) $60,000,000
B) $120,000,000
C) $300,000,000
D) $540,000,000

21. A company interviewed 21 applicants for a recent opening. Of these applicants, 7 wore blue and 6 wore white, while 5 applicants wore both blue and white. What is the number of applicants who wore neither blue nor white?

A) 6
B) 8
C) 12
D) 13

22. If $x = 5$, what is the value of the algebraic expression $2x - x$?

A) 5
B) 10
C) 15
D) 20

23. Which of the following numbers are equivalent to 2.61?

A) $\frac{261}{10}$

B) 2.061

C) $2\frac{61}{100}$

D) $2\frac{61}{1000}$

24. Which of the following equations correctly solves the word problem given below?

At a party, 6 girls and 9 boys each order a hot dog for $2 each. How much money was spent for hot dogs?

A) $2 \times 6 + 9 = \$21$

B) $2 + 6 + 9 = \$17$

C) $2 \times (6 + 9) = \$30$

D) $2 \times 6 \times 9 = \$108$

25. Which inequality is represented by the following graph?

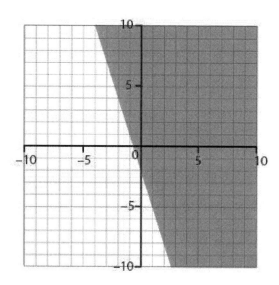

A) $y \geq -3x - 2$

B) $y \geq 3x - 2$

C) $y > -3x - 2$

D) $y \leq -3x - 2$

26. What number is equal to $(5^2 + 1)^2 + 3^3$?

A) 703

B) 694

C) 53

D) 30

27. Simplify: $\frac{7.2 \times 10^6}{1.6 \times 10^{-3}}$

A) 4.5×10^{-9}

B) 4.5×10^{-3}

C) 4.5×10^3

D) 4.5×10^9

28. A high school cross-country team sent 25 percent of its runners to a regional competition. Of these, 10 percent won medals. If two runners earned medals, how many members does the cross-country team have?

A) 8

B) 80

C) 125

D) 1250

29. A teacher has 50 notebooks to hand out to students. If she has 16 students in her class, and each student receives two notebooks, how many notebooks will she have left over?

A) 2

B) 16

C) 18

D) 32

30. 40% of what number is equal to 17?

A) 2.35

B) 6.8

C) 42.5

D) 680

31. An ice chest contains 24 sodas, some regular and some diet. The ratio of diet soda to regular soda is 1:3. How many regular sodas are there in the ice chest?

A) 1

B) 4

C) 18

D) 24

32. Which expression is equivalent to $6x + 5 \geq -15 + 8x$?

A) $x \leq -5$

B) $x \leq 5$

C) $x \leq 10$

D) $x \leq 20$

33. Which of the following equations describes the linear relationship between x and y shown in the table?

X	Y
3	11
5	15
8	21

A) $y = 2x + 5$

B) $y = 5x + 5$

C) $y = 4x + 5$

D) $y = 3x + 5$

34. If a car uses 8 gallons of gas to travel 650 miles, how many miles can it travel using 12 gallons of gas?

A) 870 miles

B) 895 miles

C) 915 miles

D) 975 miles

35. If $j = 4$, what is the value of

$2(j - 4)^4 - j + \frac{1}{2}j$?

A) −2

B) 0

C) 2

D) 4

36. The formula for distance is $d = r \times t$, where r is the rate and t is the time. How long will it take a plane to fly 4000 miles from Chicago to London if the plane flies at a constant rate of 500 mph?

A) 3.5 hours

B) 8 hours

C) 20 hours

D) 45 hours

37. How much water is needed to fill 24 bottles that each hold 0.75 liters?

A) 6 L

B) 18 L

C) 24 L

D) 32 L

38. Yanni bought a used car. He made a down payment of $3000 and then made monthly payments of $216 for three years. How much did Yanni pay for the car?

A) $10,776

B) $7806

C) $7776

D) $3678

39. The perimeter of a rectangle is 42 mm. If the length of the rectangle is 13 mm, what is its width?

A) 8 mm

B) 13 mm

C) 20 mm

D) 29 mm

40. If the volume of a cube is 343 cubic meters, what is the cube's surface area?

A) 49 m²

B) 84 m²

C) 196 m²

D) 294 m²

41. In a class of 20 students, how many conversations must take place so that every student talks to every other student in the class?

A) 190

B) 380

C) 760

D) 6840

42. A school held a raffle to raise money. If a person who bought 3 tickets had a 0.0004 chance of winning, what is the total number of tickets sold for the raffle?

A) 2400 tickets

B) 3500 tickets

C) 5000 tickets

D) 7500 tickets

43. The figure below shows a rectangle with 4 square cutouts made to each corner. What is the area of the resulting shape?

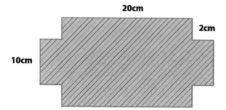

A) 142 cm²

B) 200 cm²

C) 296 cm²

D) 320 cm²

44. Melissa is ordering fencing to enclose a square garden with 5625 square feet. Which of the following is the number of feet of fencing she needs?

A) 75

B) 150

C) 300

D) 1405

45. Juan is packing a shipment of three books weighing 0.8 pounds, 0.49 pounds, and 0.89 pounds. The maximum weight for the shipping box is 2.5 pounds. How much more weight will the box hold?

A) 0.32 lb

B) 0.48 lb

C) 1.21 lb

D) 2.18 lb

46.

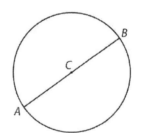

The circle above shows a walking path through a park. If the distance from A to B is 4 km, how far will someone travel when they walk along arc AB?

A) 4 km

B) 2π km

C) 8 km

D) 4π km

47. How many combinations can be made from a wardrobe that consists of 70 shirts, 2 ties, and 5 sets of cufflinks?

  A) 77

  B) 350

  C) 700

  D) 3500

48. A python coils 6 times around a round plastic bucket whose radius is 5 inches. How long is the python? (Round to the nearest whole number.)

  A) 471 inches

  B) 188 inches

  C) 94 inches

  D) 60 inches

49. In a game of musical chairs, there are 9 people playing and 7 available seats. Those who do not get a seat by the time the music ends are eliminated. What is the probability a person is not eliminated?

  A) 11%

  B) 22%

  C) 78%

  D) 89%

50. Pauline is running for class historian. All 175 students voted in the election, and she received 40% of the vote. How many students voted for Pauline?

  A) 40

  B) 70

  C) 135

  D) 438

51. Tamara is hosting a birthday party at the movie theater. Her mother gives her $50 to spend on movie tickets for her friends. The theater charges $4 per person and a $6 service charge for the order. How many friends can she invite to the party?

  A) 5

  B) 11

  C) 12

  D) 40

52. A movie runs for 92 minutes. For it to air on television, it must be edited down to 88 minutes to make room for commercials. What percent of the movie must be edited?

  A) Between 2 and 3%

  B) Between 3 and 4%

  C) Between 4 and 5%

  D) Between 5 and 6%

53. A sandwich shop offers 4 different types of meat, 3 types of cheese, 2 types of bread, and 4 condiments. If each sandwich must have 1 meat, 1 cheese, 1 type of bread, and 1 condiment, how many different sandwiches can be made?

  A) 13

  B) 32

  C) 96

  D) 300

54. A car traveled at 65 miles per hour for $1\frac{1}{2}$ hours and then traveled at 50 miles per hour for $2\frac{1}{2}$ hours. How many miles did the car travel?

  A) 200 miles

  B) 222.5 miles

  C) 237.5 miles

  D) 260 miles

55. Justine bought 6 yards of fabric to make some curtains, but she only used $4\frac{5}{8}$ yards. How many yards of fabric does she have left?

A) $\frac{3}{8}$

B) $\frac{5}{8}$

C) $1\frac{3}{8}$

D) $2\frac{5}{8}$

56. What is the perimeter of the shape?

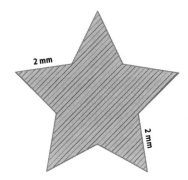

A) 2 mm

B) 4 mm

C) 10 mm

D) 20 mm

57. A 10 L container will hold how much more liquid than a 2-gallon container? (1 gal = 3.785 L)

A) 2.00 L

B) 2.43 L

C) 6.22 L

D) 8.00 L

58. Alice ran $3\frac{1}{2}$ miles on Monday, and she increased her distance by $\frac{1}{4}$ mile each day. What was her total distance from Monday to Friday?

A) $17\frac{1}{2}$ mi

B) $18\frac{1}{2}$ mi

C) 19 mi

D) 20 mi

59. A doctor advises her patient to decrease his sugar consumption by 25%. If he currently consumes 40 grams of sugar per day on average, how many daily grams of sugar should his new target be?

A) 30 g

B) 24 g

C) 16 g

D) 10 g

60. Andre welded together 3 pieces of metal pipe measuring 26.5 inches, 18.9 inches, and 35.1 inches. How long was the welded pipe?

A) 10.3 in

B) 27.5 in

C) 42.7 in

D) 80.5 in

61. What is the area of the shape below?

A) 6 mm²

B) 16 mm²

C) 64 mm²

D) 128 mm²

62. Solve: $-4x + 2 = -34$

A) -9

B) -8

C) 8

D) 9

63. Harvey types at an average speed of 45 words per minute. Approximately how long will it take for him to type a newsletter that is 4500 words in length?

A) 89 minutes

B) 100 minutes

C) 180 minutes

D) 3955 minutes

64. Ken has taken 6 tests in his English class. Each test is worth 100 points. Ken has a 92% average in English. If Ken's first 5 grades are 90, 100, 95, 83, and 87, what was Ken's score on the 6th test?

A) 80

B) 92

C) 97

D) 100

Language Skills

In questions 1 – 40, look for errors in capitalization, punctuation, or usage. If you find no mistake, mark (D) on your answer sheet.

1.

A) In 1948, the *Chicago Tribune* published an erroneous headline about the winner of the presidential election, and in 1974, it called for President Nixon's resignation after publishing the complete text of the Watergate tapes.

B) Sacagawea may be famous for her role as guide and interpreter for Lewis and Clark, but few know about the mystery surrounding her death, while some historians believe she died in 1812, others believe she lived until 1884.

C) Similar to hibernation, estivation is a state of lowered activity and energy; however, estivation is entered primarily by reptiles, amphibians, and fish to avoid the hot, dry conditions of the summer months.

D) No mistakes

2.

A) While I was baking cookies, I ate too much of the dough.

B) On Monday, either my sisters or our parents will pick me up at the bus station.

C) My teacher and the school principal have worked together for many years.

D) No mistakes

3.

A) Danny left for work after he walked the dog.

B) Left on the stove for too long, Mario realized he had burned the soup.

C) DeQuan loves eating pizza, but meat toppings make him feel queasy.

D) No mistakes

CONTINUE

4.

    A) All my teammates hope to play their best tonight.

    B) The senators from Virginia and Louisiana strongly favor the bill.

    C) I dont eat cantaloupe because I dislike the way it tastes.

    D) No mistakes

5.

    A) Of my two parents, Dad is the most old.

    B) Please read aloud the first paragraph on page 143.

    C) It is so hot today that I can scarcely bear it.

    D) No mistakes

6.

    A) Brenda and Pauletta are working late because the deadline is tomorrow.

    B) When the club members arrive, they hang their coats on hooks.

    C) Their standing right over there with their brother.

    D) No mistakes

7.

    A) Neither the administrative assistant nor her boss was scheduled to take a vacation.

    B) The cat eats it's food while the dog sleeps.

    C) The clothes that I left at the drycleaner's shop were beautifully clean when I picked them up.

    D) No mistakes

8.

    A) Kiana went to class; but Lara stayed home.

    B) Meet me at Britt-Marie's Restaurant; I love the way they cook fish there.

    C) The chairman of the board, Jessica Smith, will lead today's meeting.

    D) No mistakes

9.

    A) Let's take a pie to Susan's for Thanksgiving.

    B) My sister keeps dyeing her hair different neon colors like lime green and electric blue.

    C) Please bring me a take-out dinner from the restaurant.

    D) No mistakes

10.

    A) You and Bella shouldn't take things that aren't yours.

    B) I have about six sweaters, and the most soft one is cashmere.

    C) Of course, no one on our team wants to play poorly.

    D) No mistakes

11.

    A) I cannot accept this gift, it is far too expensive.

    B) I love raw raisins, but I hate cooked raisins in cookies or cakes.

    C) You can have either oatmeal or pancakes.

    D) No mistakes

12.

A) Robert and Kelly raced across the River in their small boats.

B) Ella, Cassie, and Cameron drove to South Carolina together.

C) Mowing the lawn, Frank discovered a family of baby rabbits.

D) No mistakes

13.

A) I brought Ms. McIlvaine the coat and told her that it was lost.

B) We're going to New Mexico so we can take hikes in the Desert.

C) Cousin Sue will be at the lake, and so will my cousins Sandy, Bonny, and Jack.

D) No mistakes

14.

A) Of the four paintings, Stanley's was the most beautiful.

B) None of us wants to owe a lot of money.

C) I don't think the outcome will affect me much so I won't worry about it.

D) No mistakes

15.

A) The hurricane and the damaged levy flooded New Orleans, Slidell, and other places.

B) Two of my teammates hopes to be star players tonight.

C) I'm having a hard time deciding what to wear where.

D) No mistakes

16.

A) When one of the cats approached her food bowl, Hollie showed her teeth and said "grrrr."

B) The automobile industry earned more than Microsoft did last year.

C) Jenny enjoys swimming in pools, but she hates swimming in lakes.

D) No mistakes

17.

A) To insure that order is preserved, the mayor will tell the police to keep the two groups of protesters apart.

B) I'm sorry, but I can't drive any farther today.

C) Is that purple jacket Shelby's or yours?

D) No mistakes

18.

A) We're going to Austin, Texas, next weekend so that we can attend my brother's graduation.

B) Trying to impress his friends, Carl ended up totaling his car.

C) Ice cream is my favorite food, it is so cold and creamy.

D) No mistakes

19.

A) I led the horse to water, but it refused to drink.

B) The cats sleep on the sofa while the dog drinks water from her bowl in the kitchen.

C) We could have went out last night, but it was raining.

D) No mistakes

20.

A) As Javi was walking to school, a gang of **mean older boys** stole his basketball.

B) The dresses that the customer wanted to return **was torn** and dirty, so Mr. Wu refused to accept them.

C) Because temperatures will drop below freezing tonight, we should stay home.

D) No mistakes

21.

A) We are going to Los Angeles on the third Wednesday in March.

B) I wish I could accept your invitation, but I am going out of town that weekend.

C) If you break that expensive glass vase, Dad will be very angry with you.

D) No mistakes

22.

A) Of my two sisters, Julie is the most responsible.

B) My warmest jacket is made of synthetic fleece.

C) Of the many artworks on display, Peter's was the most impressive.

D) No mistakes

23.

A) We are not aloud to speak in the public library.

B) I need to do some errands: I need to shop for food, and I need to pick up my dry cleaning.

C) Ursula said, "Let's hurry, so we can get to the bus station on time."

D) No mistakes

24.

A) Here is how I answered her question: "Let's not eat early, because I'm still full from lunch."

B) On Easter morning, my parent's seemed happy as they watched Ana and I enjoy the candy.

C) Adelaide said, "I wish we could go to Hawaii."

D) No mistakes

25.

A) Max left home early on Thursday morning, but he was still late for work.

B) Liz's love of praise was reflected in how happy she seemed during the birthday toasts in her honor.

C) After the bus driver spoke to the passenger, she realized that she might have acted rudely.

D) No mistakes

26.

A) Because of its distance from the sun; the planet Neptune has seasons that last the equivalent of forty-one Earth years.

B) Though Puerto Rico is known popularly for its beaches, its landscape also includes mountains, which are home to many of the island's rural villages.

C) The Boat Race, a rowing race that has been held nearly annually in London, England, since 1856, was infamously interrupted in 2012 when a protester dove in and began swimming among the boats.

D) No mistakes

27.

A) Oak trees—with proper care—can grow upward of thirty feet; providing shade for people, shelter for animals, and perches for birds.

B) I asked, "What are we doing here, anyway?"

C) We celebrate Valentine's Day in February, and we celebrate Independence Day in summer.

D) No mistakes

28.

A) "Im so relieved that the storm is over!" Robyn exclaimed.

B) The members of the orchestra played well last night, so they received a standing ovation.

C) Everybody in our class has applied to one or more colleges.

D) No mistakes

29.

A) Please close the door behind you when you leave.

B) We always give each other gifts on our shared birthday.

C) My brother and I likes the same desserts.

D) No mistakes

30.

A) My Aunt, my Mom's sister, lives in British Columbia, Canada, with her husband.

B) "Please shut up, Matty!" I said to my cat, who had been yowling all morning.

C) There are many oceans on our planet; the Pacific and the Atlantic are the two largest.

D) No mistakes

31.

A) We had already exchanged gifts by the time you arrived.

B) Of all the students in our class, Sheila was the only one who earned an A grade.

C) Yes, your right: we should always try hard to write sentences that are grammatically correct.

D) No mistakes

32.

A) We invited everyone to our wedding accept people whom neither of us knew very well.

B) Lots of people agree with me when I say that cool weather is better than a heat wave.

C) My twin cousins Sue and Sandy are the oldest cousins I have.

D) No mistakes

33.

A) We are thinking about buying a new car.

B) Of the two top students: Veronica earned an A and Heather earned an A-minus.

C) Our boss has recently hired two new employees.

D) No mistakes

34.

A) Whenever they get scared, our cats hide under the bed.

B) Before I feed the dogs, I need to finish my essay on responsibility.

C) If you are ready to leave the party.

D) No mistakes

35.

A) Mom is afraid of flying, so she listens to a relaxation CD before she flies.

B) My cat Katrina isn't the only female in our home: there's Hollie the dog, and I am female too.

C) My cat Jack likes the following items in this order: food, affection, and lying in the sunlight.

D) No mistakes

36.

A) As juveniles, African white-backed vultures are darkly colored, developing their white feathers only as they grow into adulthood.

B) I want to wear my new dress, but I don't know where I can do so—it is too fancy for most occasions.

C) Because our school colors are orange and black. I'm going to dye a few of my white T-shirts orange.

D) No mistakes

37.

A) On Saturday, June 16, we're traveling from Seattle to Victoria via ferryboat.

B) Mr. Yetto my third-grade teacher used to do magic tricks for the class.

C) The summer season is made up of June, July, and August.

D) No mistakes

38.

A) Im sure that both Rachel and Amanda are very intelligent.

B) It's true: Oklahoma City can be amazingly hot in springtime.

C) Do you truly believe that Heidi is prettier than Margaret?

D) No mistakes

39.

A) You're right: the best time to write a thank-you note is right after you receive a gift or a big favor.

B) Do you know Janet and Brian Carter? They're standing right over there with their older sister.

C) Hundreds of years ago, if you were female, your destiny was not yours to decide: your father, brother, or husband made all your decisions for you.

D) No mistakes

40.

A) Ukrainians celebrate a holiday called Malanka during which men dress in costumes and masks and plays tricks on their neighbors.

B) Everyday items like potatoes, bread, onions, and even saliva are the tools of art conservators, who work to clean and restore works of art.

C) The Akhal-Teke horse breed, originally from Turkmenistan, has long enjoyed a reputation for bravery and fortitude.

D) No mistakes

For questions 41 – 50, look for mistakes in spelling only.

41.

A) Many of these individuals struggled professionally.

B) It is important to look past labels and appearances.

C) We found her excuses suspiscious and unbelievable.

D) No mistakes

42.

A) The suspect was interogated for four hours before he confessed.

B) May I have another piece of cake?

C) The legislature rescinded the law when it was ruled unconstitutional.

D) No mistakes

43.

A) I attempted to facilitate the exchange of information between drivers.

B) There are too many stairs; I'd rather take the elevator.

C) How are you feeling on this sunny Saturday mourning?

D) No mistakes

44.

A) Please don't stare at strangers; it is rude and can make people feel uncomfortable.

B) I accidentally through my baseball threw my neighbor's window, and it shattered.

C) Let's meet at my house for a barbecue; I've been marinating some meat in a spicy sauce.

D) No mistakes

45.

A) Gabriel was an incorrigible child who would not listen to his parents.

B) My elementary school principal's name was Mrs. Woodnancy.

C) There are two bedrooms, a bathroom, and a sitting room in our hotel sweet.

D) No mistakes

46.

A) During the 1960s, many college students participated in peace marches to protest the Vietnam War.

B) Use the rains to guide your horse, but don't yank on them so hard—that can hurt your horse's mouth.

C) Please pour me a glass of lemonade.

D) No mistakes

47.

A) I awoke and realized I was still in deep morning.

B) The tenacious investigator left no stone unturned.

C) The judge described his actions as heinous.

D) No mistakes

48.

A) Are you going to dye your hair green or purple?

B) I used flour to bake a cake, and I decorated it with flowers.

C) Four independant witnesses placed Harry at the scene of the crime.

D) No mistakes

49.

A) She received a promotion because she never performed her duties in a perfunctory manner.

B) The neighbors requested a house be placed under surveillance.

C) We must remain vigilant in these times.

D) No mistakes

50.

A) She loves shopping only at hardware stores and antique shops.

B) My boss turned toward me and asked to speak with me privately.

C) A saditious organization refuses to recognize the authority of the government.

D) No mistakes

For questions 51 – 60, look for errors in composition. Follow the directions for each question.

51. Which of the following sentences is irrelevant as part of a paragraph composed of these sentences?

A) It looks like the weather might force us to move the game to next weekend.

B) Our team will be playing our biggest rival for the last game of the season.

C) The teams play each other every year, and it's a big event for the town.

D) Last year, the mayor closed down Main Street so fans could celebrate together safely.

52. Which of the following alternatives to the underlined portion of the sentence would be LEAST acceptable?

The Grand Canyon is located in northern Arizona and falls primarily inside Grand Canyon National Park, which <u>bisects</u> the Kaibab National Forest.

A) separates

B) crosses

C) intersects

D) cuts across

53. Choose the BEST word to join the thoughts together.
My job at the bakery was difficult, _____ I enjoyed every moment of it.

A) and

B) but

C) for

D) even

54. Choose the BEST word to join the thoughts together.
Most people struggle to find what they want to do with their lives, _____ Neil deGrasse Tyson knew when he was nine years old.

A) during

B) still

C) but

D) and

55. Which of these sentences expresses the idea MOST clearly?

A) However, they may never again experience the power or the excitement of their former office, retired presidents continue to enjoy many benefits as a result of their service to the United States.

B) As a result of their service as president of the United States, they may never again experience the power or the excitement of their former office, but retired presidents continue to enjoy many benefits.

C) Retired presidents continue to enjoy many benefits as a result of their service to the United States, though they may never again experience the power or the excitement of their former office.

D) None of these

56. Which of these sentences BEST fits under the topic "Animal Migration"?

A) When I was a young child, my family moved all around the world.

B) Most animal migration occurs at predictable times each year in response to seasonal changes.

C) Usually, we would live in each new country for about a year.

D) None of these

57. Which is the BEST way to revise the underlined portion of the sentence?

Spelunking involves much more than adrenaline: enthusiasts dive into unexplored caves <u>to study structures of, take photographs, and create maps</u> of the untouched systems.

A) to study structures of, take photographs, and create maps of

B) to study structures of, take photographs of, and create maps of

C) to study structures of, taking photographs of, and creating maps of

D) for studying structures, to take photographs, and for creating maps of

58. Which is the BEST way to revise and combine the underlined portion of the sentences?

Unfortunately, the belief that changelings could be convinced to leave was not just <u>an innocuous superstition. On some occasions</u>, harm came to the individual who was thought to be a changeling.

A) an innocuous superstition, on some occasions,

B) an innocuous superstition, but on some occasions,

C) an innocuous superstition; however, on some occasions,

D) an innocuous superstition: on some occasions,

CONTINUE

59. Which of the following would NOT be an acceptable way to revise and combine the underlined portion of these sentences?

First and foremost, they receive <u>an annual pension payment. The amount of the pension</u> has been reviewed and changed a number of times, most recently to reflect the salary of a high-level government executive.

A) annual pension payment, the amount of which

B) annual pension payment; the amount of the pension

C) annual pension payment; over the years since 1958, the amount of the pension

D) annual pension payment, the amount of the pension

60. Which of the following sentences is irrelevant as part of a paragraph composed of these sentences?

A) Traffic around the arena was heavy, so we were worried we'd miss the opening pitch.

B) My brother and I won tickets in a radio station contest to see his favorite team play on opening day.

C) To win the contest, you had to be the 395th caller and know the answer to a trivia question; we waited anxiously by the phone for the contest to begin.

D) My brother has followed the team since childhood, so we knew he'd be able to answer the trivia question correctly.

Answer Key
VERBAL SKILLS

1. **C)** A classroom is where teaching takes place. A park is where playing takes place.

2. **C)** A mouse, keyboard, and screen are all computer hardware, while the internet is a service.

3. **A)** Because all baseball players wear caps—which are hats—then all baseball players wear hats.

4. **B)** A freezer keeps food cold; all the others cook food.

5. **D)** Divisive means "discordant, conflict-ridden, contentious." Unifying is an antonym of divisive.

6. **D)** A joey is a baby kangaroo; a puppy is a baby dog.

7. **A)** Since her pants were too tight before and are now too loose, then Maria clearly lost weight.

8. **A)** Lively means "upbeat, energetic." The other three words refer to something lacking in positive energy.

9. **B)** To tremble is to shiver or shake.

10. **C)** Both hurricanes and tornadoes are dangerous, but there is no way to tell—based on the statements provided—which is more dangerous.

11. **D)** Energetic means "wide awake, perky." The other three words describe the need for rest.

12. **D)** Swooped means "pounced, jumped, leapt, dove." Risen is an antonym of swooped.

13. **B)** Typing is done on a computer; texting is done on a phone.

14. **C)** To hesitate is to pause or falter.

15. **B)** If all candy costs between 5 and 10 cents, then candy cannot cost less than 5 cents.

16. **B)** Ordinary means "common, regular." The other three words mean something strange or extraordinary.

17. **C)** Assurance means "promise, reassurance, confidence." Timidity is an antonym of assurance.

18. **C)** Clean and dirty are opposites; small and big are opposites.

19. **C)** While Nicole likes sandwiches, the statements do not indicate what specific type of sandwich Nicole likes.

20. **B)** If John always tells the truth, then John can never lie.

21. **C)** Create means "to make something," and the other three words refer to destroying something.

22. **D)** Entail means to "involve, need, require, necessitate." Exclude is an antonym of entail.

23. **A)** A piece is a part of the puzzle; a player is part of a team.

24. **C)** The adjective "meager" means "insufficient or inadequate."

25. **C)** We are not sure what type of animals Marlen has other than the two dogs.

26. **C)** Cheerful means happy; the other three words refer to being unhappy.

27. **C)** The adjective "dormant" indicates something that is sleeping, quiet, or inactive.

28. **C)** Ancient means "old, related to the past." The other three words refer to something new.

29. **A)** Vexation means "displeasure, annoyance, bother." Satisfaction is an antonym of vexation.

30. **B)** Feathers cover a bird; fur covers a dog.

31. **A)** To pacify someone means to cause that person to become more peaceful, or to soothe them.

32. **D)** A chameleon is a reptile, whereas the others are mammals.

33. **B)** Acclaim means "applause, praise."

34. **A)** If Max's team has never won, then his team lost today (and every day).

35. **A)** Pleased means "satisfied, experiencing pleasure." The other three words describe negative feelings.

36. **B)** Consistent means "reliable, steady, even, harmonious." Uneven is an antonym of consistent.

37. **D)** Facilitate means "assist"; obliterate means "destroy."

38. **B)** Haphazard means "disorganized, messy, or chaotic."

39. **C)** Even though Anthony went to Chicago, it is uncertain if he visited the Sears Tower.

40. **B)** Ice is a solid; all the other choices are liquids.

41. **B)** Insightful means "perceptive, shrewd, understanding, aware." Unperceptive is an antonym of insightful.

42. **D)** A pedal is one part of a bicycle; a zipper is one part of a jacket.

43. **D)** To meander is to wander, roam, or amble around on a winding, twisting route.

44. **D)** All four choices are used outside—often for gardening or yard work—but a broom is the only tool that is also often used inside.

45. **A)** To ascend means "to move upward, rise."

46. **A)** Because Max chose his favorite flavored lollipop—strawberry—Max must like strawberry-flavored lollipops.

47. **C)** Pine needles, tree trunks, and mushrooms are all related to plants, while a seagull is a mammal.

48. A) Partial means "biased, prejudiced, one-sided, unfair." Fair is an antonym of partial.

49. D) The stomach is needed for digestion; the lungs are needed for breathing.

50. C) To quench one's thirst means "to satisfy" it.

51. C) There is no indication that Walter prefers soda.

52. C) While all items are found at the ocean, only shells, sea glass, and rocks are items that people collect.

53. C) Aptitude means "ability, capacity."

54. D) A white board, desk, and chair are all pieces of furniture in a school, while a marker is a tool used in a classroom.

55. C) Revelation means "exposure, disclosure, admission, shock." Secret is an antonym of revelation.

56. B) A knife is used to slice; a fork is used to pierce.

57. A) To abolish something means "to get rid of or eliminate" it.

58. B) A medal, trophy, and award are all prizes for winning something. A certificate usually indicates an accomplishment or having completed something but does not necessarily indicate winning.

59. C) There is no way of knowing whether or not Jose likes soccer.

60. C) A beep, ring, and snort are all sounds, while a weight is an object.

QUANTITATIVE SKILLS

1. B) In this series, a new number is found by adding the two previous numbers.

1, 1, 2, 3, 5, 8, ...

$1 + 1 = 2$

$1 + 2 = 3$

$2 + 3 = 5$

$3 + 5 = 8$

The next number is $5 + 8 =$ **13**.

2. A) The diagonal of a rectangle equally divides the rectangle's area, so the shaded areas of (a) and (b) are equal. Figure (c) shows less than half of the rectangle shaded, so (c) is less shaded than (a) and (b).

(a) = (b) > (c)

3. C) The numbers in the series are decreasing by 6.

$67 - 73 = -6$

$61 - 67 = -6$

$43 - 49 = -6$

Find the missing number by subtracting 6 from the previous number.

$61 - 6 = 55$

4. **A)** The numbers in the series are decreasing by 106.

$8021 - 8127 = -106$

$7915 - 8021 = -106$

$7809 - 7915 = -106$

To find the next number, subtract 106 from the previous number.

$7809 - 106 = \textbf{7703}$

5. **C)** 75% of $24 = 0.75(24) = \textbf{18}$

6. **C)** The numbers in the series are decreasing by 2.

71, 69, ___, ___, 63, 61

$69 - 71 = -2$

$61 - 63 = -2$

To find the missing numbers, subtract 2 from the previous number.

$69 - 2 = \textbf{67}$

$67 - 2 = \textbf{65}$

7. **C)** $\frac{2}{3}$ of what number is equal to 12?

a = the number being solved for

$\frac{2}{3} \times a = 12$

$a = \frac{3}{2} \times 12 = \textbf{18}$

8. **C)** The series is geometric with a common ratio of 2 (meaning each number is multiplied by 2 to find the next number).

0.04, 0.08, 0.16, 0.32, ...

$\frac{0.08}{0.04} = 2$

$\frac{0.16}{0.08} = 2$

$\frac{0.32}{0.16} = 2$

To find the next number, multiply the previous number by 2.

$0.32 \times 2 = \textbf{0.64}$

9. **C)** The numbers in the series are increasing by 1.1.

___, 5, 6.1, 7.2, 8.3

$6.1 - 5 = 1.1$

$7.2 - 6.1 = 1.1$

$8.3 - 7.2 = 1.1$

To find the first number, subtract 1.1 from the number that follows it.

$5 - 1.1 = \textbf{3.9}$

10. **C)** $\frac{3}{5}$ of what number is 300?

a = the number being solved for

$\frac{3}{5} \times a = 300$

$a = \frac{5}{3}(300) = \textbf{500}$

11. **C)** Find the area of each figure.

(a): $A_{square} = s^2 = 10^2 = 100$

(b): $A_{rectangle} = lw = 5(2) = 10$

(c): $A_{triangle} = \frac{1}{2}bh = \frac{1}{2}(12)(3) = 18$

(a) > (c) > (b)

12. **D)** $\frac{3}{5}$ of 500 $= \frac{3}{5} \times 500 = \textbf{300}$

13. **D)** Find the perimeter of each figure. In an equilateral shape, all the sides have the same lengths.

(a): $P_{square} = 4s = 4(6) = 24$

(b): $P_{triangle} = 3s = 3(8) = 24$

(c): $P_{hexagon} = 6s = 6(3) = 18$

(a) = (b) > (c)

14. **D)** The series is geometric with a common ratio of $\frac{1}{2}$ (meaning each number is multiplied by $\frac{1}{2}$ or divided by 2 to find the next number).

4848, 2424, 1212, 606, ...

$\frac{2424}{4848} = \frac{1}{2}$

$\frac{1212}{2424} = \frac{1}{2}$

$\frac{606}{1212} = \frac{1}{2}$

To find the next number, multiply the previous number by $\frac{1}{2}$.

$606 \times \frac{1}{2} = \textbf{303}$

15. **C)** (a): 7 circles

(b): 8 circles

(c): 7 circles

(b) > (a) = (c)

16. **A)** In this series, the numbers 1 and −1 alternate with a zero between each one.

1, 0, −1, 0, 1, 0, …

The next number in the series will follow a zero, so it will be either 1 or −1. Because the number before the last zero is 1, the next number will be **−1**.

17. **B)** The numbers in the series are increasing. The difference between the values increases by 1 with each number.

13, 14, 16, 19, …

14 − 13 = 1

16 − 14 = 2

19 − 16 = 3

To find the next number, add 4 to the previous number.

19 + 4 = **23**

To find the number after that, add 5 to the previous number.

23 + 5 = **28**

18. **C)** The series is geometric with a common ratio of $\frac{1}{2}$ (meaning each number is multiplied by $\frac{1}{2}$ or divided by 2 to find the next number).

$\frac{12}{24} = \frac{1}{2}$

$\frac{6}{12} = \frac{1}{2}$

$\frac{3}{6} = \frac{1}{2}$

To find the next number, multiply the previous number by $\frac{1}{2}$.

$3 \times \frac{1}{2} = \frac{3}{2} = $ **1.5**

19. **C)** The size of an angle in a triangle is proportional to the side opposite it. ∠C is opposite the longest side, so it is the largest angle. ∠B is opposite the shortest side, so it is the shortest side.

∠C > ∠A > ∠B

20. **D)** The numbers in the series are increasing by 1.3.

1.3, 2.6, 3.9, 5.2, …

2.6 − 1.3 = 1.3

3.9 − 2.6 = 1.3

5.2 − 3.9 = 1.3

To find the next number, add 1.3 to the previous number.

5.2 + 1.3 = **6.5**

21. **D)** In this series, each digit in the four-digit number increases by 1.

1234, 2345, 3456, _____, 5678, 6789

To find the missing number, add 1 to each digit in the previous number.

3456 → **4567**

22. **A)** The numbers in the series are increasing. The difference between each value is increasing by 1.

567, 579, 592, 606, 621, _____

579 − 567 = 12

592 − 579 = 13

606 − 592 = 14

621 − 606 = 15

To find the next number, add 16 to the previous number.

621 + 16 = **637**

23. C) Simplify each expression.

(a): $3.48 \times 10^{-3} = 0.00348$

(b): $-3 \times -48 = 144$

(c): $-2 - (-4) = 2$

(a), (b), and (c) are positive.

24. A) Rewrite each value as a decimal.

(a): $30\% = 0.3$

(b): 0.3

(c) $= \frac{3}{100} = 0.03$

(a) = (b) > (c)

25. B) The numbers in the series are increasing. The difference between the values increases by 10 with each number.

$720 - 710 = 10$

$740 - 720 = 20$

$770 - 740 = 30$

$810 - 770 = 40$

To find the next number, add 50 to the previous number.

$810 + 50 = \mathbf{860}$

26. C) 21 more than 4 squared $= 21 + 4^2 = 21 + 16 = \mathbf{37}$

27. B) Simplify each expression.

(a): $\frac{2}{3} \times 42 = 28$

(b): $\frac{7}{10} \times 40 = 28$

(c): $\frac{5}{4} \times 24 = 30$

(c) > (a) = (b)

28. B) The difference between the first and third number is 8. The difference between the third and fifth numbers is also 8.

15, ____, 23, _____, 31

$23 - 15 = 8$

$31 - 23 = 8$

Divide by 2 to find the difference between each consecutive

number: $8 \div 2 = 4$. To find the missing numbers, add 4 to the previous number.

$15 + 4 = \mathbf{19}$

$23 + 4 = \mathbf{27}$

29. B) $\frac{5}{7}$ of what number is equal to 35?

a = the number being solved for

$\frac{5}{7} \times a = 35$

$a = \frac{7}{5} \times 35 = \mathbf{49}$

30. C) $\frac{1}{3}$ of $36 = \frac{1}{3} \times 36 = \mathbf{12}$

31. B) 11 less than 6 squared $= 6^2 - 11 = 36 - 11 = \mathbf{25}$

32. A) 2 multiplied by the sum of 11 and $3 = 2(11 + 3) = 2(14) = \mathbf{28}$

33. B) The numbers in the series are decreasing by 3.5.

83.5, 80, _____, 73, 69.5

$80 - 83.5 = -3.5$

$69.5 - 73 = -3.5$

To find the missing number, subtract 3.5 from the previous number.

$80 - 3.5 = \mathbf{76.5}$

34. C) $\frac{2}{3}$ of what number is equal to 150?

a = the number being solved for

$\frac{2}{3} \times a = 150$

$a = \frac{3}{2} \times 150 = \mathbf{225}$

35. C) The sum of what number and 4 is equal to 10?

a = the number being solved for

$(a + 4) = 10$

$a = \mathbf{6}$

36. C) $\frac{3}{5}$ of $100 = \frac{3}{5} \times 100 = \mathbf{60}$

37. D) Choose two consecutive odd integers (e.g., 7 and 9, 13 and 15) and subtract the lower one from the higher. The difference is always **2**.

38. D) Simplify each expression.

(a): $0 + (3 - 2) = 0 + 1 = 1$

(b): $0 \times (3 - 2) = 0 \times 1 = 0$

(c): $0 - (3 - 2) = 0 - 1 = -1$

(a) > (b) > (c)

39. A) 20% of 25% of $80 = 0.2(0.25)(80) = \mathbf{4}$

40. B) $\frac{2}{3}$ of 60 divided by $8 = \frac{2}{3} \times 60 \div 8 = 40 \div 8 = \mathbf{5}$

41. B) The numbers in the series are decreasing by 2.

$-14 - (-12) = -2$

$-16 - (-14) = -2$

$-18 - (-16) = -2$

To find the first number, subtract -2 from the second number.

$-12 - (-2) = \mathbf{-10}$

42. C) 12 more than $\frac{2}{3}$ of $33 = 12 + \frac{2}{3} \times 33 = 12 + 22 = \mathbf{34}$

43. C) 12 less than 8 squared $= 8^2 - 12 = 64 - 12 = \mathbf{52}$

44. D) Find each value. The formula for the circumference of a circle is $C = 2\pi r$, and $d = 2r$ (where r is the radius and d is the diameter).

(a): $C = 2\pi r = 2\pi(4) = 8\pi$

(b): $C = 2\pi r = \pi d = 4\pi$

(c): $C = 2\pi r = 2\pi(2) = 4\pi$

(a) > (b) = (c)

45. A) Hexagons (a) and (b) are both half shaded. Hexagon (c) is less than half shaded.

(a) = (b) > (c)

46. A) Simplify each expression.

(a): 30% of $50 = 0.3 \times 50 = 15$

(b): 50% of $30 = 0.5 \times 30 = 15$

(c): 3% of $500 = 0.03 \times 500 = 15$

(a) = (b) = (c)

47. C) A rectangular prism has four sides that are congruent. **The diagonals of those four rectangles are all congruent.**

48. B) Simplify each expression.

(a): $8 + (3 - 2) = 8 + 1 = 9$

(b): $(8 + 3) - 2 = 11 - 2 = 9$

(c): $8 - (3 - 2) = 8 - 1 = 7$

(a) = (b) > (c)

49. A) Simplify each term.

Simplify each term.

(a): $\frac{35}{35} = 1$

(b): $35^0 = 1$

(c): $35 \times 0 = 0$

(a) = (b) > c

50. A) The numbers in the series are increasing by 5.

$-8, -3, \_\_\_, 7, 12$

$-3 - (-8) = 5$

$12 - 7 = 5$

To find the missing number, add 5 to the previous number.

$\mathbf{-3 + 5 = 2}$

51. B) The diagonals of a rectangle form two sets of opposing, congruent angles.

52. A) Convert each value to a decimal.

(a): 0.6

(b): $\frac{3}{5}$ = 0.6

(c): $\frac{1}{2}$ of 1.2 = 0.6

(a) = (b) = (c)

READING

1. **B)** The passage is primarily informative. However, the author uses jokes like the one in the last paragraph to entertain readers.

2. **B)** Readers can infer that when the tongue grows cold due to contact with cold substances such as ice cream, snow cones, or iced drinks, it does not trigger "brain freeze."

3. **C)** To entertain readers, the author is referring to the following rhyme: "I scream, you scream, we all scream for ice cream."

4. **B)** As the third sentence states shows, the passage is mainly about the causes of "brain freeze." The other sentences provide details that support the main idea.

5. **D)** In paragraph 2, the author writes, "When a cold substance … presses against the roof of your mouth, it causes blood vessels there to begin to constrict." Constrict is a synonym for narrow or shrink.

6. **A)** In the last sentence, the author writes, "The duration of the pain varies from a few seconds up to about a minute." Readers can infer that "duration of the pain" means "how long the pain lasts." An ice cream headache is short, luckily.

7. **B)** In the first sentence, the author writes, "Many snakes produce a toxic fluid in their salivary glands called venom." Readers can infer from this that some snakes do not produce venom. There is no support for any of the other claims.

8. **C)** The primary purpose of the essay is to inform; its general focus is on the composition of snake venoms. It is not primarily cautionary or advisory. The author does not tell a story about a specific research scientist.

9. **D)** In the last sentence in the second paragraph, the author writes, "Some cytotoxins target specific types of cells—myotoxins affect muscles, cardiotoxins attack the heart, and nephrotoxins damage the kidneys." Readers can infer that myo refers to muscles, cardio refers to the heart, and nephro refers to the kidneys, as in nephritis (inflammation of the kidneys).

10. **C)** In the last paragraph, the author writes, "Researchers have been studying the chemical compositions of these venoms and have been making strides in using the science behind the toxins to combat major diseases such as cancer, heart disease, and Alzheimer's." Readers can infer that the author is using the phrase "making strides in using

the science" to refer to making discoveries that greatly improve medical science's ability to cure diseases.

11. **B)** The passage is mainly about the composition of snake venom. The other sentences give details from the passage.

12. **A)** In the first paragraph, the author writes, "The two key ingredients in all snake venoms are enzymes and polypeptides. Some enzymes help the snake disable its prey, and others help the snake digest its prey." Later in the passage the author goes into more detail about these processes.

13. **B)** The first paragraph tells how, in 1796, surgeon Edward Jenner invented a precursor to the modern smallpox vaccine.

14. **D)** Injecting patients with vaccines (vaccinating them) immunizes them—makes patients immune to—diseases. Here, the nouns vaccination and immunization are synonyms.

15. **D)** The primary purpose of the essay is to inform; its focus is the history of vaccines. It is not persuasive or cautionary, and it does not give advice.

16. **B)** In the second paragraph, the author writes, "Vaccines work by stimulating the immune system to produce antibodies against a particular disease .... Your immune system hangs on to the antibodies it creates; if you are exposed to the pathogen in the future, your body is ready to fight it off."

17. **D)** In the last sentence, the author writes, "Today, every state requires some immunizations for children entering public schools, though all allow medical exemptions and most allow exemptions on religious or philosophical grounds." There are no sentences supporting the other claims.

18. **A)** In the last paragraph, the author writes, "Vaccines ... have helped eradicate or almost eradicate previously widespread diseases such as whooping cough, polio, rubella, tetanus, tuberculosis, smallpox, diphtheria, and measles." Readers can infer from this and from their own experiences that, despite flu shots, many people in the United States still get sick with the flu.

19. **B)** The author writes that "jazz music was played by and for a more expressive and freed populace than the United States had previously seen." In addition to "the emergence of the flapper," the 1920s saw "the explosion of African American art and culture now known as the Harlem Renaissance."

20. **A)** The author writes that "jazz music was played by and for a more expressive and freed populace than the United States had previously seen." In addition to "the emergence of the flapper," the 1920s saw "the explosion of African American art and culture now known as the Harlem Renaissance."

21. **C)** The author opens the passage saying, "In recent decades, jazz has been associated with New Orleans and festivals like Mardi Gras, but in the 1920s, jazz was a booming trend whose influence reached into many aspects of American culture." He then goes on to elaborate on what these movements were.

22. **B)** At the end of the first paragraph, the author writes, "Ella Fitzgerald, for example, moved from Virginia to New York City to begin her much-lauded singing career, and jazz pioneer Louis Armstrong got his big break in Chicago."

23. **C)** The author writes that "jazz music was played by and for a more expressive and freed populace than the United States had previously seen." In addition to "the emergence of the flapper," the 1920s saw "the explosion of African American art and culture now known as the Harlem Renaissance."

24. **C)** In the second sentence, the author writes, "Americans … are consuming twenty more teaspoons of sugar daily than the American Heart Association's recommendation of six teaspoons for women and nine for men."

25. **A)** The text is primarily informative, although there is an underlying cautionary message about health problems that can result from consuming too much sugar.

26. **D)** This detail is not found in the passage. However, the author does mention that some processed foods contain added sugar.

27. **A)** In the first sentence, the author writes, "Sugar is an essential fuel for the human body." Readers can infer from context that the author is using the word fuel to mean "energy source."

28. **B)** In the second sentence, the author writes that the American Heart Association recommends only six teaspoons of sugar per day for women, so twenty-six is probably far too much sugar per day unless the woman in question exercises constantly throughout the day.

29. **A)** This choice addresses all of the main ideas of the passage: the flu is potentially deadly, highly infectious, and difficult to contain due to viral shedding.

30. **A)** The author uses the term measures to describe the steps that people take to prevent the spreading of the influenza virus.

31. **D)** According to the passage, "the flu is…relatively difficult to contract," and "while many people who contract the virus will recover, many others will not."

32. **C)** The final paragraph of the passage states that viral shedding is "the process by which the body releases viruses that have been successfully reproducing during the infection."

33. **C)** The second paragraph states that the flu is "relatively difficult to contract" because it "can only be transmitted when individuals come into direct contact with bodily fluids of people infected with the flu or when they are

exposed to expelled aerosol particles."

34. A) The second paragraph of the passage states that "the virus can be contained with fairly simple health measures like hand washing and face masks."

35. B) The second paragraph ends with this statement: "Larger-scale clinical studies have not provided conclusive evidence for these benefits." By "these benefits," the author means claims that turmeric can heal inflammation. The last paragraph begins with "Regardless of its true health benefits ...." The author goes on to summarize how popular turmeric has become. The reader can infer that the author does not think there is proof for turmeric's effectiveness as an anti-inflammatory health aid.

36. C) The primary purpose of the essay is to explain; its focus is on the history of turmeric, its uses, and current popularity. The essay is not persuasive or cautionary. The author's tone is mildly critical or ironic, but he or she does not seem worried that consumers will be duped by all the "buzz" about turmeric.

37. B) In the second paragraph, the author writes, "Small-scale studies have shown that curcumin, a key compound found in turmeric, can help with both skin inflammation and joint inflammation."

38. D) The passage is mainly about turmeric's current popularity among people who believe in the spice's health benefits. The other sentences provide details that support the main idea.

39. A) In paragraph 1, the author writes, "Turmeric has been used medicinally—as well as in cooking, as a dye, and in religious rituals—in India and Southeast Asia for millennia." A millennium is one thousand years, and the plural millennia refers to as least two thousand years.

40. B) In paragraph 1, the author writes, "Once the root is boiled, dried, and ground, it creates a bitter yellow powdered spice that gives Indian curry its distinctive color." The word distinctive is related to the words distinct and distinguish. Indian curry's deep yellow color distinguishes it— sets it apart—from other dishes: this color is one of Indian curry's identifying characteristics.

VOCABULARY

1. **B)** Affinity means "likeness or attraction."

2. **A)** Sustainable means "endurable, supportable, maintainable."

3. **B)** Vast means "huge, colossal, giant, enormous."

4. **C)** Adequate means "comfortable, sufficient, enough, satisfactory."

5. **C)** Irritable means "easily exasperated, touchy, testy, bothered."

6. **D)** Subsequent means "being, occurring, or carried out at a time after something else; later."

7. **A)** Proprietor means "owner, holder, possessor."

8. **B)** Throngs means "masses, swarms, mobs, groups, packs, crowds."

9. **B)** Uncharacteristically means "unexpectedly, strangely, unusually."

10. **C)** Scruffy means "grubby, shabby, sloppy, messy."

11. **A)** Notorious means "infamous, dishonorable, disreputable."

12. **C)** Obscurity means "anonymity, unimportance, insignificance."

13. **A)** Frayed means "tattered, torn, ripped."

14. **C)** Darted means "dashed, scurried, flitted, moved."

15. **C)** Integrated means "united, combined, cohesive, included."

16. **B)** Limber means "lithe, supple, agile, flexible."

17. **C)** Sufficient means "adequate, enough, appropriate, satisfactory."

18. **A)** Jolted means "jerked, surprised, shaken, stunned."

19. **C)** Delegate means "to allot, assign, allocate, designate."

20. **D)** Exalted mean "high, lofty, glorious, dignified, grand."

21. **C)** Prominent means "protruding, conspicuous, noticeable, glaring."

22. **A)** Alien means "unfamiliar, strange, outlandish."

MATHEMATICS

1. **D)** Multiply the exponents raised to a power.
$$\frac{(10^2)^3}{(10^{-2})^2} = \frac{10^6}{10^{-4}}$$
Subtract the exponent in the denominator from the exponent in the numerator.
$$10^{6-(-4)} = 10^{10}$$

2. **C)** Round each number and multiply.
$$16{,}000 \times 200 = 3{,}200{,}000 \approx$$
3,300,000

3. **D)** When adding 7 points to each test, the mean, median, and modes will all increase by 7 points.

Mean = 85; Median = 81; Mode = 84

The **range**, which is the difference between the lowest and highest score, will not change as a result of adding points.

4. **D)** The graph of $x = 3$ is a vertical line. It crosses the x-axis at 3 but **has an undefined slope**.

5. **D)** $400 \div 16 = 25$
Simplify each expression and find the expression that equals 25.
$$2(200 - 8) = 2(192) = 384$$
$$(400 \div 4) \div 12 = 100 \div 12 = 8.\overline{3}$$

$(216 \div 8) + (184 \div 8) = 27 + 23 = 50$

$(216 \div 16) + (184 \div 16) = 13.5 + 11.5 = 25$

$(216 \div 16) + (184 \div 16)$

6. **A)** Profit = income − expenses

Income = $40 for each lawn, or $40m$.

Expenses = $35 each week, or $35x$.

Profit = **$40m - 35x$**

7. **B)** The given problem is solved using subtraction: $7 - 2 = 5$ pencils. Problem B is also solved using subtraction: $10 - 6 = 4$ carrot sticks.

Selena brought 10 carrot sticks for lunch. How many carrots sticks were left after she ate 6?

8. **B)** Order the fractions by comparing the denominators.

$\frac{1}{2} > \frac{1}{3} > \frac{1}{7} > -\frac{1}{6} > -\frac{1}{5} > -\frac{1}{4}$

9. **B)** Each of the decimal numbers are expressed in ten-thousandths. The number 55 is between 47 and 162, so **0.0055** is between 0.0047 and 0.0162.

10. **D)** The given sequence is formed by subtracting 3. The new sequence would therefore start with 41 and decrease by 3 with each term: **41, 38, 35, 32, . . .**

11. **B)** The bar graph should show that 10 students prefer vanilla, 6 students prefer strawberry, and 23 students prefer chocolate ice cream. **Benjamin** completed the graph correctly.

12. **D)** A counterexample is an exception to a proposed general rule. The statement **17 + 15 = 32** is a counterexample because it shows that the sum of two odd numbers can be an even number.

13. **B)** Find all the factors of 42.

$42 = 1 \times 42$

$42 = 2 \times 21$

$42 = 3 \times 14$

$42 = 6 \times 7$

The factors of 42 are 1, 2, 3, 6, 7, 14, 21, and 42.

The prime factors are 2, 3, and 7. (1 is neither prime nor composite.)

Subtract the smallest value from the largest to find the range.

$7 - 2 = \textbf{5}$

14. **B)** Circumference of a circle:

$C = 2\pi r$.

$d = 2r$, so $C = \pi d$.

$50 \text{ ft} = \pi d$

$d = \frac{50}{\pi}$

15. **B)** Multiply each side by 2.

$4x = 3$

$2(4x) = 2(3)$

$8x = \textbf{6}$

16. **C)** Odd + odd = even → Eliminate choice A.

Either x or y can equal 0, but they do not necessarily have to be. → Eliminate choice B.

Odd × even = even → Eliminate choice D.

For the sum of two numbers to be odd, one number must be odd and the other even. → Choice **C** is correct.

17. **C)** Order the data from smallest to largest and find the middle value.

17, 26, 38, 41, **42**, 45, 46, 46, 50

18. **D)** The remainder of a division problem must be less than the divisor. The remainder cannot be **3**.

19. **B)** The numbers 66, 42, and 28 are all even numbers. Answer choices A, B, and C can all be divisible by 2. The expressions **15 × 99** has factors of 3, 5, and 11.

20. **A)** Find the amount the state will spend on infrastructure and education.

    Infrastructure = 0.2(3,000,000,000) = 600,000,000

    Education = 0.18(3,000,000,000) = 540,000,000

    Find the difference.

    600,000,000 − 540,000,000 = **$60,000,000**

21. **D)** Write an equation to find the number of people wearing neither white nor blue. Subtract the number of people wearing both colors so they are not counted twice.

    total applicants = (applicants wearing blue) + (applicants wearing white) − (applicants wearing both blue and white) + (applicants wearing neither blue nor white)

    21 = 7 + 6 − 5 + *neither*

    neither = **13**

22. **A)** Substitute 5 for *x*.

    $2(5) - 5 \rightarrow 10 - 5 = $ **5**

23. **C)** The decimal part ends in the hundredths place.

    Place the decimal over 100 →

    $2\frac{61}{100}$

24. **C)** The total number of children is described within the parentheses. Since each hot dog costs $2, that total is multiplied by 2.

    2 × (6 + 9) = $30

25. **A)** Graphing $y = -3x - 2$ gives a line with a slope of −3 and a *y*-intercept of −2. Because the symbol is greater than or equal to (≥), the line is solid and the graph is shaded above the line;

    $y \leq -3x - 2$.

26. **A)** Use order of operations to simplify the expression.

    $(5^2 + 1)^2 + 3^3 \rightarrow (25 + 1)^2 + 3^3 \rightarrow 676 + 27 \rightarrow$ **703**

27. **D)** $\frac{7.2 \times 10^6}{1.6 \times 10^{-3}}$

    Divide the decimals.

    7.2 ÷ 1.6 = 4.5

    Subtract the exponents.

    6 − (−3) = 9

    4.5×10^9

28. **B)** Work backwards and write a proportion to find the number of runners in the competition (*c*).

    $\frac{2}{c} = \frac{10}{100}$

    $c = 20$

    Substitute to find the number of runners on the team (*r*).

    $\frac{20}{r} = \frac{25}{100}$

    $r = $ **80**

29. **C)** Each student receives 2 notebooks.

    16 × 2 = 32 notebooks

    Subtract to determine the notebooks that are left.

    50 − 32 = **18** notebooks left

30. **C)** Use the equation for percentages.

    $\text{whole} = \frac{\text{part}}{\text{percent}} = \frac{17}{0.4} = $ **42.5**

31. **C)** Set up a proportion.

$\dfrac{\text{Regular}}{\text{Total}} \rightarrow \dfrac{3}{4} = \dfrac{x}{24}$

Cross multiply.

$4x = 72$

$x = \mathbf{18}$

32. **C)** Isolate the variable on the left side of the inequality.

$6x + 5 \geq -15 + 8x$

$-2x + 5 \geq -15$

$-2x \geq -20$

Reverse the direction of the inequality when dividing by a negative number.

$\boldsymbol{x \geq 10}$

33. **A)** Find the slope using the values in the table.

$m = \dfrac{y_2 - y_1}{x_2 - x_1} = \dfrac{15 - 11}{5 - 3} = \dfrac{4}{2} = 2$

Alternatively, substitute an ordered pair from the table into the equations.

$\boldsymbol{y = 2x + 5}$

$11 = 2(3) + 5$

$11 = 11$

34. **D)** Set up a proportion and solve.

$\dfrac{8}{650} = \dfrac{12}{x}$

Cross multiply.

$12(650) = 8x$

$x = \mathbf{975\ miles}$

35. **A)** Substitute 4 for j and simplify.

$2(j - 4)^4 - j + \tfrac{1}{2}j$

$2(4 - 4)^4 - 4 + \tfrac{1}{2}(4)$

$2(0) - 4 + 2 = \mathbf{-2}$

36. **B)** Substitute the given values into the equation and solve for t.

$d = r \times t$

$4000 = 500 \times t$

$t = \mathbf{8\ hours}$

37. **B)** Multiply the number of bottles by the amount each holds.

$24 \times 0.75 = \mathbf{18}$

38. **A)** 1 year = 12 months

3 years = 3 × 12 = 36 monthly payments.

Down payment + months paid × monthly payment = total paid

$\$3000 + 36(\$216) \rightarrow \$3000 + \$7776 = \mathbf{\$10{,}776}$

39. **A)** Use the equation for the perimeter of a rectangle.

$P = 2l + 2w$

$42 = 2(13) + 2w$

$w = \mathbf{8}$

40. **D)** Use the volume to find the length of the cube's side.

$V = s^3$

$343 = s^3$

$s = 7\ \text{m}$

Find the area of each side.

$7(7) = 49\ \text{m}$

Multiply by the total number of sides, 6, to find the total surface area.

$49(6) = \mathbf{294\ m^2}$

41. **A)** Use the combination formula to find the number of ways to choose 2 people out of a group of 20.

$C(20, 2) \rightarrow \dfrac{20!}{2!18!} \rightarrow \dfrac{(20)(19)}{2} = \mathbf{190}$

42. **D)** Rearrange the formula for probability to solve for the number of possible outcomes.

$P = \dfrac{\text{number of favorable outcomes}}{\text{number of possible outcomes}}$

$\text{number of possible outcomes} = \dfrac{\text{number of favorable outcomes}}{P}$

$\text{number of possible outcomes} = \dfrac{3}{0.0004} = \mathbf{7500}$

43. **D)** Find the area of the complete rectangle.

rectangle: $A = lw = (20 + 2 + 2) \times (10 + 2 + 2) = 336$ cm^2

corners: $A = 4(lw) = 4(2 \times 2) = 16$ cm^2

Subtract the area of the missing corners.

$336 - 16 = \textbf{320 cm}^2$

44. **C)** Use the area formula to find the length of one side of the square.

$A = s^2$

$5{,}625 = s^2$

$\sqrt{5{,}625} = s$

$s = 75$ ft

Multiply the side length by 4 to find the perimeter.

$P = 4s$

$P = 4(75 \text{ ft}) = \textbf{300 ft}$

45. **A)** Find the total weight of the three books.

$0.8 + 0.49 + 0.89 = 2.18$ lb

Subtract the weight of the books from the maximum weight for the shipping box.

$2.5 - 2.18 = \textbf{0.32 lb}$

46. **B)** Find the circle's radius.

$4 \text{ km} \div 2 = 2 \text{ km}$

Use the radius to find the circumference of the circle.

$C = 2\pi r = 2\pi(2) = 4\pi$

Arc AB is a semicircle, which means its length is half the circumference of the circle.

$\frac{4\pi}{2} = \textbf{2}\pi \textbf{ km}$

47. **C)** Multiply the number of outcomes for each individual event.

$(70)(2)(5) = \textbf{700}$ outfits

48. **B)** Find the circumference of the bucket.

If $r = 5$ inches, then $C = 2\pi(5) = 10\pi$ or 31.4 inches.

The python coils around the bucket six times. Multiply the circumference by 6.

$31.4 \times 6 = 188.4 \approx \textbf{188 inches}$

49. **C)** There are 7 seats and 9 people playing. There is a 7 out of 9 chance or **78%** chance a person is not eliminated.

50. **B)** Change the percentage to a decimal.

$40\% = 0.4$

Multiply the decimal by the whole (number of voters) to find the part (number of votes for Pauline).

$175 \times 0.4 = \textbf{70}$

51. **B)** Let x = the number of people to attend the party.

$4x + 6 = 50$

Solve for x.

$4x + 6 - 6 = 50 - 6$

$4x = 44$

$x = \textbf{11}$

52. **C)** Find the percent change.

$\frac{\text{original} - \text{new}}{\text{orignal}} \rightarrow \frac{92 - 88}{92} = 0.0435$

Convert to a percent.

4.35% is **between 4 and 5%**.

53. **C)** Find the number of combinations.

4 meats × 3 cheeses × 2 breads × 4 condiments = **96** different sandwiches.

54. **B)** Multiply the car's speed by the time traveled to find the distance.

$1.5(65) = 97.5$ miles

$2.5(50) = 125$ miles

$97.5 + 125 = \textbf{222.5 miles}$

55. C) Subtract the amount used from the original yards.

$6 - 4\frac{5}{8} \rightarrow 5\frac{8}{8} - 4\frac{5}{8} = \mathbf{1\frac{3}{8}}$ **yd**

56. D) There are 10 sides, and each side is 2 mm in length.

Add the length of each side to find the total.

$P = 2(10) = \mathbf{20}$ **mm**

57. B) Convert gallons to liters.

$2 \text{ gal} \times \frac{3.785 \text{ L}}{1 \text{ gal}} = 7.57 \text{ L}$

Subtract to find the difference in liters.

$10 \text{ L} - 7.57 \text{ L} = \mathbf{2.43}$ **L**

58. D) Find the daily distance by adding $\frac{1}{4}$ mile to each day.

Day	Monday	Tuesday	Wednesday	Thursday	Friday
Distance	$3\frac{2}{4}$	$3\frac{1}{2} + \frac{1}{4} = 3\frac{3}{4}$	$3\frac{3}{4} + \frac{1}{4} = 4$	$4 + \frac{1}{4} = 4\frac{1}{4}$	$4\frac{1}{4} + \frac{1}{4} = 4\frac{2}{4}$

Add each daily distance to find the total.

$3\frac{2}{4} + 3\frac{3}{4} + 4 + 4\frac{1}{4} + 4\frac{2}{4} =$

$18\frac{8}{4} \rightarrow 18 + 2 = \mathbf{20}$

59. A) Find the amount of sugar the patient will need to cut from his diet.

part = whole × percent

$40 \times 0.25 = 10$

Subtract this amount from the initial value.

$40 - 10 = \mathbf{30}$ **grams**

60. D) Add the lengths of the pipe pieces.

$26.5 + 18.9 + 35.1 = \mathbf{80.5}$ **in**

61. D) Portion the shape into squares and rectangles. Find the area of each smaller shape.

Rectangle: $A = l \times w$.

$A = 8 \times 2 = 16$

Area of the center square is $A = s^2$.

$A = 8^2 = 64$

Add the area of the four rectangles and the center square.

$4(16) + 64 = \mathbf{128}$

62. D) $-4x + 2 = -34$

Isolate x by subtracting two from each side.

$-4x = -36$

Divide by -4.

$x = \mathbf{9}$

63. B) Use dimensional analysis to determine the length of time.

$4500 \text{ words} \times \frac{1 \text{ minute}}{45 \text{ words}} =$ **100 minutes**

64. C) Ken has 6 scores that average 92%.

Total number of points: $92 \times 6 = 552$.

Total of first 5 grades: $90 + 100 + 95 + 83 + 87 = 455$.

Subtract to find the score on the 6th test.

$552 - 455 = \mathbf{97}$

LANGUAGE SKILLS

1. **B)** The comma after *death* is used incorrectly to join two complete thoughts; a semicolon should be used instead to properly join the two related, independent clauses.

2. **D)** All the sentences are correct. Choice A correctly pairs two past-tense verbs, was baking and ate. Choice B correctly pairs the plural noun *parents* with the plural verb *will pick* and correctly pairs *either* with *or*. Choice C correctly pairs the plural subject "my teacher and the school principal" with the plural verb *have worked*.

3. **B)** Choice B contains a misplaced modifier that makes it sound like Mario was left on the stove for too long.

4. **C)** The contraction don't is missing an apostrophe.

5. **A)** Choice A incorrectly uses most, a superlative, when a comparative adjective (older) should be used to compare two items ("my two parents").

6. **C)** Choice C incorrectly uses *their* instead of *they're* or *they are*.

7. **B)** Choice B contains an apostrophe error. The sentence incorrectly uses the contraction it's, meaning "it is," instead of the possessive singular pronoun *its*.

8. **A)** Choice A incorrectly uses a semicolon instead of a comma.

9. **A)** Choice C incorrectly uses take, a verb synonymous with grab, seize, or remove, in place of bring.

10. **B)** Choice B incorrectly uses *most* with a one-syllable adjective, soft. The writer should use the adjective softest.

11. **A)** Choice A correctly uses the verb *accept*, which means "to agree to take" something. However, it incorrectly uses a comma to connect two independent clauses. The writer should insert the coordinating conjunction *for* after the comma or replace the comma with a semicolon.

12. **A)** River is a common noun and should not be capitalized in this sentence.

13. **B)** Choice B incorrectly capitalizes desert, a common noun.

14. **C)** Choice C requires a comma after much to connect the two independent clauses using the conjunction *so*.

15. **B)** Choice B incorrectly pairs the plural subject two with the singular verb hopes.

16. **D)** All the sentences are correct. Choice A uses the following punctuation marks correctly: a comma, an opening quotation mark, a period, and a closing quotation mark. Choice B correctly capitalizes the proper noun Microsoft, leaving the common nouns automobile and industry in lower case. Choice C correctly connects two independent clauses ("Jenny enjoys swimming in pools" and "she hates swimming in lakes") with a comma and the coordinating conjunction *but*.

17. **A)** In choice A, the verb insure means "to cover with an insurance policy." The writer should use the verb ensure.

18. **C)** "Ice cream . . . food" and "it . . . creamy" are two independent clauses. The writer should include a coordinating conjunction like *for* or separate the clauses with a semicolon.

19. **C)** The verb went should be replaced with gone, the past participle of to go.

20. **B)** To agree with the plural noun dresses, the singular verb was should be replaced with the plural verb were to indicate all the dresses were torn and dirty.

21. **D)** All the sentences are correct. Capitalization is used correctly in choice A. In choice B, the verb accept is used to mean "to agree to take" something that is offered. In choice D, the verb break, which means "to smash into pieces," is used correctly.

22. **A)** The speaker is comparing only two people: "of my two sisters." *The most* should be replaced with the word *more*.

23. **A)** The adverb aloud means "out loud." It should be replaced with the verb allowed, which means "given permission to."

24. **B)** The apostrophe in parent's should be deleted. The apostrophe creates a singular possessive when the sentence calls for a plural noun (parents).

25. **C)** Because the bus driver and the passenger are not identified by name, using the feminine subject pronoun she is confusing to the reader. The reader cannot tell who spoke or who acted rudely. The whole sentence needs rewriting.

26. **A)** The phrase "Because of its distance from the sun" is a dependent clause, so it must be connected with the rest of the sentence by a comma, not a semicolon.

27. **A)** Providing shade is not an independent clause; therefore, it cannot be preceded by a semicolon.

28. **A)** Choice A incorrectly omits the apostrophe in the contraction I'm.

29. **C)** The subject "My brother and I" is plural, so the singular verb likes should be replaced with a plural verb, like.

30. **A)** In choice A, the common nouns aunt and mom's are incorrectly capitalized.

31. **C)** The possessive pronoun *your* should be replaced with the contraction *you're* (short for you are).

32. **A)** Accept (a verb meaning "to agree to take" something) should be replaced with its homophone, except: "We invited everyone to our wedding except people whom neither of us knew very well." Except is a preposition that means "other than."

33. **B)** "Of the two top students" is not an independent clause; it is a prepositional phrase. It must be connected to the rest of the sentence with a comma, not a semicolon.

34. **C)** This choice contains a clause, not a full sentence. It cannot stand on its own.

35. **D)** All the sentences are correct. Choice A correctly uses a comma at the end of the independent clause Mom . . . flying and before the subordinating conjunction so; it also correctly ends the sentence with a period. Choice B uses the following punctuation marks correctly: an apostrophe in isn't, a colon after home, an apostrophe in there's, a comma, and a period. Choice C uses the following punctuation marks correctly: a colon, a comma, another comma, and a period.

36. **C)** The writer should replace the period after black with a comma to connect the dependent clause "Because our school colors are orange and black" with the independent clause "I'm going to dye a few of my white T-shirts orange."

37. **B)** A comma should be inserted after Mr. Yetto and teacher to set off the appositive phrase "my third-grade teacher."

38. **A)** The contraction I'm is missing an apostrophe.

39. **D)** All the sentences are correct.

40. **A)** Plays is a singular verb and does not correctly pair with the plural subject men; "men dress . . . and play tricks."

41. **C)** The word suspicious is misspelled.

42. **A)** The verb should be spelled interrogated.

43. **C)** Mourning should be replaced with its homophone, morning: "How are you feeling on this sunny Saturday morning?" Mourning is a verb that means "grieving for a loved one who has died," and morning is a noun that means the opposite of evening.

44. **B)** The homophones through and threw should be transposed: "I accidentally threw my baseball through my neighbor's window." The past-tense verb threw means "hurled or pitched," and the preposition through (which begins the prepositional phrase "through my neighbor's window") means "in one side and out the other."

45. **C)** Sweet should be replaced with its homophone, suite: "There are two bedrooms, a bathroom, and a sitting room in our hotel suite." Sweet is an adjective that means "sugary." Suite is a noun that means "a group of connected rooms."

46. **B)** Rains should be replaced with its homophone, reins: "Use the reins to guide your horse." Rains is a plural noun in this sentence, synonymous with showers, floods, and deluges. In the corrected sentence, reins is a plural noun that means "straps that are attached to a horse's bridle; a rider uses them to control and guide the horse."

47. **A)** Morning is the early part of a day, and mourning is a grieving process someone goes through after a loved one has died.

48. **C)** Independent is misspelled.

49. **D)** No words are misspelled.

50. **C)** Seditious is misspelled.

51. **A)** The other choices all discuss the importance of the game to the town, so choice A does not belong.

52. **A)** By itself, the verb separates asks the question "Separates what from what?" The other choices all are synonyms or have similar meanings.

53. **B)** The conjunction *but* connects two contradictory ideas expressed in two independent clauses (a hard job, but an enjoyable one) with a comma.

54. **C)** The conjunction *but* connects two independent clauses with a comma and expresses contradictory ideas.

55. **C)** This sentence expresses the idea with no misplaced modifiers or misused transitions.

56. **B)** This sentence provides information about animals and migration, in accordance with the topic.

57. **B)** Only in this choice do the three phrases have a similar (parallel) structure.

58. **D)** The colon correctly signifies that the second clause builds on the first.

59. **D)** This choice creates a comma splice.

60. **A)** This sentence does not relate to the flow of information provided by the other three, which tell the story of the siblings' experience with the radio contest.

CHAPTER SIX
PRACTICE TEST TWO

Verbal Skills

1. Snake is to slithers as kangaroo is to
   - **A)** amphibians.
   - **B)** bounds.
   - **C)** marsupials.
   - **D)** pouches.

2. Which word does NOT belong with the others?
   - **A)** teeth
   - **B)** cotton ball
   - **C)** needle
   - **D)** staple

3. I love all cereal. Chuckles is a type of cereal. I love Chuckles. If the first two statements are true, the third statement is
   - **A)** true.
   - **B)** false.
   - **C)** uncertain.

4. Which word does NOT belong with the others?
   - **A)** oak
   - **B)** birch
   - **C)** maple
   - **D)** daffodil

5. Sacred means the opposite of
   - **A)** cherished.
   - **B)** fearful.
   - **C)** untouchable.
   - **D)** profane.

6. Seagull is to flock as wolf is to
   - **A)** pack.
   - **B)** canine.
   - **C)** predator.
   - **D)** deer.

7. Melissa went to the Science Museum. She examined all the exhibits but especially enjoyed the Atoms Exhibit. Melissa didn't know anything about atoms before she went to the museum. If the first two statements are true, the third statement is
   - **A)** true.
   - **B)** false.
   - **C)** uncertain.

8. Which word does NOT belong with the others?
   A) children
   B) rock
   C) plants
   D) animals

9. Gigantic most nearly means
   A) humongous.
   B) petite.
   C) dangerous.
   D) delicate.

10. Jack loves animals. He went to the pet store to look at the animals. Jack brought home a dog. If the first two statements are true, the third statement is
    A) true.
    B) false.
    C) uncertain.

11. Which word does NOT belong with the others?
    A) ostrich
    B) cow
    C) pig
    D) horse

12. Transformed means the opposite of
    A) unchanged.
    B) sweeping.
    C) mutated.
    D) shifted.

13. Sock is to foot as glove is to
    A) winter.
    B) cold.
    C) hand.
    D) toes.

14. Sleek most nearly means
    A) narrow.
    B) wet.
    C) transparent.
    D) smooth.

15. Jessica likes playing chess. Jessica likes playing checkers. Jessica does not like sports. If the first two statements are true, the third statement is
    A) true.
    B) false.
    C) uncertain.

16. Which word does NOT belong with the others?
    A) pleasant
    B) kindly
    C) cheerful
    D) rude

17. Substantial most nearly means
    A) partial.
    B) inferior.
    C) plentiful.
    D) upright.

18. Which word does NOT belong with the others?
    A) limited
    B) endless
    C) eternal
    D) lasting

19. Inertia means the opposite of
    A) stuck.
    B) bewildered.
    C) active.
    D) lifeless.

20. Key is to lock as handle is to
    A) door.
    B) safety.
    C) open.
    D) exit.

21. Fidelity most nearly means
    A) disloyalty.
    B) noncommittal.
    C) wavering.
    D) allegiance.

22. The clothing store had red, yellow, and blue shirts. Jenny wanted to buy a purple shirt for her mother. Jenny bought a shirt for her mother at the store. If the first two statements are true, the third statement is
    A) true.
    B) false.
    C) uncertain.

23. Which word does NOT belong with the others?
    A) busy
    B) complex
    C) elaborate
    D) simple

24. Deter means the opposite of
    A) encourage.
    B) dissuade.
    C) avoid.
    D) refer.

25. Sweater is to winter as swimsuit is to
    A) pool.
    B) summer.
    C) heat.
    D) clothing.

26. Briskly most nearly means
    A) energetically.
    B) slowly.
    C) methodically.
    D) carefully.

27. Benji owns five animals. Two of the animals are bunnies. One of the bunnies is brown. If the first two statements are true, the third statement is
    A) true.
    B) false.
    C) uncertain.

28. Which word does NOT belong with the others?
    A) hazy
    B) clear
    C) cloudy
    D) muddled

29. Frantic means the opposite of
    A) hysterical.
    B) desperate.
    C) calm.
    D) toxic.

30. Which word does NOT belong with the others?
    A) confident
    B) bold
    C) fearless
    D) shy

31. Airport is to planes as garage is to
    A) wheels.
    B) sheds.
    C) cars.
    D) bicycles.

32. Cacophony most nearly means
    A) harsh sound.
    B) melodious music.
    C) artificial flavor.
    D) sweet taste.

33. A dog has four puppies. Three of the puppies are male. Half of the puppies are female. If the first two statements are true, the third statement is
    A) true.
    B) false.
    C) uncertain.

34. Which word does NOT belong with the others?
    A) doubtful
    B) skeptical
    C) suspicious
    D) trusting

35. Degrade means the opposite of
    A) humiliate.
    B) respect.
    C) disfigure.
    D) vitiate.

36. Obscure is to hidden as malicious is to
    A) wicked.
    B) lonely.
    C) shy.
    D) greedy.

37. Deflated most nearly means
    A) collapsed.
    B) changed.
    C) lifted.
    D) intensified.

38. Which word does NOT belong with the others?
    A) laundry
    B) paper
    C) napkins
    D) stick

39. Jar most nearly means
    A) annoy.
    B) shake.
    C) steady.
    D) contain.

40. All seltzers are drinks. All seltzers are carbonated. All beverages are carbonated. If the first two statements are true, the third statement is
    A) true.
    B) false.
    C) uncertain.

41. Which word does NOT belong with the others?
    A) quarter
    B) nickel
    C) dime
    D) dollar

42. Illegible most nearly means
    A) printed.
    B) indecipherable.
    C) readable.
    D) understandable.

43. Which word does NOT belong with the others?
    A) combine
    B) connect
    C) join
    D) divide

44. Appointed means the opposite of
  A) rejected.
  B) anointed.
  C) unhappy.
  D) chosen.

45. Elephant is to lumbers as hummingbird is to
  A) flits.
  B) slinks.
  C) trots.
  D) squirms.

46. Scarce most nearly means
  A) frightened.
  B) opaque.
  C) rare.
  D) broken.

47. Vanessa looked at the restaurants in the food court. She ordered Chinese food. Vanessa does not like pizza. If the first two statements are true, the third statement is
  A) true.
  B) false.
  C) uncertain.

48. Which word does NOT belong with the others?
  A) sandal
  B) sneakers
  C) boot
  D) sock

49. A sun is a star in our universe. There are eight planets in our solar system. The sun is in our solar system. If the first two statements are true, the third statement is
  A) true.
  B) false.
  C) uncertain.

50. Which word does NOT belong with the others?
  A) croissant
  B) ball
  C) wheel
  D) rolling pin

51. Resilient means the opposite of
  A) weak.
  B) bulky.
  C) durable.
  D) resistant.

52. Pebble is to boulder as hut is to
  A) shack.
  B) building.
  C) colossal.
  D) mansion.

53. Beckon most nearly means
  A) dismiss.
  B) summon.
  C) push.
  D) detain.

54. The sun is a star. All stars are made of plasma. The sun is made of plasma. If the first two statements are true, the third statement is
  A) true.
  B) false.
  C) uncertain.

55. Which word does NOT belong with the others?
    A) orange
    B) grapefruit
    C) strawberry
    D) lemon

56. Solemn means the opposite of
    A) quiet.
    B) sincere.
    C) holy.
    D) cheerful.

57. Sentence is to paragraph as stanza is to
    A) essay.
    B) play.
    C) poem.
    D) line.

58. Antics most nearly means
    A) activities
    B) tasks
    C) exploits
    D) findings

59. Socks are made of fabric. Wool is a fabric. All socks are made from wool. If the first two statements are true, the third statement is
    A) true.
    B) false.
    C) uncertain.

60. Which word does NOT belong with the others?
    A) texting
    B) Instagram
    C) post office
    D) Twitter

Quantatative Skills

1. 27, 23, _____, 15, 11
   Which number should fill in the blank in the series?
   A) 19
   B) 21
   C) 18
   D) 20

2. What number is 2 more than the product of 2 and 23?
   A) 44
   B) 48
   C) 28
   D) 17

3. Examine (a), (b), and (c), and then choose the best answer.

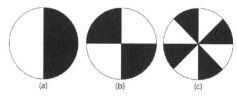
(a)   (b)   (c)

   A) (a), (b), and (c) are equally shaded
   B) (a) is more shaded than (c)
   C) (c) is more shaded than (b)
   D) (b) is less shaded than (a)

4. What number is 2 more than the quotient of 48 and 8?
   A) 8
   B) 386
   C) 42
   D) 12

5. 119, 111, 103, 95, ...
Which two numbers should come next in the series?

A) 87, 79

B) 88, 80

C) 89, 79

D) 87, 78

6. Examine (a), (b), and (c) to determine the correct answer.

(a) 2.03×10^{-8}

(b) 0.0000000203

(c) 0.00000000203

A) (a) = (c) > (b)

B) (a) = (b) > (c)

C) (a) = (c) < (b)

D) (a) = (b) < (c)

7. Examine (a), (b), and (c) to determine the correct answer.

(a) 6 hours and 30 minutes

(b) 390 minutes

(c) 6.5 hours

A) (a) and (c) are equal and less than (b)

B) (b) is less than (a) which is less than (c)

C) (a), (b), and (c) are equal

D) (a) and (b) are equal and less than (c)

8. 56, 62, ___, 74, 80
Which number should fill in the blank in the series?

A) 67

B) 69

C) 68

D) 64

9. Examine (a), (b), and (c), and then choose the best answer.

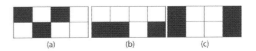

(a)   (b)   (c)

A) (a) is more shaded than (b)

B) (c) is more shaded than (a)

C) (c) is less shaded than (b)

D) (b) and (c) are equally shaded

10. $-\frac{1}{2}$, ___, ___, $\frac{1}{4}$, $\frac{1}{2}$, $\frac{3}{4}$
Which two numbers should fill in the blanks in the series?

A) $0, \frac{1}{6}$

B) $-\frac{1}{6}, \frac{1}{6}$

C) $0, \frac{1}{8}$

D) $-\frac{1}{4}, 0$

11. What number is 8 less than the sum of 11 and 2?

A) 1

B) 3

C) 5

D) 17

12. 9, 12, 16, 21, 27, ...
Which number should come next in the series?

A) 39

B) 81

C) 25

D) 34

13. Examine the circle and choose the best answer.

A) CB, AT, and CR are all equal

B) CB is equal to AB

C) AB is greater than CR

D) AB is less than BR

14. What number is the product of 2, 4, and 8?

A) 64

B) 14

C) 2

D) 4

15. What number is the square root of the product of 8 and 2?

A) 16

B) 10

C) 4

D) 256

16. 1, 3, 7, 9, 1, 3, ...
Which two numbers should come next in the series?

A) 5, 7

B) 3, 9

C) 7, 9

D) 3, 1

17. Examine (a), (b), and (c) to determine the correct answer.

(a) 0.5 × 12

(b) 0.25 × 24

(c) 0.75 × 8

A) (a) is less than (c)

B) (b) is greater than (a)

C) (a), (b), and (c) are equal

D) (a) is greater than (b)

18. ___, 147, 199, 250, 300
Which number should fill in the blank in the series?

A) 98

B) 101

C) 97

D) 94

19. Examine (a), (b), and (c) to determine the correct answer.

(a) 35%

(b) $\frac{3}{5}$

(c) 0.35

A) (a) is greater than (b) but less than (c)

B) (b) is less than (c) and greater than (a)

C) (c) is equal to (a) and less than (b)

D) (a) is equal to (c) and greater than (b)

20. 100, 121, 144, 169, ...
Which number should come next in the series?

A) 189

B) 194

C) 196

D) 200

21. Examine (a), (b), and (c), and then choose the best answer.

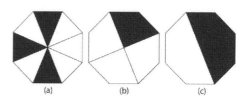

A) (a) and (b) are each less than (c)

B) (a) is less than (b)

C) (b) is greater than (c)

D) (a) is greater than both (b) and (c)

22. 3, 6, 7, 14, 15, 30, 31, ...
Which number should come next in the series?

A) 62

B) 61

C) 60

D) 32

23. Examine (a), (b), and (c) to determine the correct answer.

(a) 5 feet 2 inches

(b) 62 inches

(c) $5\frac{1}{4}$ feet

A) (a) is less than (c)

B) (b) is greater than (a)

C) (c) is equal to (b)

D) (a) is greater than (b)

24. 8, 13, 18, 23, ...

Which two numbers should come next in the series?

A) 28, 32

B) 27, 33

C) 28, 33

D) 18, 13

25. Examine (a), (b), and (c), and then choose the best answer.

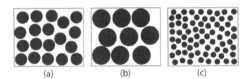

(a)   (b)   (c)

A) (a) has more circles than both (b) and (c)

B) (c) has more circles than both (a) and (b)

C) (a) has fewer circles than (b)

D) (c) has fewer circles than (a)

26. 953, 927, 901, 875, ...
Which number should come next in the series?

A) 849

B) 851

C) 859

D) 841

27. What number is $\frac{3}{5}$ of 300?

A) 180

B) 120

C) 500

D) 300

28. $2^3, 2^2, 2^1,$ ___, $2^{-1}, 2^{-2}$
Which number should fill in the blank in the series?

A) 2

B) 1

C) 0

D) −1

29. What number is $\frac{4}{3}$ of 3?

A) 6

B) 8

C) 12

D) 4

30. What number is 15 times the product of $\frac{1}{5}$ and $\frac{2}{3}$?

A) −13

B) 2

C) 17

D) 8

31. What number is $\frac{1}{3}$ of 150?

A) 50

B) 75

C) 100

D) 200

32. What number is 10 more than the quotient of 200 and 5?

A) 50

B) 55

C) 25

D) 40

33. Examine the rhombus below and choose the best answer.

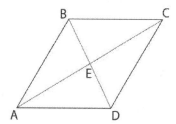

A) BD is equal to AC

B) BC is less than AD

C) BE is equal to DE

D) AE is greater than CD

34. $\frac{1}{3}$ of what number is equal to 300?

A) 100

B) 900

C) 20

D) 10

35. 12, –12, 11, –11, ____, _____, 9, –9
Which two numbers should fill in the blanks in the series?

A) 10, –10

B) –10, 10

C) 11, –9

D) –11, 10

36. What number is 6 less than the product of 9 and 4?

A) 9

B) 27

C) 5

D) 30

37. Examine (a), (b), and (c), and then choose the best answer.

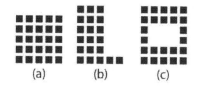

(a)   (b)   (c)

A) (a) has more squares than (b)

B) (c) has fewer squares than (b)

C) (a), (b), and (c) have an equal number of squares.

D) (b) has more squares than (a)

38. Examine (a), (b), and (c) to determine the correct answer.

(a) $\frac{1}{2} \times \frac{1}{3}$

(b) $\frac{1}{2} - \frac{1}{3}$

(c) $\frac{1}{2} \div \frac{1}{3}$

A) (c) > (b) > (a)

B) (a) = (b) = (c)

C) (c) > (a) = (b)

D) (c) < (a) = (b)

39. What number is $\frac{1}{2}$ of the average of 30 and 38?

A) 34

B) 68

C) 17

D) 15

40. What number is the sum of the quotient of 24 and 4 and the product of 4 and 2?

A) 14

B) 28

C) 40

D) 2

41. $\frac{2}{3}, \frac{3}{4}, \frac{4}{5}, \frac{5}{6}, \ldots$
Which number should come next in the series?

A) $\frac{6}{7}$

B) $\frac{11}{20}$

C) $\frac{1}{9}$

D) $\frac{7}{9}$

42. $\frac{1}{4}$ of what number is 2 times 6?

A) 3

B) 48

C) 32

D) 12

43. What number is 4 less than the average of 5, 7, and 12?

A) 4

B) 20

C) 12

D) 8

44. $\frac{2}{3}$ of what number is 4 squared?

A) 5

B) 11

C) 16

D) 24

45. 81, 27, _____, 3, 1
Which number should fill in the blank in the series?

A) 15

B) 18

C) 9

D) 6

46. Examine (a), (b), and (c), and then choose the best answer.

(a) the side of a square whose perimeter is 24

(b) the side of an equilateral triangle whose perimeter is 18

(c) the radius of a circle whose circumference is 12π

A) (a) is greater than (b)

B) (a), (b), and (c) are all equal

C) (c) is less than (a)

D) (b) is less than (c)

47. Examine the figure below and choose the best answer.

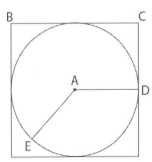

A) AD is equal to BC

B) CD is equal to half of AE

C) AE is greater than AD

D) BC is equal to AD plus AE

48. 57, 52, ___, 42, 37
Which number should fill in the blank in the series?

A) 48

B) 47

C) 47.5

D) 46

49. 3, 6, 12, 24, 48, ...
Which number should come next in the series?

A) 72

B) 96

C) 36

D) 21

50. Examine (a), (b), and (c) to determine the correct answer.

(a) -3×2

(b) $-3 + 2$

(c) $-3 \div 2$

A)   (a) < (b) < (c)

B)   (a) < (c) < (b)

C)   (b) < (c) < (a)

D)   (c) < (b) < (a)

51. Examine (a), (b), and (c) to determine the correct answer.

(a) $\sqrt{16}$

(b) $\frac{32}{8}$

(c) $-8 + 12$

A)   (a), (b), and (c) are equal

B)   (a) is greater than (b)

C)   (b) is greater than (c)

D)   (b) and (c) are equal

52. 0.74, 0.67, ___, 0.53, 0.46
Which number should fill in the blank in the series?

A)   0.59

B)   0.6

C)   0.62

D)   0.595

Reading

Skin coloration and markings have an important role to play in the world of snakes. Those intricate diamonds, stripes, and swirls help the animals hide from predators, but perhaps most importantly (for us humans, anyway), the markings can also indicate whether the snake is venomous. While it might seem counterintuitive for a venomous snake to stand out in bright red or blue, that fancy costume tells any nearby predator that approaching him would be a bad idea.

If you see a flashy looking snake in the woods, though, those markings don't necessarily mean it's venomous: some snakes have found a way to ward off predators without the actual venom. The scarlet kingsnake, for example, has very similar markings to the venomous coral snake with whom it frequently shares a habitat. However, the kingsnake is actually nonvenomous; it's merely pretending to be dangerous to eat. A predatory hawk or eagle, usually hunting from high in the sky, can't tell the difference between the two species, and so the kingsnake gets passed over and lives another day.

1. What is the author's primary purpose in writing this essay?

   A)   to explain how the markings on a snake are related to whether it's venomous

   B)   to teach readers the difference between coral snakes and kingsnakes

   C)   to illustrate why snakes are dangerous

   D)   to demonstrate how animals survive in difficult environments

2. What can the reader conclude from the passage?

   A)   The kingsnake is dangerous to humans.

   B)   The coral snake and the kingsnake are both hunted by the same predators.

   C)   It's safe to handle snakes in the woods because you can easily tell whether they're poisonous.

   D)   The kingsnake changes its markings when hawks or eagles are close by.

3. What is the best summary of this passage?

   A) Humans can use coloration and markings on snakes to determine whether they're venomous.

   B) Animals often use coloration to hide from predators.

   C) The scarlet kingsnake and the coral snake have nearly identical markings.

   D) Venomous snakes often have bright markings, although nonvenomous snakes can also mimic those colors.

4. Which statement is NOT a detail from the passage?

   A) Predators will avoid eating kingsnakes because their markings are similar to those on coral snakes.

   B) Kingsnakes and coral snakes live in the same habitats.

   C) The coral snake uses its coloration to hide from predators.

   D) The kingsnake is not venomous.

5. What is the meaning of the word *intricate* in the first paragraph?

   A) complex

   B) colorful

   C) purposeful

   D) changeable

6. What is the difference between kingsnakes and coral snakes according to the passage?

   A) Both kingsnakes and coral snakes are nonvenomous, but coral snakes have colorful markings.

   B) Both kingsnakes and coral snakes are venomous, but kingsnakes have colorful markings.

   C) Kingsnakes are nonvenomous while coral snakes are venomous.

   D) Coral snakes are nonvenomous while kingsnakes are venomous.

Taking a person's temperature is one of the most basic and common health care tasks. Everyone from nurses to emergency medical technicians to concerned parents should be able to grab a thermometer to take a patient or loved one's temperature. But what's the best way to get an accurate reading? The answer depends on the situation.

The most common way people measure body temperature is orally. A simple digital or disposable thermometer is placed under the tongue for a few minutes, and the task is done. There are many situations, however, when measuring temperature orally isn't an option. For example, when a person can't breathe through his nose, he won't be able to keep his mouth closed long enough to get an accurate reading. In these situations, it's often preferable to place the thermometer in the rectum or armpit. Using the rectum also has the added benefit of providing a much more accurate reading than other locations can provide.

It's also often the case that certain people, like agitated patients or fussy babies, won't be able to sit still long enough for an accurate reading. In these situations, it's best to use a thermometer that works much more quickly, such as one that measures temperature in the ear or at the temporal artery. No matter which method is chosen, however, it's important to check the average temperature for each region, as it can vary by several degrees.

7. Which statement is NOT a detail from the passage?

    A) Taking a temperature in the ear or at the temporal artery is more accurate than taking it orally.

    B) If an individual cannot breathe through the nose, taking his or her temperature orally will likely give an inaccurate reading.

    C) The standard human body temperature varies depending on whether it's measured in the mouth, rectum, armpit, ear, or temporal artery.

    D) The most common way to measure temperature is by placing a thermometer in the mouth.

8. What is the author's primary purpose in writing this essay?

    A) to advocate for the use of thermometers that measure temperature in the ear or at the temporal artery

    B) to explain the methods available to measure a person's temperature and the situation where each method is appropriate

    C) to warn readers that the average temperature of the human body varies by region

    D) to discuss how nurses use different types of thermometers depending on the type of patient they are examining

9. What is the best summary of this passage?

    A) It's important that everyone know the best way to take a person's temperature in any given situation.

    B) The most common method of taking a person's temperature—orally—isn't appropriate in some situations.

    C) The most accurate way to take a temperature is placing a digital thermometer in the rectum.

    D) There are many different ways to take a person's temperature, and which is appropriate will depend on the situation.

10. What is the meaning of the word *agitated* in the last paragraph?

    A) obviously upset

    B) quickly moving

    C) violently ill

    D) slightly dirty

11. According to the passage, why is it sometimes preferable to take a person's temperature rectally?

    A) Rectal readings are more accurate than oral readings.

    B) Many people cannot sit still long enough to have their temperatures taken orally.

    C) Temperature readings can vary widely between regions of the body.

    D) Many people do not have access to quick-acting thermometers.

Studies by the American Medical Association and the American Cancer Society link the prevalence of over a dozen types of cancer to smoking cigarettes: colon cancer, pancreatic cancer, kidney cancer, liver cancer, stomach cancer, throat cancer, lung cancer, and leukemia, among others, are believed to be related to heavy tobacco smoking. Even though cigarette use has been plummeting in the United States, close to 40 million people continue to smoke. This number is troubling, especially when one considers that nearly 30 percent of all cancer-related deaths in the United States can be tied to smoking. To make matters worse, cigarette-linked cancers disproportionately affect men of color, especially if they come from lower-income communities. This means that smoking continues to be not only an issue of public health, but also one of social equity.

Smoking is linked to other health problems as well. Heart disease and stroke are among the most visible, but cigarette smoke affects nearly every organ in the human body. It is correlated with birth defects, lower sperm counts, diabetes, lower bone density, tooth loss and gum disease, and more.

Continuing research reinforces the necessity of anti-smoking campaigns, both government funded and grassroots. The numbers show that such campaigns work, encouraging people to quit smoking. For the moment, however, the United States still has a long road of anti-smoking campaigning ahead.

12. Which sentence best summarizes the passage's main idea?

A) "Studies ... link the prevalence of over a dozen types of cancer to smoking cigarettes."

B) "Even though cigarette use has been plummeting in the United States, close to 40 million people continue to smoke."

C) "This number [40 million smokers] is troubling, especially when one considers that nearly 30 percent of all cancer-related deaths in the United States can be tied to smoking."

D) The fact that "cigarette-linked cancers disproportionately affect men of color" means that "smoking continues to be not only an issue of public health, but also one of social equity."

13. Which phrase from the passage has about the same meaning as "are believed to be related to" in the first paragraph?

A) "can be tied to" (paragraph 1)

B) "disproportionately affect" (paragraph 1)

C) "are among the most visible" (paragraph 2)

D) "still has a long road ... ahead" (paragraph 3)

14. Readers can infer from reading this passage that the author thinks all cigarette smokers

A) are uneducated.

B) should quit smoking.

C) are low-class people.

D) should stop smoking near their children.

15. Which of the following is NOT listed as a detail in the passage?

    A) The American Medical Association and the American Cancer Society have sponsored studies that show smoking cigarettes causes cancer.

    B) Studies show that more than a dozen kinds of cancer can be caused by cigarette smoking.

    C) Cigarette smoking is also linked to heart disease, strokes, birth defects, and diabetes.

    D) Tobacco companies advertise cigarettes on billboards and smaller signs in low-income neighborhoods.

16. What is the author's primary purpose in writing this essay?

    A) to suggest "the necessity of anti-smoking campaigns"

    B) to scare smokers into quitting cigarette smoking immediately

    C) to honor the research done by the American Medical Association and the American Cancer Society

    D) to express anger at big tobacco companies that continue to target people who do not realize how harmful smoking can be

17. In the last sentence, what does the phrase "still has a long road … ahead" mean?

    A) People should not smoke on public transportation.

    B) A cancer patient has a long, grueling treatment program to suffer through.

    C) Anti-smoking campaigns still have a lot more work to do in the United States.

    D) Even if you drive with the window open, you should not smoke while driving.

Popcorn is often associated with fun and festivities, both in and out of the home. It's eaten in theaters, usually after being salted and smothered in butter, and in homes, fresh from the microwave. But popcorn isn't just for fun—it's also a multi-million-dollar-a-year industry with a long and fascinating history.

While popcorn might seem like a modern invention, its history actually dates back thousands of years, making it one of the oldest snack foods enjoyed around the world. Popcorn is believed by food historians to be one of the earliest uses of cultivated corn. In 1948, Herbert Dick and Earle Smith discovered old popcorn dating back 4000 years in the New Mexico Bat Cave. For the Aztec Indians who called the caves home, popcorn (or momochitl) played an important role in society, both as a food staple and in ceremonies. The Aztecs cooked popcorn by heating sand in a fire; when it was heated, kernels were added and would pop when exposed to the heat of the sand.

The American love affair with popcorn began in 1912, when popcorn was first sold in theaters. The popcorn industry flourished during the Great Depression when it was advertised as a wholesome and economical food. Selling for five to ten cents a bag, it was a luxury that the downtrodden could afford. With the introduction of mobile popcorn machines at the World's Columbian Exposition, popcorn moved from the theater into fairs and parks. Popcorn continued to rule the snack food kingdom until the rise in popularity of home televisions during the 1950s.

The popcorn industry reacted to the decline in sales quickly by introducing pre-popped and unpopped popcorn for home consumption. However, it wasn't until microwave popcorn became commercially available in 1981 that at-home popcorn consumption began to grow exponentially. With the wide availability of micro-waves in the United States, popcorn also began popping up in offices and hotel rooms. However, the home still remains the most popular popcorn eating spot: today, 70 percent of the 16 billion quarts of popcorn consumed annually in the United States are eaten at home.

18. What can the reader conclude from the passage above?

   A) People ate less popcorn in the 1950s than in previous decades because they went to the movies less.

   B) Without mobile popcorn machines, people would not have been able to eat popcorn during the Great Depression.

   C) People enjoyed popcorn during the Great Depression because it was a luxury food.

   D) During the 1800s, people began abandoning theaters to go to fairs and festivals.

19. What is the meaning of the word *staple* in the second paragraph?

   A) something produced only for special occasions

   B) something produced regularly in large quantities

   C) something produced by cooking

   D) something fastened together securely

20. What is the author's primary purpose in writing this essay?

   A) to explain how microwaves affected the popcorn industry

   B) to show that popcorn is older than many people realize

   C) to illustrate the history of popcorn from ancient cultures to modern times

   D) to demonstrate the importance of popcorn in various cultures

21. Which factor does the author of the passage credit for the growth of the popcorn industry in the United States?

   A) the use of popcorn in ancient Aztec ceremonies

   B) the growth of the home television industry

   C) the marketing of popcorn during the Great Depression

   D) the nutritional value of popcorn

22. What is the best summary of this passage?

A) Popcorn is a popular snack food that dates back thousands of years. Its popularity in the United States has been tied to the growth of theaters and the availability of microwaves.

B) Popcorn has been a popular snack food for thousands of years. Archaeologists have found evidence that many ancient cultures used popcorn as a food staple and in ceremonies.

C) Popcorn was first introduced to America in 1912, and its popularity has grown exponentially since then. Today, over 16 billion quarts of popcorn are consumed in the United States annually.

D) Popcorn is a versatile snack food that can be eaten with butter or other toppings. It can also be cooked in a number of different ways, including in microwaves.

23. Which of the following is NOT a fact stated in the passage?

A) Archaeologists have found popcorn dating back 4000 years.

B) Popcorn was first sold in theaters in 1912.

C) Consumption of popcorn dropped in 1981 with the growing popularity of home televisions.

D) Seventy percent of the popcorn consumed in the United States is eaten in homes.

The bacteria, fungi, insects, plants, and animals that live together in a habitat have evolved to share a pool of limited resources. They've competed for water, minerals, nutrients, sunlight, and space—sometimes for thousands or even millions of years. As these communities have evolved, the species in them have developed complex, long-term interspecies interactions known as symbiotic relationships.

Ecologists characterize these interactions based on whether each party benefits. In mutualism, both individuals benefit, while in synnecrosis, both organisms are harmed. A relationship where one individual benefits and the other is harmed is known as parasitism. Examples of these relationships can easily be seen in any ecosystem. Pollination, for example, is mutualistic—pollinators get nutrients from the flower, and the plant is able to reproduce—while tapeworms, which steal nutrients from their host, are parasitic.

There's yet another class of symbiosis that is controversial among scientists. As it's long been defined, commensalism is a relationship where one species benefits and the other is unaffected. But is it possible for two species to interact and for one to remain completely unaffected? Often, relationships described as commensal include one species that feeds on another species' leftovers; remoras, for instance, will attach themselves to sharks and eat the food particles they leave behind.

It might seem like the shark gets nothing from the relationship, but a closer look will show that sharks in fact benefit from remoras, which clean the sharks' skin and remove parasites. In fact, many scientists claim that relationships currently described as commensal are just mutualistic or parasitic in ways that haven't been discovered yet.

24. Why is commensalism controversial among scientists?

   A) Many scientists believe that an interspecies interaction where one species is unaffected does not exist.

   B) Some scientists believe that relationships where one species feeds on the leftovers of another should be classified as parasitism.

   C) Because remoras and sharks have a mutualistic relationship, no interactions should be classified as commensalism.

   D) Only relationships among animal species should be classified as commensalism.

25. What is the meaning of the word *controversial* in the last paragraph?

   A) debatable

   B) objectionable

   C) confusing

   D) upsetting

26. What is the author's primary purpose in writing this essay?

   A) to argue that commensalism isn't actually found in nature

   B) to describe the many types of symbiotic relationships

   C) to explain how competition for resources results in long-term interspecies relationships

   D) to provide examples of the many different ways individual organisms interact

27. Which of the following is NOT a fact stated in the passage?

   A) Mutualism is an interspecies relationship where both species benefit.

   B) Synnecrosis is an interspecies relationship where both species are harmed.

   C) The relationship between plants and pollinators is mutualistic.

   D) The relationship between remoras and sharks is parasitic.

28. Epiphytes are plants that attach themselves to trees and derive nutrients from the air and surrounding debris. Sometimes, the weight of epiphytes can damage the trees on which they're growing. Which term best describes the relationship between epiphytes and their hosts?

A) mutualism

B) commensalism

C) parasitism

D) synnecrosis

29. What can the reader conclude from this passage about symbiotic relationships?

A) Scientists cannot decide how to classify symbiotic relationships among species.

B) The majority of interspecies interactions are parasitic because most species do not get along.

C) If two species are involved in a parasitic relationship, one of the species will eventually become extinct.

D) Symbiotic relationships evolve as the species that live in a community adapt to their environments and each other.

Across the globe, women are, on average, outliving their male counterparts. Although this gender gap has shrunk over the last decade thanks to medical improvements and lifestyle changes, women are still expected to live four and a half years longer than men. What is the reason for this trend? The answer may lie in our sex hormones.

Men are more likely to exhibit riskier behaviors than women, especially between the ages of fifteen and twenty-four, when testosterone production is at its peak. Testosterone is correlated with aggressive and reckless behaviors that contribute to high mortality rates—think road rage, alcohol consumption, drug use, and smoking.

Estrogen, on the other hand, seems to be correlated with cholesterol levels: an increase in estrogen is accompanied by a decrease in "bad" cholesterol, which may confer advantages by reducing the risk of heart attack and stroke.

Of course, lifestyle and diet are also components of this difference in life expectancy. Men are more likely to be involved in more physically dangerous jobs, such as manufacturing or construction. They may be less likely to eat as many fruits and vegetables as their female counterparts. And they may be more likely to consume more red meat, including processed meat. These types of meats have been linked to high cholesterol, hypertension, and cancer. Better nutrition and health decisions may eventually even the score in men's and women's life expectancy.

30. What does the second paragraph mainly concern?
    A) testosterone production
    B) young men's behavior
    C) reasons why some men die young
    D) reasons why women outlive men

31. What is the author's primary purpose in writing this essay?
    A) to warn men to stop behaving riskily and eating unhealthy foods
    B) to explain why, on average, women today outlive men
    C) to advise readers about ways to extend life expectancy
    D) to express the hope that men's life expectancy will go up

32. Which of the following statements can be considered a statement of FACT according to the passage?
    A) Sex hormones are the sole cause of the gender gap in life expectancy.
    B) Women's diets are better than men's, so women are slimmer and live longer.
    C) Because of risky behavior, most men die before they reach middle age.
    D) Worldwide, the average woman lives four and a half years longer than the average man.

33. According to the passage, what is true about women and men?
    A) In general, women care more about life expectancy than men do.
    B) In general, men care more about having fun than women do.
    C) In general, women take better care of themselves than men do.
    D) In general, men's bodies contain more sex hormones than women's do.

34. Readers can infer that in the past decade, men have been
    A) engaging in riskier behavior.
    B) eating more red meat.
    C) making positive lifestyle changes.
    D) visiting their primary care doctors more often.

35. What is the meaning of the word *correlated* in the second paragraph?
    A) associated
    B) incompatible
    C) isolated
    D) mismatched

The word *bacteria* typically conjures images of disease-inducing invaders that attack our immune systems. However, recent research is changing that perception; plenty of scholarly articles point to the benefits of healthy bacteria that actually reinforce the immune system. New research indicates that the "microbiome"—that is, the resident bacteria in your digestive system—may impact your health in multiple ways. Scientists who have been studying microbial DNA now believe that internal bacteria can influence metabolism, mental health, and mood. Some even suggest that imbalances in your digestive microbiome correlate with such disorders as obesity and autoimmune diseases.

It appears that a healthy, diverse microbiome is optimal, and one of the easiest ways to promote that is to eat an array of healthy foods. High-fiber foods, such as fruits and vegetables, can help your gut bacteria thrive. Some foods, for example, yogurt or kimchi, contain healthy bacteria that may confer health benefits when we consume them.

There is also increasing evidence that our national obsession with antibacterial products is detrimental to our microbiomes and thus our health. Children who live with pets and play outdoors seem to have lower rates of allergies, attention deficit disorder, and obesity. This line of research suggests that we can and should live in harmony with many of our bacterial neighbors (and residents) rather than fighting them.

36. Readers can infer from the passage that the author believes bacteria is

A) primarily harmful.

B) always good for us.

C) sometimes healthy.

D) one cause of obesity.

37. What does the word *conjures* mean in the first sentence?

A) charms

B) mesmerizes

C) disappears

D) brings up

38. Which sentence best summarizes the passage's main idea?

A) Most people think that bacteria causes diseases and attacks the human immune system.

B) Scientists are learning that some kinds of bacteria—especially kinds that live in our digestive systems—provide health benefits.

C) Foods such as yogurt and kimchi contain healthy bacteria, so people should eat these foods every day.

D) In the United States, people are obsessed with antibacterial products that harm our microbiomes, thereby harming our health.

39. According to the passage, what is true of children who live with pets and play outdoors?

A) They have good metabolisms, strong mental health, and sunny moods.

B) They have imbalances in their digestive microbiomes, disorders such as obesity, and autoimmune diseases.

C) They tend to eat healthy foods such as fruits, vegetables, yogurt, and kimchi.

D) They are less likely to have allergies, attention-deficit disorders, and obesity.

40. On which two systems of the human body does the author focus in this passage?

A) the nervous system and the excretory system

B) the immune system and the digestive system

C) the endocrine system and the circulatory system

D) the hormone feedback system and the cardiovascular system

VOCABULARY

1. the dirty, <u>stagnant</u> water
    - **A)** moving
    - **B)** odorous
    - **C)** still
    - **D)** active

2. a <u>serrated</u> knife
    - **A)** smooth
    - **B)** sharp
    - **C)** fancy
    - **D)** jagged

3. branches <u>hewn</u> from the tree
    - **A)** sturdy
    - **B)** chopped
    - **C)** healthy
    - **D)** huge

4. a <u>trek</u> through the forest
    - **A)** run
    - **B)** march
    - **C)** hunt
    - **D)** road

5. an <u>indigenous</u> population
    - **A)** native
    - **B)** foreign
    - **C)** strange
    - **D)** small

6. squalls and <u>tempests</u> frequently occurring
    - **A)** droughts
    - **B)** storms
    - **C)** calmness
    - **D)** earthquakes

7. her <u>cue</u> was the music
    - **A)** warning
    - **B)** inspiration
    - **C)** signal
    - **D)** pause

8. <u>expanse</u> of the ocean
    - **A)** vastness
    - **B)** depth
    - **C)** temperature
    - **D)** power

9. receiving <u>compensation</u> for their work
    - **A)** criticism
    - **B)** attention
    - **C)** payment
    - **D)** deprivation

10. being under intense <u>scrutiny</u>
    - **A)** glance
    - **B)** rules
    - **C)** examination
    - **D)** security

11. <u>reeling</u> from the bad news
    - **A)** lurching
    - **B)** crying
    - **C)** steadying
    - **D)** angering

12. the caterpillars <u>morph</u> into butterflies
    - **A)** consume
    - **B)** transform
    - **C)** review
    - **D)** preserve

13. offering boring <u>platitudes</u>
    - **A)** clichés
    - **B)** documents
    - **C)** thanks
    - **D)** longitudes

14. a terrible <u>tragedy</u>
    A) joy
    B) event
    C) drama
    D) misfortune

15. papers <u>strewn</u> everywhere
    A) piled
    B) scattered
    C) gathered
    D) written

16. a solemn <u>commemoration</u>
    A) tribute
    B) memory
    C) trial
    D) defamation

17. his <u>gruff</u> demeanor
    A) absent
    B) brusque
    C) friendly
    D) sleepy

18. their <u>presumptuous</u> attitude
    A) modest
    B) bold
    C) hyperactive

D) visible

19. a <u>glint</u> in her eye
    A) tear
    B) dim
    C) gleam
    D) color

20. the <u>sodden</u> clothes
    A) dirty
    B) sopping
    C) ugly
    D) arid

21. going to file a <u>grievance</u> with the judge
    A) complaint
    B) offer
    C) favor
    D) statement

22. these <u>unprecedented</u> events
    A) ordinary
    B) important
    C) exceptional
    D) overwhelming

Mathematics

1. How much longer is line segment *MN* than line segment *KL*?

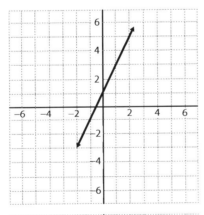

(Ruler image showing segments K—L and M———N measured in mm and inches)

A) 2 mm

B) 15 mm

C) 20 mm

D) 55 mm

2. Which number has the least value?

A) 0.305

B) 0.035

C) 0.35

D) 0.3

3. Which graph shows the solution to $y = 2x + 1$?

A)

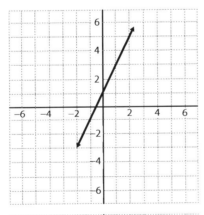

B)

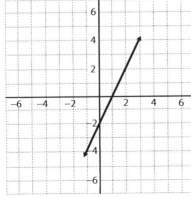

C)

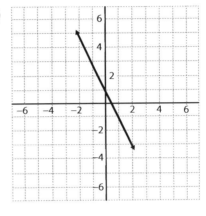

D)

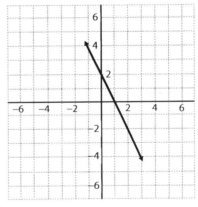

4. The graph below shows the number of months that Chicago, New York, and Houston had less than 3 inches of rain from 2009 to 2015.

Number of Months with 3 or Fewer Than 3 Inches of Rain

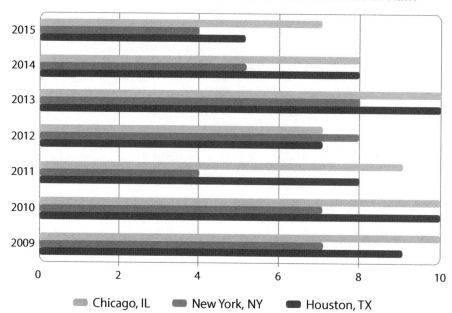

■ Chicago, IL   ■ New York, NY   ■ Houston, TX

New York had the fewest months with less than 3 inches of rain in every year except:

A) 2012

B) 2013

C) 2014

D) 2015

5. What is the greatest common factor of 45 and 22?

A) 1

B) 2

C) 9

D) 11

6. Which of the following operations is equivalent to dividing by 100?

A) multiplying by $\frac{1}{100}$

B) adding (−100)

C) dividing by $\frac{1}{100}$

D) multiplying by 0.001

7. Which of the following is equivalent to the term 5*n* for all values of *n*?

A) $5n^5 - n^4$

B) $3n + 2n$

C) n^5

D) $5 + n$

8. What is the median of all the even integers greater than 10 and less than 25?

A) 14

B) 16

C) 18

D) 20

9. How many digits are in the number four hundred twenty-three and nine thousandths?

A) 4

B) 5

C) 6

D) 7

10. Which of the following values is between $\frac{3}{4}$ and $\frac{9}{10}$?

   A) 0.92

   B) 0.55

   C) 0.80

   D) 0.72

11. Which of the following is equivalent to 1 meter?

   A) 5280 ft

   B) 0.001 km

   C) 1000 cm

   D) 3 ft

12. Which of the following is a solution to the inequality $2x + y \leq -10$?

   A) (0, 0)

   B) (10, 2)

   C) (10, 10)

   D) (−10, −10)

13. A recipe calls for $2\frac{1}{4}$ cups of flour. Which of the following measurement tools can be used to measure the flour?

   A) $\frac{1}{4}$ cup

   B) $\frac{1}{3}$ cup

   C) $\frac{1}{2}$ cup

   D) 1 cup

14. Out of 1560 students at Ward Middle School, 15% want to take French. Which expression represents how many students want to take French?

   A) 1560 ÷ 15

   B) 1560 × 15

   C) 1560 × 0.15

   D) 1560 ÷ 0.15

15. A baby weighed 7.5 pounds at birth and gained weight at a rate of 6 ounces per month for the first six months. Which equation describes the baby's weight in ounces, y, after t months?

   A) $y = 6t + 7.5$

   B) $y = 6t + 120$

   C) $y = 7.5t + 120$

   D) $y = 7.5t + 7.5$

16. Which of the following numbers is between $5\frac{1}{4}$ and $5\frac{1}{2}$?

   A) $5\frac{3}{4}$

   B) $5\frac{5}{8}$

   C) $5\frac{7}{20}$

   D) $5\frac{1}{10}$

17. Which of the following is listed in order from least to greatest?

   A) $-0.95, 0, \frac{2}{5}, 0.35, \frac{3}{4}$

   B) $-1, -\frac{1}{10}, -0.11, \frac{5}{6}, 0.75$

   C) $-\frac{3}{4}, -0.2, 0, \frac{2}{3}, 0.55$

   D) $-1.1, -\frac{4}{5}, -0.13, 0.7, \frac{9}{11}$

18. Which of the following is closest in value to 129,113 + 34,602?

   A) 162,000

   B) 163,000

   C) 164,000

   D) 165,000

19. Simplify: $\sqrt[3]{64} + \sqrt[3]{729}$

   A) 13

   B) 17

   C) 31

   D) 35

20. Two cylinders have the same base. Cylinder A has a height of x and Cylinder B has a height of $2x$. What is true regarding the relationship between the two cylinders? (The formula for the surface area of a cone is SA $= 2\pi rh + 2\pi r^2$, and the formula for the volume of a cone is V $= \pi r^2 h$.)

A) Cylinder A's surface area is $\frac{1}{2}$ that of Cylinder B.

B) Cylinder B's surface area is $\frac{1}{2}$ that of Cylinder A.

C) Cylinder A has a volume $\frac{1}{2}$ that of Cylinder B.

D) Cylinder B has a volume $\frac{1}{2}$ that of Cylinder A.

21. Which of the following is the y-intercept of the given equation?

$7y - 42x + 7 = 0$

A) $(-1, 0)$

B) $(0, -1)$

C) $(0, \frac{1}{6})$

D) $(6, 0)$

22. In a theater, there are 4,500 lower-level seats and 2,000 upper-level seats. What is the ratio of lower-level seats to total seats?

A) $\frac{4}{9}$

B) $\frac{4}{13}$

C) $\frac{9}{13}$

D) $\frac{9}{4}$

23. What is the value of 15.32×4.76?

A) 60.2432

B) 72.9232

C) 602.432

D) 729.232

24. Micah has invited 23 friends to his house and is having pizza for dinner. If each pizza feeds 4 people, how many pizzas should he order?

A) 4

B) 5

C) 6

D) 7

25. A map has a scale of 1 inch to 25 miles. What is the distance on the map between two towns that are 125 miles apart?

A) 0.2 inches

B) 1 inch

C) 5 inches

D) 25 inches

26. The average traffic light cycle at an intersection is $2\frac{1}{2}$ minutes, and 12 cars go through the intersection during each green light. If Martin must wait $7\frac{1}{2}$ minutes to cross the intersection, which of the following could be the number of cars ahead of him?

A) 4

B) 10

C) 30

D) 120

27. A computer store sells both laptops and desktops. On Sunday, the store sold three times as many laptops as desktops. If the store sold a total of 56 computers, how many more laptops did it sell than desktops?

A) 14

B) 28

C) 37

D) 42

28. Simplify: $(1.2 \times 10^{-3})(1.13 \times 10^{-4})$

   A) 1.356×10^{-7}

   B) 1.356×10^{-1}

   C) 1.356×10

   D) 1.356×10^{12}

29. The population of a town was 7250 in 2014 and 7375 in 2015. What was the percent increase from 2014 to 2015 to the nearest tenth of a percent?

   A) 1.5%

   B) 1.6%

   C) 1.7%

   D) 1.8%

30. In the fall, 425 students pass the math benchmark. In the spring, 680 students pass the same benchmark. What is the percentage increase in passing scores from fall to spring?

   A) 37.5%

   B) 55%

   C) 60%

   D) 62.5%

31. A fruit stand sells apples, bananas, and oranges at a ratio of 3:2:1. If the fruit stand sells 20 bananas, how many total pieces of fruit does the fruit stand sell?

   A) 10

   B) 30

   C) 40

   D) 60

32. Five numbers have an average of 16. If the first 4 numbers have a sum of 68, what is the 5th number?

   A) 12

   B) 16

   C) 52

   D) 80

33. Multiply: $(5+ \sqrt{5})(5- \sqrt{5})$

   A) $10\sqrt{5}$

   B) 20

   C) 25

   D) $25\sqrt{5}$

34. If the average person drinks ten 8-ounce glasses of water each day, how many ounces of water will she drink in a week?

   A) 70 oz

   B) 80 oz

   C) 560 oz

   D) 700 oz

35. Yvonne ran 4.6 miles, 4.8 miles, 5.3 miles, 5.2 miles, and 6 miles on five consecutive days. What was her average distance over the five days?

   A) 4.1 mi

   B) 4.975 mi

   C) 5.18 mi

   D) 25.9 mi

36. Robbie has a bag of treats that contains 5 pieces of gum, 7 pieces of taffy, and 8 pieces of chocolate. If Robbie reaches into the bag and randomly pulls out a treat, what is the probability that he will get a piece of taffy?

   A) $\frac{1}{7}$

   B) $\frac{7}{20}$

   C) $\frac{5}{8}$

   D) 1

37. Solve: $(50 - 12 \times 4)^2$

   A) 2

   B) 4

   C) 152

   D) 304

38. A semicircle is drawn next to the base of an isosceles triangle such that its diameter is perpendicular to the triangle's altitude. What is the area of the resulting figure shown below?

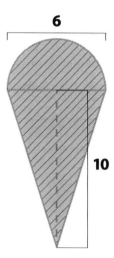

6

10

A) $30 + 4.5\pi$

B) $30 + 9\pi$

C) $30 + 36\pi$

D) $60 + 4.5\pi$

39. A restaurant offers burritos on a corn or a flour tortilla, 5 types of meat, 6 types of cheese, and 3 different salsas. When ordering, customers choose 1 type of tortilla, 1 meat, and 1 cheese. They can add any of the 3 salsas. How many different burritos are possible?

A) 180

B) 330

C) 480

D) 660

40. If the circumference of a circle is 18π, what is the area of the circle?

A) 9π

B) 18π

C) 27π

D) 81π

41. Adam is painting the outside of a 4-walled shed. The shed is 5 feet wide, 4 feet deep, and 7 feet high. How many square feet of paint will Adam need to paint the 4 sides of the shed?

A) 126

B) 140

C) 252

D) 560

42. A cyclist is moving down the sidewalk at 15 feet per second. What is his approximate speed in miles per hour?

A) 10.2 mph

B) 15.9 mph

C) 17.1 mph

D) 22 mph

43. Matt and Kendall are participating in a raffle in which one ticket will be drawn to find the winner. Matt bought 35 tickets and Kendall bought 15 tickets. If 1250 total tickets were purchased, what is the probability that either Matt or Kendall will win the raffle?

A) 0.02

B) 0.03

C) 0.04

D) 0.08

44. What number is in the hundredths place when 21.563 is divided by 8?

A) 5

B) 6

C) 8

D) 9

45. What is the probability a coin flipped 4 times in a row will be heads all 4 times?

A) $\frac{1}{32}$

B) $\frac{1}{16}$

C) $\frac{1}{8}$

D) $\frac{1}{4}$

46. A television station in City A reaches 140,000 people, and a television station in City B reaches 250,000 people. Their signals overlap in a region that includes 4% of the people in City A and 2% in City B. How many people can receive both stations?

A) 11,600

B) 12,800

C) 15,000

D) 23,400

47. Mr. Langston took out a $50,000 loan to start a new video company. He produces a video game that costs $40 to make and sells it for $60. How many copies of the game must he sell to pay off his loan?

A) 500

B) 833

C) 2500

D) 100,000

48. In baseball, a player's batting average is calculated using the formula average = $\frac{\text{hits}}{\text{at bats}}$. If Forrest has a batting average of .250 and goes to bat 4 times, how many times should he be expected to get a hit?

A) 1

B) 3

C) 4

D) 16

49. Simplify: $4(a^2 + 2a) - 3(a + 7)$

A) $4a^2 + 5a - 21$

B) $4a^2 + 11a - 21$

C) $4a^2 + 5a + 21$

D) $9a^2 + 21$

50. The weather forecast calls for an 80% chance of rain for the next two days. What is the probability it will not rain for the next two days?

A) 4%

B) 10%

C) 20%

D) 64%

51. A room is covered in tiles measuring 3 inches by 3 inches. If the size of the room is 190 square feet, how many tiles must be purchased to cover the room?

A) 21

B) 253

C) 3040

D) 9120

52. A new video game sells for $50. After a few weeks, it gets a 10% discount. All sales have a 10% sales tax added. How much will the game cost after the discount and sales tax are applied?

A) $55

B) $50

C) $49.50

D) $45

53. Evaluate the following expression for $r = 315$ and $t = -2$:

$\frac{r}{5} - 10t$

A) 43

B) 59

C) 64

D) 83

54. Beth spends $550 per month on rent, which is 25% of her budget. What is Beth's total budget?

A) $1375

B) $1650

C) $2200

D) $2500

55. Dashawn is baking two desserts for Thanksgiving dinner. One recipe calls for $2\frac{1}{2}$ cups of flour, and the other recipe calls for $1\frac{1}{3}$ cups of flour. If the flour canister had 8 cups of flour before he started baking, how much flour is left?

A) $4\frac{1}{6}$ c

B) $4\frac{3}{5}$ c

C) $5\frac{2}{5}$ c

D) $5\frac{5}{6}$ c

56. Sally has $127 in her checking account. An automatic draft takes out $150 for her electric bill. What is her balance after the automatic draft?

A) $23

B) −$23

C) −$123

D) −$277

57. A grocery store sold 30% of its pears and had 455 pears remaining. How many pears did the grocery store start with?

A) 602

B) 650

C) 692

D) 700

58. A landscaping company charges 5 cents per square foot for fertilizer. How much would they charge to fertilize a 30-foot-by-50-foot lawn?

A) $7.50

B) $15.00

C) $75.00

D) $150.00

59.

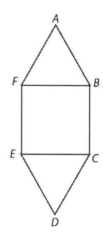

In the figure above, triangles *ABF* and *CDE* are equilateral. If the perimeter of the figure is 60 inches, what is the area of square *BCEF* in square inches?

A) 100 in²

B) 120 in²

C) 140 in²

D) 144 in²

60. Points *W*, *X*, *Y*, and *Z* lie on a circle with center *A*. If the diameter of the circle is 75, what is the sum of *AW*, *AX*, *AY*, and *AZ*?

A) 100

B) 125

C) 150

D) 300

61. Kendrick has $2,386.52 in his checking account. If he pays $792.00 for rent, $84.63 for groceries, and $112.15 for his car insurance, how much money will he have left in his account?

   A) $1,397.74

   B) $1,482.37

   C) $1,509.89

   D) $2,189.22

62. 3.819 + 14.68 + 0.0006 =

   A) 5.2846

   B) 18.4996

   C) 18.505

   D) 52.96

63. $\frac{15}{25}$ is equivalent to

   A) 0.06

   B) 0.15

   C) 0.375

   D) 0.6

64. $\frac{8}{15} \div \frac{1}{6} =$

   A) $\frac{4}{45}$

   B) $\frac{15}{48}$

   C) $\frac{16}{5}$

   D) $\frac{46}{15}$

Language Skills

In questions 1 – 40, look for errors in capitalization, punctuation, or usage. If you find no mistake, mark (D) on your answer sheet.

1.

   A) Alexa is the smartest of the three sisters.

   B) Please bring that unsafe toy away from your little brother.

   C) Are you allowed to stay out later on weekend nights than on school nights?

   D) No mistakes

2.

   A) Let's go to the movies on Saturday, OK?

   B) I am leaving for the city of seattle on Saturday, June 16.

   C) Speaker Pelosi, the leader of the House of Representatives, met with President Biden.

   D) No mistakes

3.

   A) The photographer specializes in shooting portraits and taking still lifes, but she also likes to accept more challenging assignments, such as photographing wildlife.

   B) Edward Jenner invented the world's first vaccine by infecting a young boy with cowpox, successfully protecting him from the smallpox virus.

   C) The employer decided that he could not, due to the high cost of health care, afford to offer no other benefits to his employees.

   D) No mistakes

4.

A) Even in California; January can be an excruciatingly cold month.

B) My cat is sitting in front of the computer screen.

C) If you need a ride to the party, I can pick you up on my way over there.

D) No mistakes

5.

A) I continued, "Let's wait until 8:00 p.m. to eat dinner."

B) "That is a good plan," Addie replied.

C) There was a heat wave in October, even though Summer was long over.

D) No mistakes

6.

A) I dislike hearing about real-life wars, yet I usually enjoy war movies.

B) Bubonic plague, often thought of as a concern of times past, continued to spread among rodent populations even today.

C) I'll never again fly long distance in coach, nor will I ever again fly when I have a cold.

D) No mistakes

7.

A) It rained hard during the afternoon, so I reined in my horse and turned her toward home, and we galloped for shelter.

B) Priests perform religious rites such as christenings, weddings, and funerals.

C) At the ball following the royal wedding: the queen danced with her grandson, the groom.

D) No mistakes

8.

A) Mom makes pizza dough from scratch; it contains flour, yeast, and other ingredients.

B) We always go to a picnic on Independence Day, but on Christmas we eat at home.

C) "At what time do you want to eat dinner," she asked.

D) No mistakes

9.

A) In the fight against obesity, countries' around the world are imposing taxes on sodas and other sugary drinks in hopes of curbing unhealthy habits.

B) The storm chasers, who emphasized the importance of caution in their work, decided not to go out when the sheets of rain made visibility too low.

C) Lani's mistake was dawdling during the months when she should have been paying attention to application deadlines.

D) No mistakes

10.

A) My favorite colors are different shades of blue and green: turquoise, lime green, periwinkle, bottle green, and royal blue.

B) The new member of the royal family has a sweet smile and a poised manner.

C) Advances in agricultural technology over the past five decades have led to a steady increase in the global food supply, and the population of many countries around the world are benefiting.

D) No mistakes

11.

A) Here is how I answered her question: "Let's not eat early, because I'm still full from lunch."

B) I always buy bread from the bakery down the street.

C) Go ahead and take the last slice—it's yours!

D) No mistakes

12.

A) Because caffeine keeps me awake: I can't have it in the evening, but I need one cup of coffee in the morning.

B) Many of Wharton's works have been adapted to create modern-day movies and television shows— my favorites are *The Age of Innocence* and *The Buccaneers*.

C) I usually love swimming in the ocean, but the Pacific is a little rough for me—you should see the waves in Hawaii, for example!

D) No mistakes

13.

A) Modern archaeology is helped significantly by new technologies, which allow archaeologists to search for clues without ever sticking a shovel in the dirt.

B) The assassination of President John F. Kennedy continued to fascinate Americans, with new movies, books, and television series still being released every year.

C) On Parents' Day, a public holiday in the Democratic Republic of Congo, families celebrate parents both living and deceased.

D) No mistakes

14.

A) I told my mom I would make dinner for everyone, but she said I should study instead.

B) "What a wonderful time we're going to have next weekend:" Pru said.

C) Promise to bring your famous brownies, and I will invite you to my birthday party.

D) No mistakes

15.

A) Sandra's principal reasons for choosing the job were that it would be full time and would offer benefits.

B) Because airplane seats are so uncomfortable, it is impossible for me to sleep on a long-distance flight.

C) A professor from the chemistry department is conducting a seminar on toxic chemicals.

D) No mistakes

16.
- **A)** Whenever the cats get hungry, they meow for food.
- **B)** I'm going home to change, and then I'm going to David's party.
- **C)** If you fly when you are sick, you run the risk of infecting the other passengers.
- **D)** No mistakes

17.
- **A)** I love thin-crust pizza topped with roasted red peppers and caramelized onions.
- **B)** "Do you want to join us!" Juana asked.
- **C)** When Dad was going to college, he was in his early twenties.
- **D)** No mistakes

18.
- **A)** The American Academy of Arts and Sciences includes members whose fields of study span many disciplines, like math, sciences, arts, humanities, public affairs, and business.
- **B)** The Mammoth-Flint Ridge Cave System is the largest cave system in the world, enclosing over fifty thousand acres of space and four hundred miles of passageways.
- **C)** In addition to being the subject of the largest single-artist museum in the United States, Andy Warhol's paintings are also highly desirable: some of his works have sold for over 100 million dollars.
- **D)** No mistakes

19.
- **A)** James had already been awake for nineteen hours after a twelve-hour workday; when he received the news.
- **B)** *The Chicago Tribune* is famous not only because of its wide circulation but also because of its moments in history.
- **C)** In the eighteenth century, renowned composer Wolfgang Amadeus Mozart set to music the poetry of a famous writer who shared his name: Johann Wolfgang von Goethe.
- **D)** No mistakes

20.
- **A)** My sister will be starting college in August.
- **B)** Ruby's favorite pizza is the deep-dish kind they sell at the Chicago Airport.
- **C)** Mom shops when she must, but she doesn't always love it.
- **D)** No mistakes

21.
- **A)** I offered to help her study for the test but she was too busy.
- **B)** My parents and I will fly to Austin, Texas, on May 18.
- **C)** Of all the students in our class, Pablo is the most intelligent.
- **D)** No mistakes

22.
- **A)** San Antonio, Texas, can be so amazingly hot in springtime.
- **B)** In Oregon, December, and January are the coldest months.
- **C)** Last January, it was cold in Upstate New York.
- **D)** No mistakes

23.

A) Atop the Metropolitan Museum of Art in New York City, the Iris and B. Gerald Cantor Roof Garden offers a view so remarkable, it is sometimes bemoaned as a distraction from the art that is on exhibition.

B) Although I love to travel, I dislike long plane rides; they are just too tiring, and I hate jet lag.

C) Though modern professionals discount much of Sigmund Freud's work in the field of psychology, his contributions—especially in the area of psychoanalysis—was nonetheless foundational to the mental health field.

D) No mistakes

24.

A) I can't wear my work clothes to a party; I'll take a shower, and then I'll put on my new dress.

B) Tropical rainforests are made up of many layers of plant and animal life; the lowest layer—the forest floor—gets little sunlight at all and therefore supports only minimal plant life.

C) Though the Nile River in Africa passes through eleven countries, it will be the main water source of only two of them—Egypt and Sudan.

D) No mistakes

25.

A) It's too bad, because most of her friends will be leaving town in August or September.

B) According to Greek mythology, Narcissus was a hunter who was so handsome that he not only broke the heart of a beautiful mountain nymph and also ended up falling in love with his own reflection.

C) Edith Wharton wrote mainly about wealthy people living in New York and Europe in the late 1800s; she also wrote about much humbler country folks, such as poor Ethan Frome and his family.

D) No mistakes

26.

A) You and your sister love shopping together too.

B) Don't wolf down your food so hastily—you will get a stomachache.

C) My brother's college graduation is on June 19.

D) No mistakes

27.

A) This chicken is delicious, dont you think?

B) The ceremony will begin at 11:00 in the morning.

C) Your birthday is in August, isn't it?

D) No mistakes

28.

    A)   Because the cat is blocking my view, I'm going to shoo her away; she will not be pleased.

    B)   Abby's travels in Asia provided her the opportunity to try many foods that she would not have been able to try at home in the United States: nevertheless, she ate meals of chicken feet, ants, and even tarantulas.

    C)   When skywriting, a pilot flies a small aircraft in specific formations while the plane releases puffs of vaporized oil, creating large letters that can be read from the ground.

    D)   No mistakes

29.

    A)   Because we love animals, our family has adopted a rescue dog and four rescue cats.

    B)   Danny, smelling his favorite dish in the oven, smiled as he entered the kitchen.

    C)   While we were at the hotel, we went swimming every day, and we ate many calories' worth of rich food.

    D)   No mistakes

30.

    A)   I bought him a gift, that I know he will like.

    B)   Of the two dogs, Finley seems healthier than Hollie.

    C)   I gave Maria a scarf, and she gave me a coin purse.

    D)   No mistakes

31.

    A)   In addition to the disastrous effects an active volcano can have on it's immediate surroundings, an eruption can also threaten passing aircraft.

    B)   I was considering majoring in English, but then I thought, hey, why not major in biology?

    C)   San Francisco, in Northern California, is one of the most beautiful cities in the world.

    D)   No mistakes

32.

    A)   The dog has gray fur on its face, it walks very slowly and stiffly.

    B)   Imani offered to help Jake study for the quiz, but he said he prefers studying alone.

    C)   Although it is not a good idea to consume sweets in the morning, I always add two teaspoons of raw sugar to my coffee.

    D)   No mistakes

33.

    A)   You can take either the bus nor the subway.

    B)   If William studies diligently, he will probably do well on the test.

    C)   If you're going to be on time, you'll have to leave right now.

    D)   No mistakes

34.

A) The walls of the art museum's stairwell are so beautiful: they are tiled in many shades of blue.

B) She completed her applications too late to enter college in the fall, so she will enter in the spring.

C) Hurricanes, which costs the United States roughly $5 billion per year in damages, have caused almost two million deaths in the last two hundred years.

D) No mistakes

35.

A) My sister and I love exercising together.

B) Even in California, January can be a cold month.

C) When I offered her a ride; Mazie accepted gratefully.

D) No mistakes

36.

A) Because San Francisco is so close to Oakland, the ferry ride is very short.

B) This mug, the large, pale-blue ceramic one, is my favorite cup from which to drink coffee.

C) If you can't stand the heat, get out of the kitchen.

D) No mistakes

37.

A) My sister Lani won't be starting college until next January because she filled out her applications too late.

B) If they are healthy, small dogs usually live longer than big ones, but I knew a German shepherd that lived to the age of fifteen.

C) Typically, water that has evaporated remain in the sky in cloud form for fewer than ten days before falling to Earth again as precipitation.

D) No mistakes

38.

A) I think one hundred degrees is too hot for May.

B) I'm willing to feed the dogs but I need to finish my essay first.

C) When a cat eats too fast, its stomach becomes upset.

D) No mistakes

39.

A) Because Paris is such a beautiful city, so tourists flock there all year long.

B) The custodian who works at our school has a very difficult job.

C) Here is what I love: colors that remind me of the ocean.

D) No mistakes

40.

A) The exotic pet trade is a significant concern for environmentalists and animal rights advocates around the world.

B) Freediving is sometimes combined of other underwater activities like underwater photography, underwater football, underwater hockey, and even underwater target shooting.

C) Though the term nomad is often associated with early populations, nomadic cultures continue to exist even today, especially in Europe and Asia.

D) No mistakes

For questions 41 – 50, look for mistakes in spelling only.

41.

A) The office liaison dropped off the files this morning.

B) Oh wow, I hope we don't loose the game!

C) The tension was palpable as the group awaited her decision.

D) No mistakes

42.

A) Betty was suprised when Keith offered her flowers.

B) Sometimes, a kind word is necessary.

C) Chris was wary of the quiet man sitting in the corner.

D) No mistakes

43.

A) Heather was eager to show the class her presentation.

B) John told the court he did not recognize its authority.

C) My teacher had a tendancy to speak loudly, which often upset people.

D) No mistakes

44.

A) The vampire squid has adapted to a deep ocean environment.

B) Many Americans work for the federal goverment in a variety of careers.

C) A feeling of utter astonishment fell over the professor.

D) No mistakes

45.

A) The presidential suite includes two bedrooms, two bathrooms, a living room, and a kitchen.

B) Dr. Boynton has so many patience today that she will have no time for lunch.

C) If we lose the game, we won't go on to the semifinals.

D) No mistakes

46.

A) Some careers lend themselves to controversy.

B) Effective communication is a valuable skill.

C) Deeply held beliefs significantly affect our ability to make judgments.

D) No mistakes

47.

A) The group's vote was unanimious.

B) Scientists defend their hypotheses.

C) She was a personal acquaintance.

D) No mistakes

48.

A) She changed her opinion upon receiving new information.

B) Your assumption is incorrect.

C) We drew separate conclusions.

D) No mistakes

49.

A) Some animal species protect themselves with camouflage.

B) The detail in the artwork was magnificant.

C) She chose to pursue a rigorous degree program.

D) No mistakes

50.

A) Some people choose diets that are less relient on meat proteins.

B) Discourse around renewable energy sources is commonplace.

C) He had borrowed this wonderful book from his teacher.

D) No mistakes

For questions 51 – 60, look for errors in composition. Follow the directions for each question.

51. Where should the sentence "Outdoor activities like hiking, rafting, and camping are popular, especially during the cooler months of spring and autumn" be placed in the paragraph below?

(1) The Grand Canyon is one of the most popular tourist attractions in the world, drawing upward of five million visitors every year. (2) People come from all over the world to see the massive landmark, so activities and attractions are abundant. (3) Other activities like airplane and helicopter flyovers allow visitors a broader perspective of the canyon.

A) before sentence 1

B) after sentence 1

C) after sentence 2

D) after sentence 3

52. Choose the BEST word or words to join the thoughts together.

The famously high death toll at the end of the Civil War was not exclusively due to battle losses; _____ large numbers of soldiers and civilians fell ill and died as a result of living conditions during the war.

A) in addition,

B) therefore,

C) however,

D) on the other hand,

53. Which of these sentences expresses the idea MOST clearly?

A) The public defense attorney was able to maintain her optimism despite her dearth of courtroom wins, lack of free time she had, and growing list of clients she was helping.

B) The public defense attorney was able to maintain her optimism despite her dearth of courtroom wins, lack of free time, and growing list of clients.

C) Maintaining her optimism, the public defense attorney was able to despite her dearth of courtroom wins, the free time she lacked, and the list of clients she was growing.

D) The public defense attorney was able to maintain her optimism despite the losses she had experienced, the free time she lacked, and her growing client list.

54. Choose the group of words that BEST completes this sentence.

Though organized firefighting groups existed as early as ancient Egypt, the first fully state-run brigade was created by Emperor Augustus of Rome _____ as the nation's official police force.

A) which also functioned

B) and also functioned

C) also functioning

D) that also functioned

55. Which of these sentences expresses the idea MOST clearly?

A) In 1977, Jerry R. Ehman detected a signal that seemed to come from a source outside the Earth's atmosphere, using a powerful radio telescope, which played for over a minute.

B) In 1977, Jerry R. Ehman, using a powerful radio telescope, detected a signal that seemed to come from a source outside the Earth's atmosphere, which played for over a minute.

C) In 1977, using a powerful radio telescope, Jerry R. Ehman detected a signal that seemed to come from outside the Earth's atmosphere, which played for over a minute.

D) In 1977, Jerry R. Ehman, using a powerful radio telescope, detected a signal, which played for over a minute, that seemed to come from outside the Earth's atmosphere.

56. Choose the word or group of words that BEST completes this sentence.

In today's professional baseball leagues, strict regulations have standardized the design of bats; in the early days of baseball, _____, players often shaped their own bats, leading to a wide range of shapes, sizes, and weights.

A) although

B) on the other hand

C) nevertheless

D) in consequence

57. Which sentence does NOT belong in a paragraph made up of these sentences?

A) Presidents receive several benefits upon retirement, many of which are afforded by the Former Presidents Act of 1958.

B) First and foremost, they receive an annual pension payment.

C) In addition to their pension, retired presidents and their families are also entitled to ongoing Secret Service protection, which lasts until the death of the president.

D) Interestingly, Richard Nixon was the only president ever to relinquish his right to ongoing Secret Service security.

58. Which of these sentences BEST fits under the topic "Understanding Art"?

A) As recently as the last two centuries, many cultures have turned to folklore and superstition to explain odd occurrences and behaviors.

B) While some argue that art is an imitation of life, others believe that, just as often, life ends up imitating art.

C) In ancient cultures, mythology explained the weather, the elements of nature, and even the creation of the universe.

D) In the folk traditions of European countries, one creature takes the blame when individuals begin acting strangely: the changeling.

59. Where should the sentence "Some of humanity's biggest accomplishments were achieved first in science fiction" be placed in the paragraph below?

(1) Jules Verne wrote about humanity traveling to the moon over a century before it happened. (2) Scientists Robert H. Goddard and Leo Szilard both credit his work—on liquid-fueled rockets and atomic power, respectively—to the futuristic novels of H.G. Wells. (3) Gene Roddenberry, the creator of *Star Trek*, dreamed up replicators long before 3-D printers were invented.

A) before sentence 1

B) after sentence 1

C) after sentence 2

D) after sentence 3

60. Choose the word that BEST completes this sentence.

For example, in the film *The Breakfast Club*, the five main characters, _____ are all from different social circles at one high school, learn to look past labels and appearances and find that they have a lot in common.

A) whom

B) who

C) which

D) and

Answer Key
VERBAL SKILLS

1. **B)** A snake slithers along the ground; a kangaroo bounds across the land.

2. **B)** Teeth, needles, and staples are all sharp, while a cotton ball is soft.

3. **A)** Because I love all cereal, then I would love Chuckles—a type of cereal.

4. **D)** A daffodil is a flower; all the others are types of trees.

5. **D)** Sacred means "holy, protected, not to be disturbed." Profane is an antonym of sacred.

6. **A)** A seagull is one member of a flock; a wolf is one member of a pack.

7. **C)** It is unclear why Melissa especially enjoyed the Atoms Exhibit; she could already know a lot about atoms, or she could have learned about them for the first time.

8. **B)** A rock does not grow, but the other answer choices do.

9. **A)** Something that is gigantic is huge or humongous.

10. **C)** Even though Jack loves animals, there is no way of knowing if Jack got an animal at the pet store and if he did whether or not that animal was a dog.

11. **A)** While all four are animals, an ostrich is a bird with two legs. The others are mammals with four legs.

12. **A)** Transformed means "radically changed or converted." Unchanged is an antonym of transformed.

13. **C)** A sock covers a foot; a glove covers a hand.

14. **D)** Something that is sleek is smooth, glossy, and shiny.

15. **C)** There is no indication whether Jessica likes sports; just because she likes board games does not mean she doesn't also like sports.

16. **D)** Rude means "showing a lack of manners or consideration." The other three words refer to being friendly or agreeable.

17. **C)** Substantial means "a lot or plentiful."

18. **A)** Limited means "having defined boundaries," and the other three words refer to something that is never-ending.

19. **C)** Inertia means "inactive, asleep, passive, quiet." Active is an antonym of inertia.

20. **A)** A key opens a lock; a handle opens a door.

21. **D)** Fidelity is allegiance or a commitment to someone or something.

22. **B)** If Jenny wants to buy a purple shirt for her mother and the store only has red, yellow, and blue shirts, she will not buy a shirt.

23. **D)** Simple means "clear, uncluttered." The other four words describe something complicated.

24. **A)** Deter means "discourage, prevent, put off." Encourage is an antonym of deter.

25. **B)** A sweater is worn in the winter; a swimsuit is worn in the summer.

26. **A)** Briskly means "energetically, quickly."

27. **C)** There is no way of knowing what color the bunnies are.

28. **B)** Clear means "easily seen through," and the other three words refer to something difficult to understand or see.

29. **C)** Frantic means "panicky, desperate, worried, frenzied." Calm is an antonym of frantic.

30. **D)** Shy means "easily frightened." The other three words refer to having courage.

31. **C)** An airport houses planes; a garage houses cars.

32. **A)** Cacophony is the opposite of harmony; it is a combination of harsh, unpleasant noises that sound terrible together.

33. **B)** If three of the four puppies are male, then one of the puppies is a female. Therefore, the statement "half of the puppies are female" is false.

34. **D)** Trusting means "someone who trusts or believes." The other four words describe someone who is disbelieving.

35. **B)** Degrade means "humiliate, shame, disgrace, mortify." Respect is an antonym of degrade.

36. **A)** Obscure means "hidden"; malicious means "wicked."

37. **A)** Deflated means "collapsed, let down."

38. **D)** A stick is breakable, but the other answer choices are foldable.

39. **B)** To jar is to jolt or shake.

40. **B)** All seltzers are carbonated, but the statements do not say whether other beverages are carbonated.

41. **D)** While all four are forms of US currency, the dollar is usually made from paper; the rest are types of coins.

42. **B)** Something that is illegible is impossible to read or indecipherable.

43. **D)** Divide means "separate, disconnect." The other four words refer to joining things together.

44. **A)** Appointed means "chosen, selected, allotted, arranged." Rejected is an antonym of appointed.

45. **A)** An elephant lumbers through the jungle; a hummingbird flits through the air.

46. **C)** Something that is scarce is hard to find or rare.

47. **C)** Just because Vanessa chose to order Chinese food does not mean that she does not like pizza.

48. D) Sandals, sneakers, and boots are shoes; socks are clothing.

49. C) Just because a sun is in our universe doesn't mean it is in our solar system.

50. A) A croissant is a type of food; balls, wheels, and rolling pins all roll.

51. A) Resilient means "hardy, strong, tough, durable." Weak is an antonym of resilient.

52. D) A pebble is a small rock, while a boulder is a huge one; a hut is a small building, while a mansion is a huge one.

53. B) To beckon someone means "to call or summon" them.

54. A) If all stars are made of plasma and the sun is a star, then it is made of plasma.

55. C) Orange, grapefruit, and lemon are all citrus fruits; strawberries are berries.

56. D) Solemn means "sincere, serious, glum, sacred." Cheerful is an antonym of solemn.

57. C) A sentence is part of a paragraph; a stanza is part of a poem.

58. C) Antics are playful tricks or exploits. Choice C, "exploits," is a synonym for "antics."

59. C) There is no way to know for sure if the socks are not wool, and wool is a fabric.

60. C) While all four answer choices are ways to distribute information or communicate, the post office is not electronic.

QUANTITATIVE SKILLS

1. A) The numbers in the series are decreasing by 4.

27, 23, _____, 15, 11

$23 - 27 = -4$

$11 - 15 = -4$

Find the missing number by subtracting 4 from the previous number.

$23 - 4 = \textbf{19}$

2. B) 2 more than the product of 2 and $23 = 2 + (2 \times 23) = 2 + 46 = \textbf{48}$

3. A) Write the shaded part of each circle as a fraction.

(a): shaded area $= \frac{1}{2}$

(b): shaded area $= \frac{2}{4} = \frac{1}{2}$

(c): shaded area $= \frac{4}{8} = \frac{1}{2}$

(a) = (b) = (c)

4. A) 2 more than the quotient of 48 and $8 = 2 + (48 \div 8) = 2 + 6 = \textbf{8}$

5. **A)** The numbers in the series are decreasing by 8.

119, 111, 103, 95, ...

$111 - 119 = -8$

$103 - 111 = -8$

$95 - 103 = -8$

To find the next two numbers, subtract 8 from the previous number.

$95 - 8 = \mathbf{87}$

$87 - 8 = \mathbf{79}$

6. **B)** Write each term in scientific notation.

(a): 2.03×10^{-8}

(b): $0.0000000203 = 2.03 \times 10^{-8}$

(c): $0.00000000203 = 2.03 \times 10^{-9}$

(a) = (b) > (c)

7. **C)** Convert each expression into minutes.

(a): 6 hours and 30 minutes = (6 × 60) + 30 = 390 minutes

(b): 390 minutes

(c): 6.5 hours = 6 hours and 30 minutes = 390 minutes

(a) = (b) = (c)

8. **C)** The numbers in the series are increasing by 6.

56, 62, ____, 74, 80

$62 - 56 = 6$

$80 - 74 = 6$

To find the missing number, add 6 to the previous number.

$62 + 6 = \mathbf{68}$

9. **B)** Rectangles (a) and (b) are both $\frac{3}{8}$ shaded. Rectangle (c) is $\frac{4}{8}$ shaded.

(c) > (a) = (b)

10. **D)** The numbers in the series are increasing by $\frac{1}{4}$.

$-\frac{1}{2}$, ____, ____, $\frac{1}{4}$, $\frac{1}{2}$, $\frac{3}{4}$

$\frac{1}{2} - \frac{1}{4} = \frac{1}{4}$

$\frac{3}{4} - \frac{1}{2} = \frac{1}{4}$

To find the missing numbers, add $\frac{1}{4}$ to the previous number.

$-\frac{1}{2} + \frac{1}{4} = \mathbf{-\frac{1}{4}}$

$-\frac{1}{4} + \frac{1}{4} = \mathbf{0}$

11. **C)** 8 less than the sum of 11 and 2 = (11 + 2) − 8 = **5**

12. **D)** The numbers in the series are increasing. The difference between each value is increasing by 1.

$12 - 9 = 3$

$16 - 12 = 4$

$21 - 16 = 5$

$27 - 21 = 6$

To find the next number, add 7 to the previous number.

$27 + 7 = \mathbf{34}$

13. **B)** All radii in a circle are the same length, so **CB is equal to AB**.

14. **A)** The product of 2, 4, and 8 = 2 × 4 × 8 = **64**

15. **C)** The square root of the product of 8 and 2 = $\sqrt{8 \times 2}$ = $\sqrt{16}$ = **4**

16. **C)** In this series, the numbers 1, 3, 7, and 9 repeat.

1, 3, 7, 9, 1, 3, ...

The missing numbers will complete the repeating pattern.

1, 3, 7, 9, 1, 3, **7**, **9**

17. **C)** Simplify each expression.

(a): $0.5 \times 12 = 6$

(b): $0.25 \times 24 = 6$

(c): $0.75 \times 8 = 6$

(a) = (b) = (c)

18. **D)** The numbers in the series are increasing. The difference between each value is decreasing by 1.

___, 147, 199, 250, 300

$199 - 147 = 52$

$250 - 199 = 51$

$300 - 250 = 50$

To find the first number, subtract 53 from the next number in the series.

$147 - 53 = $ **94**

19. **C)** Rewrite each value as a decimal.

(a): $35\% = 0.35$

(b): $\frac{3}{5} = 0.6$

(c): 0.35

(c) = (a) < (b)

20. **C)** This series shows consecutive perfect squares.

100, 121, 144, 169, ...

$100 = 10^2$

$121 = 11^2$

$144 = 12^2$

$169 = 13^2$

The next number is $14^2 = $ **196**.

21. **A)** Write the shaded part of each octagon as a fraction.

(a): $\frac{3}{8}$

(b): $\frac{1}{4} = \frac{2}{8}$

(c): $\frac{1}{2} = \frac{4}{8}$

(c) > (a) > (b)

22. **A)** In this series, the numbers alternate between increasing by a factor of 2 and increasing by adding 1.

3, 6, 7, 14, 15, 30, 31, ...

$\frac{6}{3} = 2$

$7 - 6 = 1$

$\frac{14}{7} = 2$

$15 - 14 = 1$

$\frac{30}{15} = 2$

$31 - 30 = 1$

The last given number in the series is found by adding 1 to the previous number. To find the next number, multiply the last number given by 2.

$31 \times 2 = $ **62**

23. **A)** Convert each term into inches.

(a): 5 feet 2 inches = 5 ft $\times \frac{12 \text{ in}}{1 \text{ ft}} = $ 60 in + 2 in = 62 inches

(b): 62 inches

(c): $5\frac{1}{4}$ feet = 5.25 feet = 5.25 ft $\times \frac{12 \text{ in}}{1 \text{ ft}} = $ 63 inches

(c) > (a) = (b)

24. **C)** The numbers in the series are increasing by 5.

8, 13, 18, 23, ...

$13 - 8 = 5$

$18 - 13 = 5$

$23 - 18 = 5$

To find the next two numbers, add 5 to the previous number.

$23 + 5 = $ **28**

$28 + 5 = $ **33**

25. **B)**

(a): 19 circles

(b): 9 circles

(c): 70 circles

(c) > (a) > (b)

26. **A)** The numbers in the series are decreasing by 26.

953, 927, 901, 875, ...

$927 - 953 = -26$

$901 - 927 = -26$

$875 - 901 = -26$

To find the next number, subtract 26 from the previous number.

$875 - 26 = $ **849**

27. **A)** $\frac{3}{5}$ of $300 = \frac{3}{5} \times 300 = $ **180**

28. **B)** In this series, the exponents are decreasing by 1.

$2^3, 2^2, 2^1, $ ___, $2^{-1}, 2^{-2}$

To find the missing number, subtract 1 from the exponent.

$2^{1-1} = 2^0 = $ **1**

29. **D)** $\frac{4}{3}$ of $3 = \frac{4}{3} \times 3 = $ **4**

30. **B)** 15 times the product of $\frac{1}{5}$ and $\frac{2}{3}$ $= 15 \times (\frac{1}{5} \times \frac{2}{3}) = 15 \times (\frac{2}{15}) = $ **2**

31. **A)** $\frac{1}{3}$ of $150 = \frac{1}{3} \times 150 = $ **50**

32. **A)** 10 more than the quotient of 200 and $5 = 10 + (200 \div 5) = 10 + 40 = $ **50**

33. **C)** In a rhombus, the diagonals bisect each other, so BE is equal to DE.

34. **B)** $\frac{1}{3}$ of what number is equal to 300?

$a = $ the number being solved for

$\frac{1}{3} \times a = 300$

$a = $ **900**

35. **A)** In this series, every other number is decreasing by 1 and the signs of the numbers are alternating.

12, −12, 11, −11, ___, ____, 9, −9

The missing numbers are **10** and **−10**.

36. **D)** 6 less than the product of 9 and $4 = (9 \times 4) - 6 = 36 - 6 = $ **30**

37. **A)** (a): 25 squares

(b): 20 squares

(c): 24 squares

(a) > (c) > (b)

38. **C)** Simplify each expression.

(a): $\frac{1}{2} \times \frac{1}{3} = \frac{1}{6}$

(b): $\frac{1}{2} - \frac{1}{3} = \frac{3}{6} - \frac{2}{6} = \frac{1}{6}$

(c): $\frac{1}{2} \div \frac{1}{3} = \frac{1}{2} \times \frac{3}{1} = \frac{3}{2}$

(c) > (a) = (b)

39. **C)** $\frac{1}{2}$ of the average of 30 and 38

$= \frac{1}{2}(\frac{30 + 38}{2}) = \frac{1}{2} \times 34 = $ **17**

40. **A)** The sum of the quotient of 24 and 4 and the product of 4 and 2 = $(24 \div 4) + (4 \times 2) = 6 + 8 = $ **14**

41. **A)** In the series, both the numerator and denominator are increasing by 1.

$\frac{2}{3}, \frac{3}{4}, \frac{4}{5}, \frac{5}{6}, $ ----

To find the next number, add 1 to the numerator and denominator in the previous number.

$\frac{5 + 1}{6 + 1} = \frac{6}{7}$

42. **B)** $\frac{1}{4}$ of what number is 2 times 6?

$a = $ the number being solved for

$\frac{1}{4}(a) = 2 \times 6$

$\frac{1}{4}(a) = 12$

$a = $ **48**

43. A) 4 less than the average of 5, 7, and 12 = $\frac{5 + 7 + 12}{3} - 4 = 8 - 4 = \mathbf{4}$

44. D) $\frac{2}{3}$ of what number is 4 squared?

a = number being solved for

$\frac{2}{3}(a) = 4^2$

$\frac{2}{3}(a) = 16$

$a = \mathbf{24}$

45. C) The series is geometric with a common ratio of $\frac{1}{3}$ (meaning each number is divided by 3 to find the next number).

81, 27, _____, 3, 1

$\frac{27}{81} = \frac{1}{3}$

$\frac{1}{3} = \frac{1}{3}$

To find the missing number, multiply the previous number by $\frac{1}{3}$.

$27 \times \frac{1}{3} = \mathbf{9}$

46. B) Find each value.

(a) $P_{\text{square}} = 4s$

$24 = 4s$

$s = 6$

(b) $P_{\text{equilateral triangle}} = 3s$

$18 = 3s$

$s = 6$

(c) $C = 2\pi r$

$12\pi = 2\pi r$

$r = 6$

(a) = (b) = (c)

47. D) AD and AE are both radii of circle A, so AD plus AE is equal to the diameter of the circle. BC is also equal to the diameter of the circle.

48. B) The numbers in the series are decreasing by 5.

57, 52, ____, 42, 37

$52 - 57 = -5$

$37 - 42 = -5$

Find the missing number by subtracting 5 from the previous number.

$52 - 5 = \mathbf{47}$

49. B) The series is geometric with a common ratio of 2 (meaning each number is multiplied by 2 to find the next number).

3, 6, 12, 24, 48, ...

$\frac{6}{3} = 2$

$\frac{12}{6} = 2$

$\frac{24}{12} = 2$

$\frac{48}{24} = 2$

To find the next number, multiply the previous number by 2.

$48 \times 2 = \mathbf{96}$

50. B) Simplify each expression.

(a): $-3 \times 2 = -6$

(b): $-3 + 2 = -1$

(c): $-3 \div 2 = -\frac{3}{2}$

(a) < (c) < (b)

51. A) Simplify each term and expression.

(a): $\sqrt{16} = 4$

(b): $\frac{32}{8} = 4$

(c): $-8 + 12 = 4$

(a) = (b) = (c)

52. B) The numbers in the series are decreasing by 0.07.

0.74, 0.67, ___, 0.53, 0.46

$0.67 - 0.74 = -0.07$

$0.46 - 0.53 = -0.07$

To find the missing number, subtract 0.07 from the previous number.

$0.67 - 0.07 = \mathbf{0.6}$

READING

1. **A)** The passage indicates that a snakes' "intricate diamonds, stripes, and swirls help the animals hide from predators, but perhaps most importantly (for us humans, anyway), the markings can also indicate whether the snake is venomous."

2. **B)** The final paragraph of the passage states that the two species "frequently [share] a habitat" and that a "predatory hawk or eagle, usually hunting from high in the sky, can't tell the difference between the two species, and so the kingsnake gets passed over and lives another day."

3. **D)** This summary captures the main ideas of each paragraph.

4. **C)** The first paragraph states that "while it might seem counterintuitive for a venomous snake to stand out in bright red or blue, that fancy costume tells any nearby predator that approaching him would be a bad idea." The coral snake's markings do not allow it to hide from predators but rather to "ward [them] off."

5. **A)** The passage states that "intricate diamonds, stripes, and swirls help the animals hide from predators," implying that these markings are complex enough to allow the animals to blend in with their surroundings.

6. **C)** The second paragraph states that "The scarlet kingsnake, for example, has very similar markings to the venomous coral snake with whom it frequently shares a habitat. However, the kingsnake is actually nonvenomous."

7. **A)** This detail is not stated in the passage.

8. **B)** In the first paragraph, the author writes, "But what's the best way to get an accurate reading? The answer depends on the situation." She then goes on to describe various options and their applications.

9. **B)** The author indicates that "the most common way people measure body temperature is orally" but that "there are many situations...when measuring temperature orally isn't an option." She then goes on to describe these situations in the second and third paragraphs.

10. **A)** The final paragraph states that "agitated patients...won't be able to sit still long enough for an accurate reading." The reader can infer that an agitated patient is a patient who is visibly upset, annoyed, or uncomfortable.

11. **A)** The second paragraph of the passage states that "Using the rectum also has the added benefit of providing a much more accurate reading than other locations can provide."

12. **C)** The passage is mainly about the "troubling" fact that 40 million people in the United States still smoke, even though most people know that heavy smoking shortens people's lives. The other sentences give details from the passage.

13. **A)** The author uses various phrases to describe the cause-effect relationship between cigarette smoking and serious illnesses. Other words and phrases the author uses include "link," "cigarette-linked cancers," "is linked to," and "correlated with."

14. **B)** Words and phrases such as "40 million people continue to smoke," "troubling," "30 percent of all cancer-related deaths in the United States can be tied to smoking," and "the necessity of anti-smoking campaigns" show that the author thinks all smokers should quit—the sooner the better.

15. **D)** The passage does not contain this detail. The passage does not mention advertising.

16. **A)** In the last paragraph, the author states that "Continuing research reinforces the necessity of anti-smoking campaigns, both government funded and grassroots. The numbers show that such campaigns work, encouraging people to quit smoking." Clearly, the author is strongly in favor of "anti-smoking campaigns."

17. **C)** In the last sentence, the author writes, "the United States still has a long road of anti-smoking campaigning ahead." Readers can infer that by "a long road" the author means "a lot of hard work left to do."

18. **A)** The author states that "popcorn continued to rule the snack food kingdom until the rise in popularity of home televisions during the 1950s" when the industry saw a "decline in sales" as a result of the changing pastimes of the American people.

19. **B)** The author states, "For the Aztec Indians who called the caves home, popcorn (or momochitl) played an important role in society, both as a food staple and in ceremonies." This implies that the Aztec people popped popcorn both for special occasions ("in ceremonies") and for regular consumption ("as a food staple").

20. **C)** In the opening paragraph the author writes, "But popcorn isn't just for fun—it's also a multimillion-dollar-a-year industry with a long and fascinating history." The author then goes on to illustrate the history of popcorn from the ancient Aztecs, to early twentieth century America, to the present day.

21. **C)** The author writes, "The popcorn industry flourished during the Great Depression when it was advertised as a wholesome and economical food."

22. **A)** This statement summarizes the entire passage, including the brief history of popcorn in ancient cultures and the growth in the popularity of popcorn in America.

23. **C)** The author writes, "However, it wasn't until microwave popcorn became commercially available in 1981 that at-home popcorn consumption began to grow exponentially. With the wide availability of microwaves in the United States, popcorn also began popping up in offices and hotel rooms."

24. **A)** The author writes, "But is it possible for two species to interact and for one to remain completely unaffected?...In fact, many scientists claim that relationships currently described as commensal are just mutualistic or parasitic in ways that haven't been discovered yet."

25. **A)** The author writes that "there's another class of symbiosis that is controversial among scientists" and goes on to say that "many scientists claim the relationships currently described as commensal are just mutualistic or parasitic in ways that haven't been discovered yet." This implies that scientists debate about the topic of commensalism.

26. **B)** The author writes that "as these communities have evolved, the species in them have developed complex, long-term interspecies interactions known as symbiotic relationships." She then goes on to describe the different types of symbiotic relationships that exist.

27. **D)** The author writes, "Often, relationships described as commensal include one species that feeds on another species' leftovers; remoras, for instance, will attach themselves to sharks and eat the food particles they leave behind. It might seem like the shark gets nothing from the relationship, but a closer look will show that sharks in fact benefit from remoras, which clean the sharks' skin and remove parasites."

28. **C)** The author writes, "A relationship where one individual benefits and the other is harmed is known as parasitism."

29. **D)** The author writes, "The bacteria, fungi, insects, plants, and animals that live together in a habitat have evolved to share a pool of limited resources...As these communities have evolved, the species in them have developed complex, long-term interspecies interactions known as symbiotic relationships."

30. **C)** The first sentence in the second paragraph states the paragraph's main idea, the behavior of young men: "Men are more likely to exhibit riskier behaviors than women, especially between the ages of fifteen and twenty-four, when testosterone production is at its peak."

31. **B)** The primary purpose of the essay is to explain or give reasons; its focus is the gender gap in life expectancy, as the first sentence states. It is not advisory or cautionary, and it does not express the author's hopes.

32. **D)** In the first paragraph, the author writes, "Across the globe, women are, on average, outliving their male counterparts. Although this gender gap has shrunk over the last decade, ... women are still expected to live four and a half years longer than men." The passage does not support any of the other statements.

33. C) In the second paragraph, the author implies that young women do not behave as riskily as young men do. In the third paragraph, the author states that men "may be less likely to eat as many fruits and vegetables as their female counterparts. And [men] may be more likely to consume more red meat, including processed meat. These types of meats have been linked to high cholesterol, hypertension, and cancer." In general, the author describes women as more sensible than men when it comes to physical safety and a healthy lifestyle.

34. C) In the first paragraph, the author writes that the "gender gap has shrunk over the last decade thanks to medical improvements and lifestyle changes." Readers can infer from this that the average man has a healthier lifestyle than he did over ten years ago.

35. A) In the third paragraph, the author writes, "Estrogen ... seems to be correlated with cholesterol levels: an increase in estrogen is accompanied by a decrease in 'bad' cholesterol." Readers can infer that correlated means "linked or associated."

36. C) In the first paragraph, the author states that "recent research is changing [the perception that bacteria causes diseases and attacks the immune system]; plenty of scholarly articles point to the benefits of healthy bacteria that actually reinforce the immune system."

37. D) The first sentence reads, "The word *bacteria* typically conjures images of disease-inducing invaders that attack our immune systems." Readers can infer that by "conjures images," the author means "brings up images" (in other words, causes people to imagine).

38. B) As the second sentence states, the passage is mainly about healthy bacteria. The other sentences provide details from the passage.

39. D) In paragraph 3, the author writes, "Children who live with pets and play outdoors seem to have lower rates of allergies, attention deficit disorder, and obesity."

40. B) Readers can infer that bacteria affects the immune system and the digestive system more than other systems in the body.

VOCABULARY ANSWER KEY

1. C) Stagnant means "still, motionless, quiet, stationary."

2. D) Serrated means "jagged, saw-like, toothed."

3. B) Hewn means "cut, chopped, felled, axed, hacked."

4. B) A trek is a "walk, hike, journey, trudge, march."

5. A) Indigenous means "native, original, homegrown, local."

6. B) Tempest means "storm, blizzard, commotion, disorder."

7. **C)** Cue means "signal to begin an action."

8. **A)** Expanse means "span, spread, breadth, vastness."

9. **C)** Compensation means "reward, reimbursement, payment, benefit."

10. **C)** Scrutiny means "inspection, examination, inquiry."

11. **A)** Reeling means "lurching, stumbling, swaying."

12. **B)** Morph means "transform, alter, switch, change."

13. **A)** Platitude means "cliché, tired expression or idea, commonplace."

14. **D)** Tragedy means "disaster, calamity, catastrophe."

15. **B)** Strewn means "scattered, spread, thrown."

16. **A)** Commemoration means "tribute, remembrance, celebration."

17. **B)** Gruff means "bad-tempered, grumpy, impatient."

18. **B)** Presumptuous means "arrogant, rude, presuming, bold."

19. **C)** Glint means "flash, sparkle, shine, gleam."

20. **B)** Sodden means "soaking, saturated, drenched, wet."

21. **A)** Grievance means "complaint, criticism, accusation."

22. **C)** Unprecedented means "unparalleled, exceptional, unique."

MATHEMATICS

1. **C)** Line segment *MN* begins at 35 mm and ends at 70 mm, so 70 − 35 = 35 mm.

   The length of line segment *KL* is 15 mm.

   Find the difference.

   35 mm − 15 mm = **20 mm**

2. **B)** Compare decimals from left to right. Three of the numbers have a 3 in the tenths place, while one has a zero. The number with the least value is **0.035**.

3. **A)** Use a table to find coordinates of $y = 2x + 1$.

x	y
0	1
1	3
2	5

   Plot the coordinates (0, 1), (1, 3), and (2, 5). Connect the points with a line. **The graph is choice A.**

4. **A)** In **2012**, New York had more months with less than 3 inches of rain than either Chicago or Houston.

5. **A)** Find the prime factorization of each number.

$45 = 3 \times 3 \times 5$

$22 = 2 \times 11$

The two numbers have no prime factors in common. Because 1 is a factor of every number, their greatest common factor is **1**.

6. **A)** $n \div 100 = \frac{n}{100}$

$n \times \frac{1}{100} = \frac{n}{100}$

Dividing by 100 produces the same result as **multiplying by $\frac{1}{100}$**.

7. **B)** Combine like terms.

$5n = 3n + 2n$

8. **C)** List all the even integers greater than 10 and less than 25 in ascending order. The median is the value in the middle.

12, 14, 16, **18**, 20, 22, 24

9. **C)** Four hundred twenty-three and nine thousandths is written as 423.009. It has **6 digits.**

10. **C)** Convert each fraction to a decimal.

$\frac{3}{4} = 0.75$

$\frac{9}{10} = 0.90$

The value **0.80** is between 0.75 and 0.90.

11. **B)** There are 1000 meters in 1 kilometer, so 1 meter = **0.001 km**.

12. **D)** Substitute each set of values and determine if the inequality is true.

$(0, 0) \rightarrow 2(0) + 0 \leq -10$ FALSE

$(10, 2) \rightarrow 2(10) + 2 \leq -10$ FALSE

$(10, 10) \rightarrow 2(10) + 10 \leq -10$ FALSE

$\mathbf{(-10, -10)} \rightarrow 2(-10) + (-10) \leq -10$
TRUE

13. **A)** $2\frac{1}{4}$ is divisible by $\frac{1}{4}$, so the $\frac{1}{4}$ cup can be used to measure the flour; $\frac{1}{4} \times 9 = 2\frac{1}{4}$.

14. **C)** Use the formula for finding percentages. Express the percentage as a decimal.

part = whole × percentage

part = **1560 × 0.15**

15. **B)** 1 pound = 16 ounces

Birth weight → 7.5 × 16 = 120 ounces

Gained 6 ounces per month, or 6t.

Current weight = monthly gain + birth weight

$y = 6t + 120$

16. **C)** Convert each fraction to a decimal.

$5\frac{1}{4} = 5.25$

$5\frac{1}{2} = 5.5$

Convert each answer choice to a decimal to find a value between 5.25 and 5.5.

$5\frac{7}{20} = 5.35$, which is between 5.25 and 5.5.

17. **D)** Write each value in decimal form and compare.

A) $-0.95 < 0 < \underline{0.4 < 0.35} < 0.75$
FALSE

B) $-1 < -0.1 < -0.11 < 0.8\overline{3} \underline{\,\leq 0.}75$
FALSE

C) $-0.75 < -0.2 < 0 < 0\overline{66} \underline{\,\leq 0.55}$
FALSE

D) $-1.1 < -0.8 < -0.13 < 0.7 < 0.\overline{81}$
TRUE

18. **C)** Round each value to the nearest thousand.

$129{,}113 \approx 129{,}000$

$34{,}602 \approx 35{,}000$

Add.

$129{,}000 + 35{,}000 = \mathbf{164{,}000}$

19. **A)** Simplify each root and add.

$\sqrt[3]{64} = 4$

$\sqrt[3]{729} = 9$

$4 + 9 = \mathbf{13}$

20. **C)** Cylinder A: Surface Area → $SA = 2\pi rx + 2\pi r^2$; Volume → $V = \pi r^2 x$.

Cylinder B: Surface Area → $SA = 4\pi rx + 2\pi r^2$; Volume → $V = 2\pi r^2 x$.

Cylinder A has half the volume of Cylinder B.

21. **B)** Substitute 0 for x and solve for y.

$7y - 42x + 7 = 0$

$7y - 42(0) + 7 = 0$

$y = -1$

The y-intercept is at **(0, –1)**.

22. **C)** total seats = 4,500 + 2,000

$\dfrac{\text{lower seats}}{\text{all seats}} = \dfrac{4,500}{6,500} = \mathbf{\dfrac{9}{13}}$

23. **B)** Multiply the values without the decimal points, then move the decimal so that the final answer has 4 values to the right of the decimal.

$1532 \times 476 = 729{,}232 \rightarrow \mathbf{72.9232}$

24. **C)** $23 \div 4 = 5.75$ pizzas

Round up to **6 pizzas.**

25. **C)** Write a proportion and solve.

$\dfrac{1 \text{ inch}}{25 \text{ miles}} = \dfrac{x}{125 \text{ miles}}$

Cross multiply.

$25x = 125$

$x = \mathbf{5}$

26. **C)** A light cycle lasts $2\frac{1}{2}$ minutes and Martin is waiting $7\frac{1}{2}$ minutes. Divide to determine how many cycles.

$7.5 \div 2.5 = 3.$

If each cycle lets 12 cars proceed, the most cycles he waits is 3.

Multiply the number of cars in each cycle: 2(12) = 24 and 3(12) = 36.

The only answer between these values is **30**.

27. **B)** Let x = the number of desktops sold.

The store sold three times as many laptops as desktops.

Let $3x$ = number of laptops.

The number of laptops plus the number of desktops is 56.

$x + 3x = 56$

$4x = 56$

$x = 14$

There were 14 desktops sold and 14(3) = 42 laptops sold.

Subtract to find how many more laptops than desktops sold.

$42 - 14 = \mathbf{28}$

28. **A)** Multiply the decimal values.

$1.2 \times 1.13 = 1.356$

Add the exponents.

$-3 + (-4) = -7$

$(1.2 \times 10^{-3})(1.13 \times 10^{-4}) = \mathbf{1.356 \times 10^{-7}}$

29. **C)** Use the formula for percent change.

$\text{percent change} = \dfrac{\text{amount of change}}{\text{original amount}}$

$\dfrac{7375 - 7250}{7{,}250} \approx 0.017 = \mathbf{1.7\%}$

30. **C)** Use the formula for percent change.

$\text{percent change} = \dfrac{\text{amount of change}}{\text{original amount}}$

$\dfrac{(680 - 425)}{425} \rightarrow \dfrac{255}{425} \rightarrow 0.60 = \mathbf{60\%}$

31. **D)** Assign variables and write the ratios as fractions. Cross multiply to solve.

Let x = number of apples

$$\frac{\text{apples}}{\text{bananas}} = \frac{3}{2} = \frac{x}{20}$$

$60 = 2$

$x = 30$ apples

Let y = number of oranges

$$\frac{\text{oranges}}{\text{bananas}} = \frac{1}{2} = \frac{y}{20}$$

$2y = 20$

$y = 10$ oranges

Add the number of apples, oranges, and bananas to find the total.

$30 + 20 + 10 = $ **60 pieces of fruit**

32. **A)** The average of 5 numbers is 16.

$$\frac{\text{sum}}{5} = 16$$

Solve for the sum.

$16 \times 5 = 80$

Subtract to find the 5th number.

$80 - 68 = $ **12**

33. **B)** Use the FOIL method to multiply binomials.

$(5 + \sqrt{5})(5 - \sqrt{5})$

$5(5) - 5(\sqrt{5}) + \sqrt{5}(5) - \sqrt{5}(\sqrt{5})$

$25 - 5\sqrt{5} + 5\sqrt{5} - 5$

$25 - 5 = $ **20**

34. **C)** 1 week = 7 days

$10 \times 8 \times 7 = $ **560 oz**

35. **C)** Find the total distance.

$4.6 + 4.8 + 5.3 + 5.2 + 6 = 25.9$

Divide by the number of days.

$25.9 \div 5 = $ **5.18 mi**

36. **B)** $P = \dfrac{\text{number of favorable outcomes}}{\text{number of possible outcomes}}$

The total number of possible outcomes is $5 + 7 + 8 = 20$.

There are 7 pieces of taffy, which is the favorable outcome.

$P = \dfrac{\text{number of favorable outcomes}}{\text{number of possible outcomes}}$

$= \dfrac{7}{20}$

37. **B)** Use order of operations (PEMDAS) to solve the equation.

Parentheses (multiply, then subtract)

$12 \times 4 = 48$

$50 - 48 = 2$

Exponents

$2^2 = $ **4**

38. **A)** Add the area of the semicircle and the area of the triangle.

semicircle: $A = \dfrac{\pi r^2}{2} = \dfrac{\pi(3)^2}{2} = 4.5\pi$

triangle: $A = \dfrac{1}{2}bh = \dfrac{1}{2}(6)(10) = 30$

total area = **30 + 4.5π**

39. **C)** Use the fundamental counting principle. Think of the salsa as a yes or no option.

$(2)(5)(6)(2)(2)(2) = $ **480**

40. **D)** Use the formula for circumference of the circle to find the radius.

$C = 2\pi r$

$18\pi = 2\pi r$

$r = 9$

Use the radius to find the area.

$A = \pi r^2$

$A = \pi(9)^2$

$A = $ **81π**

41. **A)** Find the area of all sides of the shed.

Two walls measure 5 feet by 7 feet. Two walls measure 4 feet by 7 feet.

$A = 2l_1w_1 + 2l_2w_2$

$A = 2(5 \text{ ft})(7 \text{ ft}) + 2(4 \text{ ft})(7 \text{ ft})$

$A = 70 \text{ ft}^2 + 56 \text{ ft}^2 = $ **126 ft²**

42. **A)** Use dimensional analysis to convert feet to miles and seconds to hours.

$$\frac{15 \text{ ft}}{\text{sec}} \times \frac{3600 \text{ sec}}{1 \text{ hr}} \times \frac{1 \text{ mi}}{5280 \text{ ft}} \approx \textbf{10.2 mph}$$

43. **C)** The probability that Matt or Kendall will win is the number of winning tickets (successful outcomes) over the total number of tickets in the raffle (total outcomes).

$$= \frac{\text{number of favorable outcomes}}{\text{total number of possible outcomes}} =$$

$$\frac{35 + 15}{1250} = \textbf{0.04}$$

44. **D)** Divide and find the digit in the hundredths place.

$$21.563 \div 8 = 2.6\textbf{9}5375$$

45. **B)** Find the probability of multiple independent events, and multiply the probability of each separate event.

$$\frac{1}{2} \times \frac{1}{2} \times \frac{1}{2} \times \frac{1}{2} = \frac{\textbf{1}}{\textbf{16}}$$

46. **A)** Determine the number of people in each area that are in the overlap.

City A's area: $140,000 \times 0.04 = 5600$

City B's area: $250,000 \times 0.02 = 5000$

Total the overlap area.

$5600 + 5000 = \textbf{11,600}$

47. **C)** Selling price − cost = profit

$\$60 − \$40 = \$20$

He took out a \$50,000 loan. Divide to determine how many copies he must sell.

$\$50,000 \div \$20 = \textbf{2500 copies}$

48. **A)** Substitute the known values in the formula and solve for the number of hits.

$$\text{average} = \frac{\text{hits}}{\text{at bats}}$$

$$0.250 = \frac{\text{hits}}{4}$$

$$\text{hits} = \textbf{1}$$

49. **A)** $4(a^2 + 2a) − 3(a + 7)$

Use the distributive property.

$4a^2 + 8a − 3a − 21$

Combine like terms.

$\textbf{4}a^\textbf{2} + \textbf{5}a − \textbf{21}$

50. **A)** Each day there is a 80% chance it will rain, there is a 20% chance it will not rain.

Probability it will not rain = 20% × 20% or 0.2 × 0.2 = 0.04

Convert to a percent; 0.04 = **4%**.

51. **C)** Convert the size of the room to square inches. (1 foot = 144 square inches)

$190 \times 144 = 27,360$ square inches

Area of each tile → 3 in × 3 in = 9 in²

Divide the total area by the area of each tile.

$27,360 \div 9 = \textbf{3040 tiles}$

52. **C)** Convert 10% to a decimal and find the discount.

$50 \times 0.1 = \$5$

Original price − discount = discounted price

$\$50 − \$5 = \$45$

Convert the tax percent to a decimal and calculate the sales tax.

$\$45 \times 0.1 = \$4.50$

Add the sales tax to the discounted price.

$\$45 + \$4.50 = \textbf{\$49.50}$

53. **D)** Substitute the given values and simplify.

$$\frac{r}{5} - 10t$$

$r = 315$ and $t = −2$

$$\frac{315}{5} - 10(−2) = 63 + 20 = \textbf{83}$$

54. **C)** Use the percent proportion and solve for the whole.

$$\frac{\text{part}}{\text{percent}} = \text{whole}$$

$$\frac{550}{0.25} = \textbf{2200}$$

55. **A)** Find the total amount of flour used.

$2\frac{1}{2} + 1\frac{1}{3} = 2\frac{3}{6} + 1\frac{2}{6} = 3\frac{5}{6}$

Subtract the total used from 8 cups to find the remaining amount.

$8 - 3\frac{5}{6} = \frac{48}{6} - \frac{23}{6} = \frac{25}{6} = \mathbf{4\frac{1}{6}}$

56. **B)** Subtract to find the new balance.

$127 + (-150) = \mathbf{-23}$

57. **B)** Let p = the original number of pears.

Convert 30% to a decimal.

$30\% = 0.3$

The store has sold $0.30p$ pears.

Write an equation for the original number minus the number sold equal to 455.

$p - 0.30p = 455$

$p = \frac{455}{0.7} = \mathbf{650}$ **pears**

58. **C)** Find the area of the lawn.

50 feet × 30 feet = 1500 square feet

Multiply the total number of square feet by the charge per square foot.

$1500 \times 0.05 = \mathbf{\$75.00}$

59. **A)** Sides of an equilateral triangle are all the same length. Sides of a square are all the same length. The triangles and the square share a side, so all the lines in the figure are the same length.

Use the perimeter to find the length of one side.

60 inches ÷ 6 = 10 inches

Use the formula for area of a square; $A = s^2$.

10 in × 10 in = **100 in²**

60. **C)** All the points lie on the circle, so each line segment is a radius.

radius = $\frac{\text{diameter}}{2} = \frac{75}{2} = 37.5$

The sum of the 4 lines is 4 times the radius.

$4r = 4(37.5) = \mathbf{150}$

61. **A)** Subtract the amount of the bills from the amount in the checking account.

792.00 + 84.63 + 112.15 = 988.78

2,386.52 − 988.78 = **$1,397.74**

62. **B)** Add zeros so that each number is expressed in ten-thousandths.

3.8190 + 14.6800 + 0.0006 = **18.4996**

63. **D)** Reduce the fraction; divide to change the reduced fraction to a decimal.

$\frac{15}{25} = \frac{15 \div 5}{25 \div 5} = \frac{3}{5}$

$3 \div 5 = \mathbf{0.6}$

64. **C)** To divide fractions, multiply by the reciprocal.

$\frac{8}{15} \div \frac{1}{6} = \frac{8}{15} \times \frac{6}{1} = \frac{48}{15} = \frac{48 \div 3}{15 \div 3} = \mathbf{\frac{16}{5}}$

LANGUAGE SKILLS

1. **B)** The verb bring should be replaced with take: "Please take that unsafe toy away from your little brother." Bring means "to carry [something] from one place to another," and take means "to remove [something] from someone or move it from one place to another."

2. **B)** The place name Seattle (a city in the state of Washington) should be capitalized—it is a proper noun.

3. **C)** Because it is a negative, no other inaccurately discounts the first negative (not) and creates a double negative ("could not afford no other"); it should be changed to any other.

4. **A)** The semicolon after California should be replaced by a comma. The phrase "even in California" is not an independent clause, so a semicolon is incorrect.

5. **C)** The common noun summer, the name of a season, should not be capitalized. Months' names (like October) are proper nouns, but seasons' names (spring, summer, fall, and winter) are common nouns.

6. **B)** Continued is a past-tense verb; however, the present tense (continues) is needed to align with the time mentioned later in the sentence (even today).

7. **C)** The prepositional phrase "At the ball following the royal wedding" is not an independent clause, so it should be followed by a comma, not a colon.

8. **C)** The comma should be replaced with a question mark: "At what time do you want to eat dinner?" The speaker in the sentence (she) is asking a question.

9. **A)** Countries' is a plural possessive but should be acting as a plural subject; the correct form of the word is countries ("around the world").

10. **C)** An agreement error exists in this sentence. Because the people "of many countries" are benefiting, multiple populations are benefiting: "the population[s] of many countries."

11. **D)** There are no errors in the sentences.

12. **A)** The phrase "Because caffeine keeps me awake" is not an independent clause, so it should be followed by a comma, not a colon.

13. **B)** Because of the language used later in the sentence ("still being released every year"), a present-tense verb is needed here ("continues to fascinate").

14. **B)** The colon should be replaced with a comma or an exclamation point: "What a wonderful time we're going to have next weekend," Pru said. Or: "What a wonderful time we're going to have next weekend!" Pru said.

15. **A)** Principal is a homophone for the more appropriate word principle, meaning "main" or "primary."

16. **D)** All the sentences are correct. There are no errors in usage, punctuation, or capitalization.

17. **B)** The exclamation point should be replaced with a question mark since Juana is asking a question: "Do you want to join us?" Juana asked.

18. **C)** The phrase "Andy Warhol's paintings" creates a dangling modifier; "the subject of the largest single-artist museum" is Andy Warhol, not his paintings.

19. **A)** The semicolon after workday should be replaced with a comma. The phrase "when he received the news" cannot stand on its own, so it needs a comma to connect with the independent clause "James had already been awake for nineteen hours after a twelve-hour workday."

20. **B)** As a common noun, airport should not be capitalized.

21. **A)** There are two independent clauses in this sentence connected by the coordinating conjunction but. A comma is needed following the word test.

22. **B)** An extra, unnecessary comma is inserted after December. It should be deleted because there are only two items in this series connected by the word and.

23. **C)** Was is a singular, past-tense verb that does not agree with the plural subject (contributions); for agreement, was should be changed to were.

24. **C)** Will be is a future-tense verb; the sentence is a general statement of fact and should be written in present tense ("it is the main water source").

25. **B)** To create the correlative conjunction, *not only* should be followed by the words *but also*.

26. **D)** There are no errors in the sentences.

27. **A)** The contraction don't is missing an apostrophe.

28. **B)** *Nevertheless*, a transitional word signifying contradiction, is used incorrectly here. To improve the sentence, a different transition word or phrase (like indeed or while there) should be used instead.

29. **D)** All the sentences are correct. There are no errors in usage, punctuation, or capitalization.

30. **A)** The comma after gift is unnecessary and incorrect. That introduces a restrictive relative clause. Because it is essential information in the sentence, it does not require a comma to connect to the independent clause "I bought him a gift."

31. **A)** It's is a contraction of the phrase it is; this context requires the possessive form (its . . . surroundings).

32. **A)** This sentence is a comma splice. The writer should add the coordinating conjunction and after the comma to connect the two independent clauses.

33. **A)** In choice A, *either* is incorrectly paired with *nor*. The correct construction is either / or.

34. **C)** Costs is a singular verb that does not agree with the subject of this sentence (hurricanes).

35. **C)** The semicolon after ride should be replaced with a comma to connect the dependent clause "When I offered her a ride" to the independent clause "Mazie accepted gratefully."

36. **D)** All the sentences are correct. There are no errors in usage, punctuation, or capitalization.

37. **C)** Remain is a plural, present-tense verb that does not agree with its subject, water.

38. **B)** This sentence is a comma splice. The writer should insert a comma after dogs to connect the two independent clauses using the coordinating conjunction *but*.

39. **A)** "Because Paris is such a beautiful city" is a dependent clause. Only a comma is necessary to connect it to the independent clause "tourists flock there all year long," and the conjunction *so* should be deleted.

40. **B)** The preposition *of* is incorrect. The writer should use the preposition with to complete the prepositional idiom combined *with*. This change will also properly communicate the intended meaning (that two things are combined with each other).

41. **B)** The adjective loose should be replaced with the verb lose: "Oh wow, I hope we don't lose the game!" Lose means the opposite of win, and loose means the opposite of tight.

42. **A)** The word surprised is misspelled.

43. **C)** Tendency is misspelled.

44. **B)** The word government is misspelled.

45. **B)** Patience should be replaced with its homophone, patients: "Dr. Boynton has so many patients today that she will have no time for lunch." Patience is a noun, synonymous with tolerance, serenity, and persistence. Patients is a plural noun that means "sick or injured people who a medical professional examines and treats."

46. **D)** No words are misspelled.

47. **A)** The word unanimous is misspelled.

48. **D)** No words are misspelled.

49. **B)** The word magnificent is misspelled.

50. **A)** The word reliant is misspelled.

51. **C)** The new sentence refers to "outdoor activities like hiking, rafting, and camping." Sentence 3 mentions "other activities like airplane and helicopter flyovers," so introductory information about "outdoor activities" would fit well before sentence 3.

52. **A)** *In addition* is the appropriate introductory phrase to signify the additive relationship between the two clauses.

53. B) In this version, all items in the list are nouns (dearth, lack, and list), followed by prepositions (of) and objects of the prepositions (wins, time, and clients).

54. B) "And also functioned" introduces the second part of a compound verb phrase ("was created . . . and also functioned").

55. D) Modifying relationships are clear in this sentence: the phrase "which played for over a minute" correctly modifies signal.

56. B) The phrase "on the other hand" appropriately signifies the opposing ideas in the two pieces of information.

57. D) This choice provides unnecessary information that detracts from the main idea expressed by the other three sentences (the benefits received by retired presidents).

58. B) This sentence addresses art; the other three sentences address mythology or folklore.

59. A) The new sentence introduces the idea that science fiction inspires human accomplishments. The paragraph lists various human accomplishments inspired by science fiction works. So the new sentence should precede sentence 1, beginning the paragraph.

60. B) The subject form of the relative pronoun *who* should appear here. The word functions as a subject, not an object, so whom would be incorrect. In general, *which* is not used to refer to people.

Made in the USA
Middletown, DE
21 July 2024

57815387R00130